37.95

Getting Signed!

An Insider's Guide to the Record Industry

George Howard

Edited by Jonathan Feist

Berklee Media

Associate Vice President: Dave Kusek
Director of Content: Debbie Cavalier
Business Manager: Linda Chady Chase
Technology Manager: Mike Serio
Marketing Manager, Berkleemusic: Barry Kelly
Senior Designer: David Ehlers

Berklee Press

Senior Writer/Editor: Jonathan Feist
Writer/Editor: Susan Gedutis
Production Manager: Shawn Girsberger
Marketing Manager, Berklee Press: Jennifer Rassler
Product Marketing Manager: David Goldberg
Production Assistant: Louis O'choa

ISBN 0-87639-045-9

1140 Boylston Street
Boston, MA 02215-3693 USA
(617) 747-2146

Visit Berklee Press Online at
www.berkleepress.com

DISTRIBUTED BY

HAL•LEONARD®
CORPORATION
7777 W. BLUEMOUND RD. P.O. BOX 13819
MILWAUKEE, WISCONSIN 53213

Visit Hal Leonard Online at
www.halleonard.com

Printed in the United States of America at Patterson Printing.

12 11 10 09 08 07 06 05 04 5 4 3 2 1

Dedicated to all of the artists with whom
I have the pleasure of working.
Without you, there would be…

Contents

Acknowledgments

Thanks to Berklee's Peter Spellman for the initial encouragement; Debbie Cavalier for the belief; and Jonathan Feist, editor as artist/artist as editor. Jill Christiansen, from whom I've learned (and continue to learn) more about the music business than anyone else. All of the "From the Field" experts who took the time to contribute their expertise so that others could learn from them. Ken Goes for getting me on the right track. George W. Howard III for the legal advice. Austine Howard for reminding me to always keep an open ear. Adam Maffei for the encouragement. Ian Moss for keeping me in line. And Marci Johnson for the patience and support.

Introduction

Why This Book Now?

As I write this, the music industry is changing around me. From the covers of magazines and the mouths of pundits, the demise of the record industry is being trumpeted, loudly. On some level, it's true. The record industry as we know it appears to be going away.

Now, don't expect an apocalyptic flash, and then—poof—no more records, no more record stores, no more record labels. Instead, it will gradually metamorphise. I believe we're well into the metamorphic stage now.

It is an interesting time to write a book about how to get signed to a label. The perception is that labels are all stuck in outmoded business models that exploit artists while enriching themselves. The reality, though, is that these days, very few labels are making as much money as they used to. And, yes, artists throughout the years have entered into draconian contracts, which stripped them of their artistic control and their royalties. While these practices are largely part of history, there remains a constant hum of discontent from artists towards their record labels.

So, who would possibly want to be signed to one of these dinosaurs? And why write a book of strategies on how best to enter into a contract with a label, if they are soon to be extinct? Good questions, and the answers largely rely on how you define the word "label." Certainly, what passes for a label today will not be the same as what passes for a label in five years. We are at a fulcrum point in history, and new paradigms and infrastructures keep springing up to challenge the current—failing—business models. In business, as in nature, vacuums are abhorred. So, as the "labels" of today crumble under the weight of downloading, difficult retail conditions, narrow radio formats, fickle consumers, and all of the other problems they face, new entities will begin (and are beginning) to emerge that shift the old paradigms. Perhaps these new entities will rely more on the Internet for distribution, or perhaps sustain their infrastructure through taking percentages of revenue from artists—such as a piece of their merchandise or ticket sales income—which were once sacrosanct.

Whatever the future brings, there will be infrastructures—call them "labels," if you will—that work to promote, market, and distribute artists' material. This is why I write. Whether or not these infrastructures will be referred to as labels is irrelevant. They will perform functions that artists need in order to succeed. Artists will want their support, and will be willing to part with some of the money from their record sales in order to gain access to this support. Fundamentally, artists just want to create. Anything that gets in the way of this creative process will be given short shrift, or more likely, be ignored completely. This is why it is so rare to see a successful artist-run label. Those that are successful are usually just a label in name only, and actually run by another (typically larger) entity. Only a handful of artists have managed to continue to make compelling, vital music while running a label. Ani Defranco's Righteous Babe and John Prine's Oh Boy labels spring to mind. But even these are run by artists in conjunction with others, who largely handle the day-to-day activity of running a label so that the artists can focus on creating.

A few years ago, you saw artists, *en masse*, rising up to eschew record companies and their "odious" practices, and beginning to create and market their art on their own terms. It did not take long for most of these artists to realize that, fundamentally, they really didn't want to run a label. They wanted to create. On the other hand, they didn't want to return to the label system they had left. Today, many feel that somewhere between the two extremes is the answer.

Still, with this sort of "in-between label," you have issues of economy of scale. Setting up an infrastructure in order to service just one artist is not good business. It is better to build an infrastructure and then use it to its full capacity by servicing multiple artists. Therefore, these entities often strive to find like-minded musicians to plug into their infrastructures. In other words, they sign additional artists. Of course, they don't do this out of pure altruism; they need economic recompense for their efforts. So, some sort of economic model is instated. Ironically, these resemble the economic models currently employed by today's labels. In short, these neo-infrastructures do not differ radically from traditional labels. The means of marketing and distribution may differ, and there may be gradations when it comes to contracts, but pulling off the mask, you will see that they are in essence labels. Again, this is why I write.

My sincere hope is that the entities of the future (some of whom may very well be the labels that exist today, if they are able to adapt) will strive to do right by their artists, and aspire to create long-term value for their companies by investing (for the long haul) in artists who can have careers and affect the culture in a positive manner for years to come. I hope too that these entities will find ways in which to compensate these artists appropriately for their cultural contributions without stripping them of their own long-term value by taking their entire copyrights or publishing. We shall see. My guess is that some will accomplish this and others won't. But that is how it has always been.

There will always be artists looking for the help of these entities—which for simplicity's sake, I'll call "labels" in this book. Artists need their help for three reasons. First, because labels, on some level, represent the dream. They are the first tangible step to the dream that if you have talent and charisma, your music can topple mountains and leave you basking in the glow of victory—as long as you find the right company to get you started. Second, on a more pragmatic level, artists will simply realize that by relinquishing a percentage of their copyrights or royalties, they will receive greater returns, and their careers will progress more quickly and efficiently. Third, artists want and need to create, and simply are not willing—or able—to do the things required to promote, market, and distribute their music on their own.

All of this, I believe, gives license for the pages that follow. It is a sort of users' guide to the record industry. I have tried to distill what I've learned as a participant and student of the record industry. As an A&R person for many years, I was responsible for listening to demo tapes and determining who had the goods, for purposes of determining who should be offered a record contract. As a record label president, I was responsible for determining how best to market the artists who made the cut, and seeing all aspects of the industry and how they related to each other.

I have been in the trenches, working with developing artists as well as more established ones, signing artists, and struggling to find ways to bring their art into the public's consciousness, by any means necessary.

This book is my travel-log. I do not pretend to have the most experience of anyone in the industry, nor do I feel qualified to speak about all genres of music. But I do understand the process that must occur for an artist not just to get a record deal, but to build a career. This is what I hope to impart.

Ultimately, the book is about connecting. Connecting with your songs, connecting with your community, connecting with the industry, and ultimately, connecting with the right label, which will help you to connect with your record-buying constituency.

As a technologist, I believe fervently that the Internet and other technology can be actualized as wonderful tools to help a musician's career. (An excellent book on the subject is Peter Spellman's *The Musician's Internet.*) For these tools to work effectively, they must be assimilated into a larger plan of connection. Therefore, I don't discuss it much. To be blunt, I don't think a single artist has been signed because of their presence on the Internet. Of course, in conjunction with all of the other activities that must precede getting a record deal, easily summed up as "hard work," the Internet, and technology in general, can be a wildly helpful tool, and it has been partly responsible for many artists getting deals. I do discuss how tools such as e-mail lists and home recording systems can leverage your abilities as an artist, and help you get signed.

People constantly ask me what I think of the industry as it faces its varied challenges. They ask how artists can succeed and survive. I think about all of the challenges, but I also think of the opportunities being brought about by the same technology that is creating the obstacles. The ability to burn CDs, while wreaking havoc on the industry, is also a boon to artists who want to sell CDs at their shows. The technology for distributing music online (without paying for it, which thus deprives many artists from their rightful royalties) is a result of the same technology that allows artists to create studio quality demos for a fraction of the price that it would have cost only a few years ago. So I remain resolutely hopeful that what has been causing the industry some difficulty is also leading to further possibilities for helping musicians communicate their art.

If you make a real emotional connection with those who hear your music, and are able to sustain your fan base through your talent and hard work, then over time, you will be able to have a career that is fulfilling, from both an artistic and monetary perspective. I hope that this book helps you to attain this.

About This Book

This book is divided into three parts, which will assist you at different stages of your career and quest for a deal. The first assumes that you have some songs and belief in yourself, but little else. It will help you figure out where to begin. The second part is for artists who have not only written some songs and come to the conclusion that they must be heard, but have taken the additional step of recording a demo of their songs. These chapters will help you put your demo to use, and show how to build your core team—managers, booking agents, and lawyers—who will help you advance your career and your quest for a record deal. Part 3 is for the artists who have some sort of infrastructure already in place, such as a manager or agent, and want to extend the reach of their music via a distribution deal or publishing. Additionally, this part takes a hard look at what to expect once you do achieve the goal of finding a record label, and examines the types of deals that you will be presented with.

I'd advise even experienced artists to read the early chapters and refresh yourself on the basics—especially if you have been having difficulty getting your foot in the door. Similarly, I'd advise beginning artists to read the later sections, so you can see where you're going. The workshops in each chapter will guide you through completing the tasks that will dramatically increase your chances of getting signed, and of generally strengthening your chances of having a successful career in music.

PART I

The Demo

BREAKING THROUGH:
History, Attitude, and Your Demo

There is a process to everything—an order in which things take place. One order is not necessarily better than the other, but there is always a starting point. The starting point in your journey towards getting a record deal is to fi st believe, with ultimate conviction, that your music is undeniably great and that it must be heard by others. When you have that level of confi ence—not a second before—you can then begin the process of letting others know about your music.

Your second step is to produce a great demo.

I'm not going to discuss how to write great songs, choose a band name, or find a reliable bass player. There are other books about those topics, and while I'm somewhat skeptical of books that tell you how to write great songs, I'm sure their authors are skeptical about books that tell you how to get a record deal. Seeing as how I like the view from my glass house, I will put my stone back in my pocket, and focus on what I know: what it takes to get a record deal. I will just assume that you've got the best songs and the best bass player, and now you're ready to start letting the world know it.

Conventional wisdom says that to show the world your greatness, you must f rst get signed to a label. While this is certainly one way, musicians who think that simply producing a demo and sending it off to a label will result in a deal are sorely mistaken. The reality is, an unsolicited demo—one not specif cally requested by a label—will very likely do nothing at all for you.

As a matter of fact, the major labels do not even open unsolicited demo tapes. They simply return them unopened.

Even independent labels who do accept unsolicited demos (and not all of them do) do not give them the same attention they do to demos which are either requested or received from someone they know (that someone could be a manager, a lawyer, or another artist they work with). As the following chapters will show, the f rst stop for a demo is really never a label. Rather, it is used to begin building a community or team of supporters for your music who will have the connections, power, and knowledge to not only get your demo into the right people's hands, but also to make your demo stand out to the labels and not just end up in a pile.

The process of letting the world know that you are great necessarily begins with believing that you yourself are great. Without this conviction, you will simply not have the fortitude to make it through the myriad obstacles that stand in your way. All the great ones—some of whom we will look at in detail in chapter 2—had to overcome a litany of diff culties in order to have their music heard, and you will too. What the great ones had, and what you too must have, is a belief that your music must be heard and nothing will keep it from happening. Only then can you move on to the next stage, actually putting a demo together so others can hear it.

What is a Demo?

The question that I'm asked almost as frequently as "How do I get a record deal?" is, "How good does my demo need to be?" The answer, as you might guess, is that it must be undeniably great. Talk about an answer that creates more questions, huh.

Let's look at the questions behind the question. What you are really asking, when you ask how good your demo needs to be, is:

- Does it have to be professionally recorded (i.e., a lot of money spent)?
- Does it need to have artwork or photos in the packaging or can it just be a burned CDR with the song titles written on the sleeve?
- Does it need a barcode?
- Do the songs need to be copyrighted before the demo is sent out?
- How many songs should go on the demo?
- Should I include lyrics?

In order to answer these questions, you must f rst understand what the word "demo" means. It is an abbreviation for "demonstration." Get it? The demo must demonstrate—in as clear a manner as possible—what you are capable of. All A&R people understand the limitations around which most demos are recorded. (We will discuss shortly what exactly A&R people do.) While it's lovely to get a demo that is so fully formed that you feel you can just slap the record label's logo on it and put it in the marketplace, most of the time, the demo is the band's calling card that intimates what is possible.

You must not consider the demo to be more than a calling card or introduction to your band. There are many, many "studio geniuses" who spend all of their time perfecting their recordings only to fina ly emerge from their dank lairs to realize they have no one to play their masterpieces for. Working too long in a vacuum to make a perfect demo is the equivalent of not having a demo at all. A demo is really just one part of the equation, when it comes to getting a record deal. It alone—regardless of how great it is—will not get you a record deal. If you focus on the demo to the exclusion of other things, such as playing live, building a community around your music, getting press reviews, and getting some local radio play, you will probably not get a record deal.

I think you need to leave some room, so that the person listening at a record company can imagine what it will become. It's good if you make it sort of an obvious demo so that the A&R person can feel like they have something to do with the process.

—Paul Q. Kolderie, Producer/Engineer

The Demo: A Multi-Purpose Tool

View your demo as a multi-purpose tool, like those things you see on late-night TV that get dents out of your car and change your child's diaper. Yes, the most obvious use for this tool is to send it to record labels to get a record deal. Pragmatically, however, you will use it for many other things, long before you should bother sending it to labels. For instance, you will use your demo to try to get gigs, you will service it to local radio stations, you will slip it to the writers of the local arts paper, and you will f nally level that shaky table by putting one under the short leg so you can enjoy a meal without hot Ramen noodles dripping into your lap.

Before you can do any of these things, of course, you must record the demo. Before you record, you must select your best songs for it. And then you need to present it in a way that compels the receiver to listen. In short, you've got your work ahead of you, if you really want to create an effective demo. The following chapters take an in-depth look at how you can do just that.

1

What is a Label?...and what the hell does A&R stand for anyway?

"Was that the A&R guy?" "I think that woman back there does A&R for Sony." "The label says they're going to send out their head A&R person to our next show. We've got to tighten our set list." "That damn A&R guy is so out of it. He comes stumbling into the studio in his Armani suit, tries to get all 'real' with us like he's our bud, sits on the couch just nodding and not saying anything, and then finally says, 'Sounds pretty good, guys, but I don't hear a hit. Wanna get some sushi?' I hate our A&R guy."

All this and more have been uttered using the strange personal noun "A&R." If you're in a band and you're thinking about getting signed, you have doubtless heard of these two letters joined by an ampersand, over and over. But what does it stand for? What functions, beyond A&R, does a record label perform? If you hope to get signed, you must understand what an A&R person is and does, and how they and other players fit into record labels.

This chapter is broken into two sections. The first gives a description of what A&R is and how it has evolved through the years. The second section looks at record labels in a broad sense and examines the roles of the people who work at them. Knowledge is power in this business. Understanding how labels work and what their goals are will help you find the "love match" that is your label.

What is A&R?

What "A&R" literally stands for and what it functionally stands for are often two different things. In some ways, A&R is an anachronism—something that once had a clear meaning, but over time, has grown increasingly blurry and hard to define. It doesn't really apply the way it once did.

So a bit of explanation and history is in order. Understanding both the traditional and the current roles of A&R will give you a better chance of achieving your goal: getting a record deal.

A for Artist, R for Repertoire

First, A&R stands for "artist and repertoire." What the hell does that mean, you're probably asking. You thought an A&R person was the one who could get you signed to a record label. In a way, you're correct. A&R people are (in theory) those responsible for finding *artists* for the label. That's what the "A" in "A&R" stands for. They will (again, in theory) listen to demo tapes, go to clubs, network with managers and lawyers, and so on, in order to find the artist or band that they can then champion and ultimately get signed to the label. So, they are a key link in the chain. But as this book will show, they are really just one of many links, and not even necessarily the most immediate or direct route to getting signed. But I'm getting ahead of myself.

Performers and Songwriters

Sure, "A" is for artist. But what is this "repertoire" I speak of? In order to answer this question, we must now get in our "wayback" machines and go to that strange and exotic musical era before Bob Dylan and the Beatles. If this is hard for you to imagine, think of the Austin Powers' movies and go back in time just a few more years.

The Beatles were obviously a massively important band on a number of levels—maybe the most important rock band ever. (If, for some strange reason, you're not familiar with the Beatles, immediately put this book down and go buy *Abbey Road* and *Revolver*.) And Bob Dylan remains one of the most influential artists of all time. (While you're shopping for Beatles albums, pick up Dylan's *Blonde On Blonde* and *Blood On The Tracks*.) One thing they had in common was that they were great performers that also wrote their own songs. And while the Beatles and Dylan are the most well known early performers who also wrote their own material, I would be remiss if I didn't note that they were not the first or only ones to do so. Artists such as Little Richard, Chuck Berry, Buddy Holly, Fats Domino, Jerry Lee Lewis, Smokey Robinson, the Beach Boys, Duane Eddy, and Del Shannon all composed their own material and performed it fantastically. So fantastically, in fact, that they influenced countless others . . . such as Dylan and the Beatles.

Prior to these artists, there was an entire industry devoted to composing songs for others to perform. Very few performers actually wrote their own songs. Sounds strange, doesn't it? It's hard to imagine Eminem being told by someone from the record company that with his unique vocal phrasing and delivery, he should go to talk to writer X about generating some material for him. And yet, pre-Beatles and Dylan, that's exactly the way it worked for most artists.

Elvis Presley, for instance, wrote virtually none of the songs that he sung (and even the ones he is credited with writing, rumor has it, he did not). Ditto for Frank Sinatra. You think he sat around between games of craps, massages from Ava Gardner, and generally making fun of poor Sammy Davis Jr., and penned "Fly Me to the Moon?" Think again.

In fact, there was an entire industry of people who sat in offices and wrote songs to be performed by people like Sinatra (if they were lucky). Perhaps you've heard of some of these songwriters: Leiber & Stoller, Goffin & King, Doc Pomus, and others. If not, have a look at the album credits on recordings by people like Elvis Presley, Diana Ross, Bobby Darrin, or the Shirelles. Have you heard the expression Tin Pan Alley or read about the Brill Building? These were actual places where songwriters came to work in the morning, tried to come up with catchy melodies and lyrics, ate lunch, tried to get popular singers to perform ("cover") their songs, had a quick martini on the way to the train, and went home, only to return another day to do it again. Where do I sign up?

So, you had, in one camp, the performers—people with wonderful, expressive voices, who often looked very good in their pants. And then in the other camp, at places like Tin Pan Alley (so named because cheap pianos were described as sounding like tin pans), you had a somewhat anonymous group of people who wrote songs (or "repertoire") the same way others make shoes: as a craft. Someone had to put these two camps together. This is the "R" in "A&R." The A&R people were responsible for finding material or "repertoire" for these great voices, and they would often go to these songwriters in order to pair up a song with a singer.

For a time, a performer was to songwriting as a pitcher is to batting: you just didn't want him doing it. But things changed with Dylan, the Beatles, the Rolling Stones, the Beach Boys, and others. These artists did write their own material, as well as perform it, and they also sold a phenomenal number of records. These sales validated the idea that performers could actually write popular songs. In so doing, they influenced aspiring performers everywhere and gave them license to believe that they too were capable of writing their own material.

This started a revolution in the industry and changed it forever. Today, not only is it acceptable for performers to write their own songs, but it is almost mandatory. Largely because of Dylan and the Beatles, today's artists are judged and perceived not just on how they perform a song, but how well they write the songs too.

What is the Role of A&R Now?

Though far more artists today write and perform their own material, A&R people still must make the connection between the "A" *and* the "R." There are still many great performers who can't write well, and there are many great writers who can't sing or perform. In fact, it is very rare for both parts to come together in a single performer or band. A&R people must invest a significant amount of time to try to put these pieces together. That is why many first records by artists have "covers" on them. The A&R person (or someone else at the record label) feels that the artist's own material isn't fully developed, so they suggest that the artist "cover" another person's song.

There are, of course, more nuanced and subtle ways to work with the artist to help them develop their repertoire, and while that has largely become the role of the producer, A&R people still are part of the process. A&R people work closely with artists to flesh out what the artist hopes to accomplish through their music. In large part, A&R people try to focus on the artist. They highlight the artist's strengths—which, not surprisingly, are frequently what the A&R person believes are the artist's most saleable attributes. In this manner, A&R people look first to sign artists whose strengths are already mature, as these artists have the greatest sales potential with the least amount of costly development time. Short of finding the ultra-rare fully formed artist, A&R people look for artists who are closest to being fully formed, and then help them to develop. This can involve helping with song selection, choosing producers, working on the live show—anything that an artist must do to sell the most records.

Since we're doing our history lesson here, I will mention the best known A&R person: John Hammond. You say you've heard of him, but can't think why. Well, here are a few reasons: Bob Dylan, Billie Holiday, Robert Johnson, Aretha Franklin, and Bruce Springsteen. Yep, he "discovered" them all. This is why you usually hear his name preceded by the words, "legendary A&R man," as in, "legendary A&R man John Hammond signed Bob Dylan to Columbia Records in 1961." Of course, his involvement didn't end with just signing the artists to the label. He also worked with them to find the right material for them to record.

In country music, there are still a tremendous number of writers who don't perform, and performers who don't write. There is a (long) street in Nashville that houses "Music Row." Like Tin Pan Alley, Music Row is where songs are written by people who rarely—if ever—perform themselves. Instead, they shop them to artists, A&R people, and producers, hoping that someone likes it enough to record on their album.

POP QUIZ

Quick, who wrote the country standard "Crazy?" If you answered Patsy Cline, go to the back of the room. It was, in fact, written by Willie Nelson, who came to Nashville with a truckload of songs and a very distinctive voice. It took some time before people warmed to the idea of him singing his own songs. During that time, he wrote for others.

So, there is a thumbnail sketch of what the "A" and the "R" stand for. It's important for you, as a performing artist, to understand the mindset of most A&R people. The "R" is as important as the "A." A&R people are looking for great performers, and want them to perform great material. If they can write their own songs, all the better. If not, it is the A&R person's job to help them find material, or help them develop their songs to be marketable. At the end of the day, whether they know it or not, all A&R people want to be John Hammond.

What Is a Record Label? Majors Vs. Indies

Now, let's examine the record labels in general. There is no such thing as a typical record label. They are all different. There is, of course, a spectrum, which at one end has the "major" labels like Sony and Universal, and on the other end, is the one-person dorm room operation, pressing up CDs for their friend's band. In between, there exist the majority of labels. Most are smaller than the majors but bigger than the guy in the dorm room. These labels are often collectively referred to as "indies," short for "independent" labels.

Any label that is not distributed by a major distribution company is considered an indie. Within this large category, it is important to distinguish between established, professional indies and those dorm-room labels, which are really hobbies. This is not to say that the latter aren't important or relevant. They are, and in fact, some of the majors of today were started in settings not much more grandiose than a dorm room. (Some of the most successful labels out there now actually *were* started in dorm rooms.) But understanding the difference will help you make the best choices when you are trying to find the right record company to sign with.

The Majors

As of this writing, there are five major labels: Universal, EMI, Sony, Warner Music Group, and BMG. Underneath each of these parent companies are many labels that are distributed (that is, have their records put in stores) by the above companies' proprietary distribution arms. For instance, Capitol Records is owned and distributed by EMI (which is a British company). RCA (home of Elvis Presley) is owned and distributed by BMG, which is a German company. Columbia, which released, among many others, records by Miles Davis and Bob Dylan, is owned and distributed by Japan-based Sony. Even Reprise, which was started by Frank Sinatra, and releases records by great artists such as Neil Young and Green Day, is owned by Warner Bros., which is now owned by AOL. It's all a bit complicated, and kind of irrelevant. The majors all compete for the greatest market share. They try to be the one that sells the most records, and trade the title of "holder of greatest market share" back and forth every couple of years.

THE MAJORS, C. 2003

- Universal
- EMI
- Sony
- Warner Music Group
- BMG

The majors are similar in that they are all multinationals (meaning they run their businesses in countries throughout the world), they all have their own distribution companies, they all have their own publishing companies, and they all have massive back catalogs of titles that they continue to sell into the marketplace. These individual elements combined under one company's roof are very potent and ultimately distinguish the label as a "major." Any record company that does not fit the above criteria or is not distributed by a label that fits the above criteria is said to be an "independent" or an "indie."

Not very long ago, there were more than five of these companies, but through consolidation, we have arrived where we are today. More than likely, there will be further consolidation. One of the majors will be bought by one of the others, and we will have four majors. Or perhaps some company outside the entertainment business, such as Microsoft, will buy one of the majors, thereby radically changing the landscape.

Why would one major buy another? In large part, they (like all companies) are looking for ways in which they can operate most efficiently. To that end, they want to build infrastructures that can sustain and support the records that go through that infrastructure. The thinking is that once an infrastructure is in place, it should be able to accommodate (within reason) a large number of records. This is an important point, as it underscores what it is that all labels need, and why, ultimately, they acquire other labels: they need product.

Commercially Released Music is Product

Now, "product" is an evil word, and in a perfect world, it would never be used as a synonym for music (or any art). But as offensive as it is, you need to get used to the idea that what is "art" to you is "product" to the record company. The degree to which your art is considered "product" varies from label to label, but most (not all) labels are working with economic imperatives. In order to sustain their infrastructures, they need to sell products. Those products are, of course, your art. Sorry.

You can think of this in two ways:

1. "I don't want my art considered product on any level. Therefore, I will not sell records, but will keep it purely as a poetic venture and give the CDs away to friends and family." There is nothing wrong with this choice, and in fact, it is the most appropriate choice for most people.
2. Accept that having your CD released into the marketplace makes it, on some level, a piece of product, like any other thing that is released into the marketplace. This doesn't mean that your CDs have the same amount of cultural import as, say, breakfast cereal. But what it does mean is that you are playing a part in the capitalist society of supply-and-demand. That's okay, and I would posit, lends you an incredibly powerful opportunity to co-opt and subvert the very system that supports your art, if you so choose.

Not to get too deep into my more anarchic views, but one way to view it, if you have problems thinking of your music as product, is to consider that rather than contributing to the cultural wasteland by adding more worthless material crap into the world—or worse, deciding not to contribute at all and just kvetch relentlessly about the shoddy state of the world—you have a third opportunity: to actually change and use and subvert the system from within. By this, I mean that if you write, record, and release music that really impacts the culture in a positive way, you are doing something wonderfully powerful. Of course, determining how you affect the culture in a positive way is a broad subject, but arguments can be made that everyone from Bob Dylan to Public Enemy to U2 have been able to do this on a large scale. Many more have done it on a smaller, more intimate, and personal scale. Affecting the culture in a positive way does not mean that you must be political. You can affect it by giving voice to the disenfranchised or by just releasing music that helps someone relax at the end of the day.

So, the world, and more relevantly, record companies, need this product. People buy it to make their lives better. Record companies need product to stay in business and to support their infrastructure that allows them to keep releasing records.

In short, record companies need you and your music. Without you, they have no purpose or means of staying in business. Never forget this. Record companies need you. They make it seem like you need them (and in some ways you do), but more and more, the dynamics of this relationship are changing, and they need you more than you need them. Understanding this is the key to success in the short term, and success over a career.

Record Label Architecture

Let's look at this infrastructure that your art supports. Understanding how companies work will help you determine the best manner in which to align yourself with one of these companies.

The infrastructures of all record labels are similar. The difference with the majors is just that the number of people doing the jobs is greater than at the indies. The jobs are the same because the goal is the same: sell records. So what are these jobs?

- **A&R.** Responsible for finding artists and helping them develop their material for release. The A&R person is like the door—the person that must be unlocked in order for the artist to walk through the wood paneled halls of a record label.
- **Marketing (including product managers).** Responsible for exposing you and your music to the public, in order to drive consumers to the store. They do this by developing advertising, "POP" (point-of-purchase materials, such as posters), consumer outreach through postcards/e-mails (many labels have dedicated Web/Internet marketing staff), convention appearances, touring ideas (but usually *not* booking the tours), video production, and whatever else they can dream up. Not all labels have product managers, but when they do, these people work directly with the artist (or the artist's manager) as a day-to-day contact. They work closely with the A&R person and the artist/manager to design marketing plans, create packaging ideas to give to the production (read, graphics/design) people, and, importantly, make sure these marketing plans are executed. These people are an important chain link to your ultimate success. When you get signed, make friends with them.
- **Publicity.** Responsible for getting your CDs written about in magazines, newspapers, and so on. Also responsible for trying to get you TV appearances, interviews while on tour, and other press exposure.

- **Promotion.** Responsible for getting your music played on the radio, setting up interviews for you at radio stations, and often, getting your video played.
- **Sales.** Responsible for either selling your CD directly into retail accounts or working with the distribution company to help them sell your CD into accounts.

That is really the nuts and bolts of it. Obviously, there are other people working at these companies. There are presidents, CEOs, COOs, Business Affairs people (lawyers who draft contracts between the artist and label, clear samples, and so on), and CFOs, all of whom, in some ways, hold your destiny in their hands—especially the CFOs, who will tell the CEOs and COOs whether or not you're making any money for the company.

If you are not making money for the company, eventually, inevitably, these CEOs or CFOs will tell the A&R person that you will not be making any more records for the company, and tell marketing that the company will not be spending any more money trying to sell your records. All of those people listed above will then stop working on your behalf. Of course, this is the glass-half-empty scenario (even though far more records never make money for companies than those that do). A more optimistic one is that the CFO tells the CEO and president that you're making piles of money for the company, and the company pushes the A&R person to get you in the studio ASAP to record a follow-up, and instructs the sales and marketing staff to increase their sales and marketing budgets in order to really push this thing over the edge. Ah, bliss.

Sometimes, all of these jobs are handled by only a couple of people—sometimes one. When I started my first label, I signed the bands, recorded the records, wrote the marketing plans, called the press and radio and retail, boxed up the packages, and worked on the Web site. In fact, outside of a handful of labels (majors and indies), very few companies can afford an infrastructure in which these different jobs are handled by individual people. Just realize, whether you sign to a major label or a one-person operation, that the job functions outlined above must get done on some level, by someone, in order to give you the best chance of success.

Independent Promotion: More Indies

There are also industries built around freelancers who provide many of these services. Confusingly, these freelancers are also referred to as "indies" in the industry. This is because they are not on the staff of the label exclusively. In other words, they are independent of any one label and work for various labels. Often, you have promotion or publicity indies working for majors. Indies can be hired to do publicity, promotion, retail, video plugging, and anything else you can think of that might help to bring attention to a release.

While it would seem that the majors and bigger indie labels, because of their larger staffs, don't need to hire publicity or promotion indies, they are typically the biggest utilizers of indies. Their in-house people often have too much on their plate, or often don't have the range of expertise needed for more specific projects. For example, if a label releases a record from a Latin band, and that label has not released many Latin records in the past, they are better off hiring an indie who is an expert in the Latin music world than hiring staff to only work the handful of Latin records they release.

For smaller labels, indies are more a matter of necessity. It is almost impossible for a record company that consists of just one or two people to adequately promote and market their records to their fullest potential. They too will turn to indies to augment their own efforts. Obviously, indies aren't free, and the label must have the financial wherewithal to pay the indie. Many can't afford them. This is why you often see the insidious Catch-22 of a label not having enough money to pay an indie to promote the record because the record isn't selling enough because it's not being promoted adequately. This happens all the time, and it is very sad. This is why it is critical to your success to understand very clearly what your band's needs are, and to determine which label can fulfill those needs. Similarly, it is the job of the record company (or responsible record company) to work only with bands that they can adequately promote with their means and infrastructure.

Summary

Understand, as we enter an era of rapid change for the record industry, the term "label" will soon not apply the way it once did. But whatever you call it, the company that works on your behalf must fulfill three basic necessities:

1. They must engage in the ownership (partial or otherwise) of the music they release, even if only for a limited time.
2. They must have some ability to market and promote this music.
3. They must have some ability to make this music available for sale, either via traditional methods (such as working with a distributor to get them into stores), or through "new" methods, such as the Internet.

Any company or entity that fulfills these three criteria is behaving like a "label," regardless of what it calls itself.

Again, the better you understand how labels work to sell records, the better your chances of getting signed. Labels want to succeed, and any band that shows that they have the potential for success will have a good chance of getting a record deal. Yes, writing great songs and performing them flawlessly is the single most important thing you can do to show a label that you have a chance to succeed, but more and more, that alone will not get you a record deal.

It is the countless other things that you must do that will push the label over the edge. You must be able to help them sell records. Labels get presented with many bands that write great songs and perform them brilliantly, only to pass on signing them because they are lacking the critical other elements that the label determines are needed for success. We will discuss these elements in the following chapters. Understanding what these labels do, and how their infrastructures work is the first step in understanding how you can make yourself most appealing to a record label, beyond just the "A" and the "R."

Workshop

Examine twenty CDs that resemble the music you strive to create. Choose artists whose music inspires and influences your own. Determine what labels they were released on and in what year. (This information is usually found on the back of the CD or on the CD itself).

Then do some research to see if you can determine which of these labels (a) still exist, (b) are a major or an indie, and (c) whether or not they are accepting demos. (Remember, majors don't accept unsolicited demos.)

The best way to find this information is by visiting the label's Web site. (If the label doesn't have an easily found Web site, it means they are either out of business or probably not a label you'd want to sign with. I mean come on, it's the twenty-first century, get a Web site.)

2

Three Case Studies in Breaking Through: Nirvana, Def Jam, and Bob Dylan

The Essential Quality in an Artist

Fundamentally, as an artist, you have to believe in yourself. This belief will help you to persevere, and also help you make connections with others who share your vision.

While every success story is different, you will find that most successful artists share the sense that their music *must be heard*. This chapter describes the early days of two successful artists and one visionary label, showing how their sense of self-identity helped shape their destiny.

Study and cultivate this mindset in yourself. It is imperative for your success. It is the *sine qua non* of getting a record deal. It is this belief that allows artists to persevere during the inevitable difficult times. It is what motivates artists to get to know the business and its participants in their milieu. Additionally, it is the quality that attracts other visionaries to you—the ones who hold the keys to the kingdom of record labels. This mindset will, in short, prepare you for the arduous journey that you have ahead of you.

We begin by considering how a typical (perhaps, stereotypical) label approaches new signings. It's not pretty. Then, three case studies show the artists' perspective in attracting their initial labels' attention. These studies reveal the mindset necessary to overcome the difficulties all artists face when looking for a label.

The Problem

In order to understand why this belief is so important, you must first understand the roadblocks you will face when confronting typical record labels. First, know this: whatever is currently popular in the world of music is exactly what A&R people are trying to sign—particularly at the majors, and most (not all) of the larger independent labels. Nothing gets green-lighted faster than an artist who can easily be contextualized as something similar to some other popular, money-making artist, whether that band or genre is any good or not. Never forget that.

Now, I would hazard to guess that most artists believe that their music is unique—as they should, as they must. This fights against the fact that labels typically look for trends rather than originality, and leads to a troubling impasse.

How Artists Really Get Signed: A Signing Drama

The reality is that one of the first things A&R people must do, when trying to pitch their company on a band that they are keen on signing, is to put the artist in some kind of context that can be understood quickly, easily, and decisively. What is the easiest way to do this? Compare the band to another one, of course. And if they want to convince their company to sign this band, do you think that they will compare the band to one that (a) isn't popular, or—worse—(b) no one has ever heard of? Doesn't happen.

Dig, if you will, my picture.

A&R Person: Hey Mr.-label-executive-guy-who-controls-the-purse-strings, you gotta hear this band. We should sign them. They're going to be huge!

Exec: Oh yeah? Wait, do you still work here?

A&R Person: Yeah, you know, I was fired from here like four years ago, went to a few other labels, and then you guys hired me back. Rad! But really, you gotta hear this band, they're going to be huge!

Exec: Oh, well, it seems like you never left, but then again, I can never tell you "creative" people apart. So, tell me about this band.

A&R Person: They're going to be huge! They've got a buff lead singer, and monster hooks.

Exec: What do they sound like?

At this point, the conversation can go one of two ways.

Option 1

A&R Person: They sound like a cross between [insert obscure critic's fave] and [insert obscure band from twenty years ago]. I think we should get [insert au courant NYC DJ] to do some remixes. It could be huge!

The exec, while looking as though he is hearing this, and perhaps even nodding attentively, is actually thinking, "Did I eat lunch yet? I can't remember. I feel like I might have, but I really can't remember. It seems like I have something stuck in my teeth, but that could be that bagel from breakfast. Maybe not, maybe it's bread from a sandwich, but I don't remember eating a sandwich. I could have sworn we fired this guy. Maybe I'll check into that and fire him tomorrow."

And what he is hearing is:

"Mumblemumblemumblemumble. . . ."

But what he says is:

Exec: Well, send a copy to my secretary, I'll try to give it a listen.

What do you think the odds are that that band is going to be signed? What do you think the odds are of that A&R person keeping his job?

Now, let's look at option number 2. We'll pick up from the key moment.

Option 2

Exec: What do they sound like?

A&R Person: A cross between [current band that sold 130,000 copies this week] and [band that just won a Grammy for best new artist—even though it's their fourth record, which sold 3,000,000 copies] and Led Zeppelin. [It's never a bad idea to compare anyone at anytime to Led Zeppelin.]

Exec: *Really*? I'd like to hear that. Do you, uh, have an office or a stereo, or, uh, come on, let's go get some sushi, and you can play it for me on my car system. That's where I do all my serious listening, anyway.

They walk off as the sun sets, and the exec avuncularly swings his arm around the young A&R fellow's shoulders, tussles his hair, and says, "I don't know who fired you the first time, but I'm going to find out and let you fire him tomorrow."

This is why it is so hard for bands that don't fit into easily categorized piles to get a deal. Few A&R people would dare risk losing their job at a record company by trying to introduce an artist that can't be easily contextualized.

The Solution

So how does it happen? How does an artist who doesn't fit neatly into a pre-established successful category get signed? It happens, as we will see, because certain artists who get signed—especially those whose music is truly unique—have the belief that their music must be heard. This belief guides them through the labyrinth, and allows them to smash down the walls that keep the pretenders out. (Not the band. *They* certainly had this quality, and Chrissie Hynde will mess you up, if you don't believe it.)

This belief is also what enables artists to find and attract those in the business who have visionary characteristics—the rare A&R people or record label presidents/founders or powerful managers—who can see the potential in the iconoclasts. They are able to see this potential because they too are iconoclastic.

In short, there are magnetic attributes that surface in people with extraordinarily strong convictions. They attract each other. The case studies below illustrate this process.

Case 1: Nirvana

How Nirvana got their record deal

You think Seattle is a cold and gray place? The state of the record business in 1987 (the year Nirvana was signed to Sub Pop) made Seattle look like a tropical island. Here's a list of the top ten songs from *Billboard's* Top 40 chart for that year:

1. "Faith" by George Michael
2. "Livin' On A Prayer" by Bon Jovi
3. "Alone" by Heart
4. "With Or Without You" by U2
5. "La Bamba" by Los Lobos

6. "I Wanna Dance With Somebody (Who Loves Me)" by Whitney Houston
7. "Nothing's Gonna Stop Us Now" by Starship
8. "I Still Haven't Found What I'm Looking For" by U2
9. "Didn't We Have It All" by Whitney Houston
10. "I Know You Were Waiting (For Me)" by Aretha Franklin & George Michael

I'm not here to make aesthetic judgements, so I won't comment too much about what many of these songs have in common. Rather, I bring them up to highlight the abject discrepancy between what was popular at the time compared to the music that Nirvana made. Given the state of music in 1987, no one could have ever imagined that in just about a year, this scruffy little rock band from some Seattle suburb would turn the music business upside down. To do so, they had to attract the attention of someone at a record label first. Easy, right? They *were* Nirvana. Well …

As we saw from the previous chart, the music that Nirvana was making and the music popular in the mainstream could not have been more different. And yet, we all know what happened. "Smells Like Teen Spirit," and its accompanying video, truly revolutionized the music marketplace. It solidified and nationalized a new genre (grunge). Without Nirvana, all sorts of bands may never have been signed, made records, nor had the opportunity to affect the culture: Pearl Jam, Foo Fighters, Everclear, and many others.

Let's now look back to the time before Nirvana exploded into the mainstream on the Geffen (DGC) label. In a way, what Cobain says, recalling his time before starting a band, sums up much of what I'm trying to convey.

> *I had this feeling all the time—I always knew I was doing something special.… I knew it was better, even though I couldn't prove it at the time. I knew I had something to offer, and I knew eventually I would have the opportunity to show people that I could write good songs—that I could contribute something musically to rock and roll.*[1]

Do you think Cobain believed in his ability? I think so.

Cobain had these insistent thoughts in that hotbed of creativity, Aberdeen, Washington, a remote, lower-class logging town. And yet,

[1]Azerrad, Michael. *Come As You Are.* Main Street Books, 1993. p. 23.

Cobain somehow managed—even in this creative wasteland—to find ways to get his music out. He gravitated to the only band in the area that he felt an affinity for—the ultra-heavy Melvins—and began hanging around with them, while he honed his guitar and songwriting skills. Additionally, through his connection with the Melvins, he was able to occasionally escape Aberdeen for the far more hospitable Olympia, Washington.

Olympia is a college town, with a large bohemian contingency, many venues for bands to perform, a great indie radio station (KAOS), as well as a record label that so represented Cobain's ethos that he eventually tattooed its name and "K" logo on his forearm.

Nirvana—as they were now called, after wisely ditching their first name, Fecal Matter—recorded a demo tape in January of 1988 at Reciprocal Recordings in Seattle. It was not a coincidence that they chose to record there, as some of Cobain's favorite bands had done so as well.

The owner of Reciprocal, Jack Endino, engineered the early Nirvana demo tapes. He played them for Sub Pop head and founder Jonathan Poneman. It is not surprising or coincidental that Endino played the Nirvana demos for Poneman. In fact, two EPs (records longer than a single, but shorter than a full album) that Endino had previously recorded were for the bands Soundgarden and Green River, which were released by Sub Pop. Clearly, Endino and Poneman had a rapport. And Cobain, who was aware of the scene that he aspired to become a part of, wisely chose to find a way—however tangentially—to make a connection to it by selecting this studio to record his demo.

Sub Pop is a Seattle-based label that, at the time, was specializing in a relatively specific genre of music that came to be known as "grunge." This music, in some ways, reflected the regional climate of Seattle: dark, thick, somewhat gloomy. The label became known for releasing records by artists that defined this type of sound. Nirvana was making music that fit—and soon defined—the description of this sound. At the time, Sub Pop was actively looking for artists to help grow their label, and Cobain realized this.

Cobain believed that his music had to be heard. This need forced him to assess how to get it heard. He educated himself about the industry that he wanted to be a part of, and found ways to connect his music to it. He did not simply let his undeniable talent stay in his room unheard. Instead, he learned who the players were, and directed his energies towards appealing specifically to them.

While Poneman debated whether or not to sign the band (among others, his partner, Bruce Pavitt, was not immediately convinced), Endino duped copies for his friends, and Cobain sent copies out to labels that he admired

(SST, Alternative Tentacles, Touch & Go). Rumor has it that Cobain sent no fewer than twenty demo tapes to Touch & Go alone. No one responded.

Eventually, Sub Pop decided to test the waters, and asked Nirvana to record a single for them. There were no contracts issued by Sub Pop, just a request. Due to Sub Pop's limited budgets at the time, they were only able to press one thousand copies of the single. Those thousand copies soon became collector's items, as the single began getting great word-of-mouth reviews and local radio airplay.

Even with the growing buzz, Sub Pop wouldn't pay for Nirvana to record a full-length album, so the band managed to find an outsider to put up the money it cost to record their first album, *Bleach*, with Endino again engineering the session. Sub Pop released *Bleach* in June of 1989. The band began touring and winning fans rapidly. Soon, Sub Pop formalized their relationship with Nirvana by officially signing the band. The rest, as they say, is . . . oh *Nevermind*.

What we see from this case study is that while Cobain's musical talent ultimately played a huge role in Nirvana's success, it wasn't this talent alone that got him signed. We also see that he was forced to really persevere—funding his own demos and finding backers, while the label waffled, in order to bring his music to a larger stage. Additionally, it was his desire to have his music heard that drove him—gave him the fuel—to contextualize it and find other participants in the business who he hoped would grant him entrée into the record industry.

Are you doing the same for your music?

Case 2: Def Jam Recordings

The importance of the visionary at the label

The brief history of Nirvana's pathway to finding a label clearly shows how crucial perseverance and belief in your music are. However, there are other, equally important factors that were responsible for allowing Nirvana's originality and creativity to emerge on a wide scale via a recording contract. Obviously, a record deal is a marriage, in some senses. Two partners feel that they are uniquely compatible and come together. The artist and the label must find a commonality in order for a signing to occur. Sometimes, this commonality is simply the belief, by the label, that the artist will make them money. Much of the time, however, there are other factors involved. We saw, by looking at Nirvana, that determining which labels will embrace the type of music you make is of crucial import. Similarly, there is no disputing the fact that Nirvana and Sub Pop sharing a rough geographic proximity was instrumental to the two coming together. Additionally, we saw that even these qualities aren't necessarily enough. Ultimately, it took Sub Pop's visionary Jonathan Poneman to consummate the relationship and give license to Kurt Cobain's musical genius.

Nirvana's case study gave us the perspective of the artist, and what an artist must do to get a record deal. I now want to flesh out the concept of how important the role of the visionary or innovator at the label is in terms of getting a record deal. As an artist, you necessarily are a person of unique vision. You should aspire to seek out others who have this quality. Doing so will enable you to break through many of the walls of complacency that are so frequently encountered when trying to get a deal.

Have a quick look at what was on the top of the charts when Public Enemy—one of Def Jam Recordings' most important signings—was started in 1982:

1. "I Love Rock 'n' Roll" by Joan Jett & The Blackhearts
2. "Ebony and Ivory" by Paul McCartney/Stevie Wonder
3. "Eye of the Tiger" by Survivor
4. "Centerfold" by The J. Geils Band
5. "Maneater" by Daryl Hall & John Oates

....ahhhh! I can't go on—someone make it stop....

Okay, sorry, it was just that I got the chorus from "Eye of the Tiger" stuck in my head. The closest thing to rap in the whole Top 40 for that year is, uh...well, would you consider Tommy Tutone's "867-5309/Jenny" (#29) a rap song? No, me neither. Would you consider it a song at all? You get my drift. There was no rap. And yet, at this time, Def Jam was well on their way to becoming one of the most profitable and significant labels in history. How did this happen?

A very brief history of rap is required to answer this question. In the late 1970s, artists like Afrika Bambaataa, Grandmaster Flash, and the Sugar Hill Gang performed at block parties and dances in New York City. They largely rapped over disco or funk records and synthesizer beats. Eventually, a record was pressed using this method of song creation. The song "Rapper's Delight" by the Sugar Hill Gang used Chic's "Good Times" as its backing track.

Around this time, Robert "Rocky" Ford was writing a story on break beats and rapping DJs for *Billboard*. His story was the first national coverage of hip-hop. Ford became so intrigued by the burgeoning genre that he decided to produce a rap record of his own. Having met a young concert promoter named Russell Simmons while researching his *Billboard* story, he turned to him for advice regarding who he should consider recording for his release. Simmons took Ford to see Kurtis Blow, an early rap pioneer who had employed Simmons' younger brother as a DJ. Ford was not only convinced that Blow was the artist to record; he was also convinced that Simmons should manage Blow.

Simmons pressed up copies of the record and passed them out at clubs, and was buoyed by the response. Through research, he and Ford determined that PolyGram would be the ideal label for the record. They began telling retailers that they could order the record from PolyGram even though PolyGram at this point had not signed Blow and had no records. Surprisingly, this strategy worked. Retailers began trying to order the records, and eventually, PolyGram became curious about this artist who they had supposedly signed. Soon, Mercury (a PolyGram subsidiary) signed Blow. In so doing, Kurtis Blow became, in 1979, the first rapper on a major label.

Encouraged by the success, Russell Simmons began to expand his management roster, and signed on his younger brother Joey's group, Run-D.M.C. He produced their first record, and soon negotiated a deal for Run-D.M.C. to sign to the indie Profile. Their debut became the first rap record to go gold.

By 1983, with the success of Run-D.M.C., Kurtis Blow, and a handful of other early rappers, a viable industry—which included record labels, distributors, and promotion people—was growing around rap music. The logical progression for Simmons, who had gone from promoter to manager, was now to venture into the label business.

It was an unlikely pairing that led to the formation of his label. Simmons, impressed by a record by T. La Rock & Jazzy J, noticed that it was on a label called Def Jam. He made some inquiries and eventually met the man behind Def Jam. Rick Rubin was a 19-year old NYU student who was running the label out of his dorm. (I wasn't kidding when I said that massively important labels get started in dorm rooms!) The pair were a good team. Simmons was an entrepreneur who had experience promoting concerts and managing artists, while Rubin was closer to the production (beat-making) side of things, and understood the importance of marketing. Importantly, they shared a vision that the inchoate genre of music they were developing could have widespread appeal far beyond the urban centers. They created a logo for their company modeled after the Technics 1200 turntable—the one used by the vast majority of DJs—and thereby gave visual notice that the company both understood and was a part of the culture. The label had their initial taste of success with LL Cool J's "I Need a Beat" in 1984, which led to a distribution deal with CBS (now Sony).

Soon, Simmons and Rubin had created a kind of family around their label. The artists on the label knew and attracted others. In this way, the sound and style of the label was codified while the credibility was maintained. In fact, it was D.M.C. who brought Public Enemy—perhaps Def Jam's most important signing—to the attention of Def Jam. D.M.C. was from the same town as Public Enemy, making it nearly inevitable that he would know of their music. Once he had heard their talent, he alerted Rubin and Simmons.

Such connectivity through being part of the milieu or community is essential. It is the most effective way to expose your music in a real manner to that community's labels.

It was also significant that one of Def Jam's artists was instrumental in turning on the label to a new group. People at labels often look to their artists for sources of new signings. When a label signs an artist, they are buying into that artist's aesthetic judgment. Since the label feels that the music the band they have signed is a good fit, they will be predisposed to listen to a band if they are supportive of another band. So, try to make friends.

In short, it was a combination of original thinkers like Rubin and Simmons, combined with an original artist like Public Enemy, that allowed for the love connection. One without the other, and perhaps Public Enemy would not had been able to affect the music and culture in the ways they did—from being the soundtrack to the Spike Lee movie *Do the Right Thing*, to the kid in *Terminator 2* wearing a Public Enemy T-shirt. Public Enemy and Def Jam connected because like-minded individuals recognized a common goal.

When you are looking for the ideal label to support your music, you must have a grasp of what the label is about. Certainly, the majors have become somewhat generic when it comes to their aesthetic values—signing whatever will make the most money. And yet, even within the majors, there are A&R people who have strong visions and base their signings upon them. It is your job to know which people have visions that jibe with your type of music. This is crucial to remember, as you seek to find the right label.

Ask yourself where your music fits. Which labels are putting out records that are similar to your music? Which people may see that your art, in all of its originality, can connect with an audience and transcend all of the barriers of cookie-cutter A&R mentality? You will have a far greater chance of success if you can surround yourself with others who have a similar creative bent. How do you figure out where these people are? Well, as we will see in the remainder of the book, the prime challenge ahead of you is to build a web of connections from which to draw support, exposure, and information. As your music begins to spread, you will be exposed to more and more people who know other people. If you spread your net wide enough, and your music is good enough, you will eventually find someone with the vision to know just what to do with your music. It will, of course, help if you are as great as PE. "Bring the noise," indeed.

Case 3: Bob Dylan

How Dylan got his record deal

On Dylan's underrated, post-motorcycle-accident album, *John Wesley Harding*, he sings, of the titular character, "He was never known to make a foolish move." In some ways, this line can be seen as Dylan singing about himself. Is it true or not? Well, this last case study will show that, at least when it comes to getting a deal, it is true.

One caveat, before we discuss Dylan. I know many people who have entire walls of their homes stacked floor to ceiling with books and articles on Dylan, so it is safe to say that this is a story told many times. It should also be noted that many of these books contradict each other, as do many people who are interviewed. Dylan, as we will see, has a real penchant for making his trail an elusive one. I have tried to grab the essence of the specific period of time around his signing in as accurate a manner as possible. That said, there are many inconsistencies in the Dylan lore.

Dylan's middle-class childhood in Minnesota, with his time spent listening to hillbilly radio and loving Hank Williams, quickly morphed into an obsession with the inchoate spirit of rock 'n' roll. As rock became more of a mainstream phenomenon, it lost some of the early rebellious appeal it had for Robert Zimmerman (as he had not yet changed his name). Dylan, always being ahead, had moved away from rock as it had moved away from him. In college, at the University of Minnesota, Dylan embraced the emerging folk ethos. He began playing in 1960 at a local coffeehouse called the Ten O'Clock Scholar. He was occasionally billed as Bob Dillon (after Matt Dillon from the TV show *Gunsmoke*; he later changed the spelling to "Dylan").

It is important to note a few things here about Dylan's early development. The first is that he found a community in which to perform his music. Dinkytown, Minnesota is never going to be considered a hotbed of culture and creativity (sorry, Dinkytown residents), yet Dylan managed to find a place in which he could expose people to his music and gain feedback. The second point here is that Dylan understood the importance of persona. He knew somehow that his music was more likely to be embraced if he was seen to be an embodiment of that music. He understood the very real connection that audiences, A&R people, and others in the industry make between the person singing the songs and the songs themselves. His matched his persona to his musical output.

Like Cobain and Def Jam, Dylan did not invent his particular image or genre; rather, he refined and perfected it. While it had been Hank Williams, and later, the early rock 'n' rollers that started him on his path, it was really Woody Guthrie who lit a fire under his heels. Guthrie—with his folk ethos and rock 'n' roll spirit—was everything Dylan loved rolled into one.

Like all good acolytes of any religion, Dylan had a pilgrimage to make. In January of 1961, Dylan arrived in New York City to pay respects to his spiritual mentor. He played for Guthrie, who was hospitalized at the time.

This journey to New York to visit Guthrie resulted in Dylan not only finding his hero, but finding his own spiritual home. He followed his muse, and it had led him to his ideal musical environment. Consciously or otherwise, Dylan realized that he needed to be part of a musical community that was more active than what he had found in Minnesota.

Once in Greenwich Village, Dylan inhabited it with a vengeance. He played somewhere virtually every night: The Café Wha?, the Lion's Den, the Commons, the Folklore Center, Gerde's Folk City. He slept where he could—clubs, couches, and floors.

While he was refining his image and persona through his invented biography and his emulation of Woody Guthrie, he was not integrating seamlessly into the Greenwich Village folk world of the time. He didn't quite play by the established rules and mores of the scene at the time. Nevertheless, he worked to ingratiate himself with those in it. For example, Dylan asked Joan Baez, one of the stars of the early folk scene, if he could play her a song, after a chance meeting. He then suggested that she might want to record it.

It was not just Baez that Dylan tried to "network" with. In fact, it was another artist, Carolyn Hester, who had already managed to secure a record deal, who led to Dylan securing his own.

Hester asked Dylan to play harmonica on her record, which was being produced by John Hammond. The day of the recording session, coincidentally or otherwise, the *New York Times* ran a positive review of a Dylan performance. Whether it was the review, the performance during the recording session, his growing reputation, the fact that Hammond's son—a 19-year-old Dylan fan—had told his father about him, or all of the above, very soon thereafter, Bob Dylan was a Columbia recording artist. He remains a Columbia recording artist to this day.

While it seems obvious in hindsight that Dylan was going to get signed, given his ridiculous talent, there was quite a process that he went through on his way to a record deal. This process involved Dylan not only defining and redefining his musical style and persona, but also required him to move across the country in order to find a milieu in which his music had a chance to be embraced. This required him to network within this community with not just the other performers, but the club bookers, writers, and all others, whom he believed might be able to help him achieve the goal of getting a deal. While all this took perseverance, it ultimately took real belief in himself and his work to bear the struggles and the rejection (both the Elektra and Folkways labels passed on him before Columbia signed him), which is endemic to this process.

Summary

So there you have it. Three very different case studies from different times and different genres.

Yet there were obvious similarities between them, the most significant being that each believed that their musical vision was undeniably great and should be exposed on a wider level. This belief fueled their determination to make their success possible.

The remainder of this book presents pragmatic concepts and tools to help you get signed. It cannot give you the one thing you need beyond all others—the belief that what you are doing is undeniably great must come from within. But when you combine this belief with the practical approaches I suggest, you will truly have a chance to seal the deal.

Workshop

Which successful artists in your music's genre started out in your own geographic area? What can you find out about them? Where did they do their early recording or performing? Do you know someone who knows someone who knows them? How can you make contacts in this circle?

3

Demo Track Selection and Sequencing: Start with the Songs

Before you even think about recording songs, you must choose which ones to include on your demo. This is not as simple as it sounds. Picking your songs effectively means you must first understand and appreciate how your demo will be listened to. Once you have this insight, you will see how important it is that your demo is presented clearly and concisely. The good news is that you only have to choose three or four songs. The bad news is that you better choose wisely because you don't have much time.

How A&R People Listen to Demos

When A&R people listen to an unsolicited demo—one that does not arrive by personal acquaintance, as in a manager, lawyer, or other artist—the listening circumstances are far less than ideal. A&R people rarely sit in vacuum-sealed rooms with no distractions. Instead, our phones are ringing, people are walking into our offices asking us questions, and we're trying to eat some kind of lunch.

> *Demo listening sessions occur when the stack of demos reaches a certain height, usually measured by its likelihood of toppling over.*
>
> **—Peter Lubin, Veteran A&R Executive**

We certainly wouldn't be *just* listening to demo tapes. A&R people seem to always have to be doing more than one thing. Eating lunch is so far down on the list of priorities that if we have enough time to eat, then we're probably already feeling guilty, and when we're feeling guilty, we are more likely to try to make progress on some of the other things that are making us feel guilty—like those huge stacks of unlistened-to demos. Most likely, we are grumpy, because at this point, with the way the record business is, everyone in it is grumpy. And certainly, we are focusing on something else, like writing e-mail.

So your demo better be pretty amazing, if it's going to pull us away from all of these distractions and make us go, "Hold on a second, what is that?" If there is something so potent that it knocks through all the distraction, we really will shut everything else out and listen.

Additionally, the process that most A&R people use to listen to demos isn't as asinine as it seems, at first. In fact, this process gives the demo a fair and realistic chance, and it allows us to be forthright and honest with its creator. And while this may not be as "nice" as if I said that we give our undivided attention to every demo, it actually is a much more compassionate and kind way of assessing what we're listening to, in the long run.

Hear me out. If you think that listening to demos in the manner described above is disrespectful to the music's creator, or that it doesn't give the songs a fair chance, try thinking of it this way. A&R people actually care about the people that make demos. Artists are our lifeblood. Without you, there would be no music to sell. For that reason alone, we are far more predisposed to listen—even if it's only with half an ear—than the person who is in the car with the radio on and the kids screaming. We are also more predisposed to listen than are the people who program the radio stations. Radio programmers don't want to (or are not allowed to) play anything that would scare off potential listeners (and hence advertisers), and therefore, they can never program anything that isn't familiar to the average listener—that is, anything new. And A&R people are more likely to listen than are the poor reviewers for *Rolling Stone*, who have to choose one of the 700 albums they receive each week to review. Because

There is no common process for listening to demos. It can take a long time, particularly with material that finds its way here without an introduction. I listen in the office, but am often distracted. I listen at home, but am often distracted. I listen in the car—even though I live in New York and am rarely in a car—and find it to be the least distracting venue of all. The lower part of the brain is occupied with things like steering and braking, leaving the upper reaches of the brain free to concentrate on the music. The best listening experience I know.

—David Bither, Senior Vice President, Nonesuch Records

they have to sell magazines, they are almost definitely going to write about someone that people have heard about. Do you see what I'm saying? There's so much music out there. People aren't going to listen unless it's something they already know or unless it absolutely cuts through.

Of course, it is not just A&R people that listen in this manner. Do you really think that the guy who books the local club is going to turn off the lights, lock the doors, unplug the phone, light some incense, recline in a supine position, place the headphones on his head, and then press play and eagerly await the dulcet tones of your demo? Come on. This just isn't going to happen. Therefore, the same rules apply to virtually everyone (except your mom) who will be listening to your demo.

The way most A&R people listen to demos is reflective of the way the real world listens (or doesn't listen). If it's able to cut through and get an A&R person's attention while we're in the middle of dozens of other things, that means it may also be able to get the attention of a radio programmer or a reviewer, and ultimately, the public.

The Importance of Song Sequence: Put Your Best Song Forward

This is why it is so crucial to choose the right songs to include on your demo—and more specifically, to choose the right song to go first on your demo. Ideally, you will have a hard time determining which song should be first because all of your songs are great, but choose you must.

Let me say this loudly, ahem: You must pick your strongest, hookiest, most immediate, most representative song to be first on your demo.

This seems obvious but I can't tell you the number of demos that I've received where the third or fourth song, or even the second, is far better and more immediate than the first. Nine times out of ten, I never get to those later songs. The sad reality is that if the first song doesn't grab me, it's "game over," and on to the next demo.

I imagine there are many reasons why people choose not to put their strongest or most immediate song first. Perhaps it has something to do with setting a mood or showing the dynamic range of the band. But I guarantee you that if you have fifteen minutes of Pink Floyd spacey psychedelia at the beginning of the demo, you are going to piss off anyone who is trying to gauge what is going on with the band. Now, of course, if what you do is Pink Floydesque psychedelia, then by all means, have at it from track number 1. However, if you are a pop band, please, please do not hide your three-minute pop songs behind fifteen minutes of vague psychedelia.

Also, don't confuse what I'm saying. If you are an artist that writes subtle, low-key music, that is fine. I'm not suggesting that you must have some sonic wallop at the beginning of a demo in order to get the listener's attention. Just put the song that most immediately reflects what it is that you do at the beginning. I will *occasionally* get to track 2 of a demo. But I will only get to track 2 if there was something captivating about track 1, and I will only discover something captivating about track 1 if it happens quickly. (That's how I know that track 2 is sometimes better than track 1, smarty-pants. Now get back to your LSAT prep course.) This may sound harsh or un-artistic, but the reality is you must introduce what it is that you do as quickly as humanly possible.

How quickly does this have to happen, you ask? Well, when you are considering whether a song should be first, make sure that it sums up and conveys what you do in the first ninety seconds of the song. That's right buddy, ninety seconds, and preferably sooner. Sounds like not a lot of time, but count it off. The bonobo monkey can start a family in less time than that. Ninety seconds certainly should give you plenty of time to convey what you do.

As you go about the process of selecting songs for your demo, look closely to see which ones really fulfill this mandate. For instance, if your band has a great vocalist with a terrific range, and that is what separates your band from all the rest, then by all means, make sure this vocal is evidenced within the demo's first ninety seconds. If you are the greatest guitar player in the world, and your pyrotechnics set you apart from all of the other guitar players, then make sure you play something that will knock my socks off in the first ninety seconds of the first song. If you are a rapper who is able to convey all the evils of the postmodern age in your rhymes, and that is what makes you different from all the other rappers out there, then what do you do? That's right, tell me about these ills in the first ninety seconds of the first song. And, by all means, if you are a pop band who writes great hooky choruses, then, as the man said, "Don't bore us, get to the chorus." And if that man were me, he'd add "...in the first ninety seconds of the first song."

As I write this, unfortunately, I feel very much like "the man"—the enemy of the artist and creativity. I don't like this feeling, especially because it's so untrue. This advice is not meant to cheapen or degrade your art or to make it seem as though I think there is some formula to writing a song that has an impact. It is certainly not meant to put a moratorium on creativity or originality. It's just that if you do something that is really creative or original in the first ninety seconds of your demo, you will stand a far greater chance of having your whole demo listened to than will someone who either is not original or creative, or worse, saves their originality or creativity for minute number 7 of track number 4.

If all of this seems very un-artistic and like it is reducing your music to product, I must remind you that by the act of sending your demo to record labels, you are buying into the culture that defines your music as product. If you don't want to accept this, then don't submit your demo. If you choose to submit it, just realize what your opportunity time is. It will give you the best chance to get a record deal, which will then allow you to do what most artists want to do: create great art that will affect the culture in a positive way. In order to have this opportunity, you must reduce your art to a manageable, bite-sized demo that is easily digestible by the average, harried A&R person, club booker, reviewer, or whoever.

How Many Songs, and Why?

Once you've determined which song begins the demo, you need only worry about choosing two or three more that have the same qualities as the first. This doesn't mean that you should have two or three identical songs on the demo. In fact, it's a good idea to mix it up a bit with tempo, dynamics, and other things that show that you are not completely one-dimensional. However, remember, the demo is not an album, and it should not have some sort of narrative arc (again, unless song-cycles or concept albums are what you do; Lord knows we need more interconnected songs about the difficult socio-political relations between hobbits and elves). All of the songs need to stand on their own, and they need to be clear, concise examples of what your music is all about.

> *Less is more.*
>
> *Three great songs can be enough reason to contact an artist and ask for more, see a show, etc.*
>
> **—David Bither**
> **(Nonesuch)**

Why Less is More

Not only do you not need more than two or three more songs for the demo, but if you include more, you may in fact be hurting your chances of getting a deal. Here's why. If I get hooked on the first song, I'm going to listen to the second song. Even if the second song doesn't do anything for me, I'm going to forgive it for being lame and move on to the third song, because I got hooked by the first song (which so rarely happens). And even if the third song is lame, I'm still going to be rooting for the band or the artist because the first song got me.

Rooting for the band or artist is critically important because it means that I may go the next step: making contact and requesting more songs. (One thing to be clear on, here, is that if that song that hooked me had been second instead of first, I promise you that I never would have gotten to the second song.)

Once I'm hooked and I try to get in touch with you, we begin to develop a relationship. I cannot overstate how crucial this relationship element is to getting signed. This is why the number of songs you put on your demo has a very direct connection to your chances of getting to the "relationship" stage. Think about it. If you put twelve songs on a demo and the only one I like is the first, no matter how much I love that first song, if the other eleven are no good, I'm going to be forced to think it was a fluke, and will toss the demo. I probably won't reach out to you, and therefore, there is no chance to begin having a relationship. However, if the demo only has three our four songs on it, and I love the first song and don't care for the other two or three, I will probably still reach out to you to hear more. This gives us a chance to speak (or e-mail), which gives you a chance to sell yourself to me in other ways, like telling me about live shows. In short, it allows for a deeper connection to start.

There's a lesson here: Leave them wanting more. When you are selecting songs to record for your demo, remember that you don't need more than four songs, and three will do. If there's something great in that first song, regardless of what the other two or three songs on the demo sound like, you've got a good shot of getting a call. If there are twelve mediocre songs, no one's going to get beyond the first song anyway. If the first song is great and so are songs 2, 3, and 4, well, we're on our way to making a deal. A little bit truly goes a long way here. Just make sure that you present it quickly, emphatically, and concisely.

There are two schools of thought
regarding how stylistically diverse
your demo should be.
One that says it is vitally important
to commit to one style and mine it
as deeply and completely as possible.
Another would argue that it is
equally valid to explore
as many styles as the artist can
successfully command.
I think, at least initially,
the first argument probably wins out.

—Peter Lubin, A&R

FROM THE FIELD **Jeff Price**
Co-Founder, General Manager,
President of spinART Records

How many demos to you get on an average week—solicited or otherwise?

About twenty to fifty.

Are there any sine qua non's that an artist must have before they even think about looking for a record deal?

Yes, be willing to tour, understand how things work so we can set realistic expectations, have patience, and be willing to sleep on floors and eat Taco Bell. Owning a van is a plus.

How many songs does a demo need?

Three to five.

Any tips on which songs to put on the demo?

A well-written song, which might not work on radio but does highlight songwriting, instrumental proficiency, as well as the "single."

How "professional-sounding" does the demo need to be?

Just get across what represents the band. A great song can be recorded on a Tascam 4-track but still stand out.

Is there any particular order the artist should put the songs in?

Start with a song that is catchy yet unique (if ya got one).

What should the artist send you?

A CDR and a bulleted fact sheet. Do not give us descriptions of the music. We're looking for info like your age, where you are from, do you tour, what markets you have hit, any sales under your belt, a URL address for more info, etc. Make sure your name, phone number, and e-mail address are on the actual CDR or cassette.

Workshop

What's the best thing about your band—the element that separates you from all the rest? Is it your lead singer's range? Your ability to write good melodies? Your rhythm section?

Look at all your songs, and determine which one best presents this in the first ninety seconds. If none of them do, work on a new arrangement that does, or even write something new.

Choose your five best songs—the ones that best represent your band's strengths. Determine which one has the most immediate impact. Do this by playing them for friends, or better, judging audience reaction at shows.

Three of these songs should make it onto your demo. Which order works best?

4

Recording Your Demo: Getting It Down

Once you've chosen the songs, it's just a matter of committing them to some sort of recordable medium, and you will be on your way to completing your demo. The goal is to produce your actual demo CDs in the most efficient way possible. This requires you to wrestle the beast with two heads: sound quality and cost.

> *The thing about a demo is that it should be done quickly and cheaply.*
> *You're trying to catch the idea.*
> *It should be done like a sketch, not a painting.*
> *You should be able to record a presentable demo with three or four songs for between $2,000 and $5,000.*
>
> **—Paul Q. Kolderie, Producer/ Engineer**

Remember, the demo demonstrates what the artist is all about. It isn't a fully formed record, and when you are creating it, you must keep the differences in mind. They are lower budget, simpler, and shorter than the recordings you make to be released commercially. Sound quality does not have to be as high. Knowing this allows you to focus your search for the appropriate recording options.

There was a time, and it wasn't that long ago, when if you wanted to record a demo that was on a sonic level above putting a boom box in the middle of a room and pressing record and play at the same time, you had very, very few options. You could toil for years trying to squeeze sonic fidelity out of a home 4-track recorder that—for most types of music—is not capable of creating demos of good enough audio quality to submit to labels. If you happened to be an heiress or date an heiress, you could spend the money to build a high caliber home studio. Or, you could do what most did, and still do: go into a studio to record.

Today, there are more and better options, but the one that is most often chosen is still the latter. In this chapter, we will look at the process of recording a demo in a professional studio and in a home studio to determine which is the best option for you.

You have to be willing to put up the cash for the project. Get another job if you have to. I meet so many talented people that sit around year after year waiting for someone to drop by with a briefcase full of money, whining about not being able to do anything because they don't have a deal. Why should any label invest hundreds of thousands of dollars in you if you won't even come up with a fraction of that? Never expect anyone to champion your music more than you do. If you let them, it won't be your project anymore. It's your music—you should be willing to take the risk. If not . . . keep it as a hobby.

—David Henry, Producer and Studio Owner

The Recording Studio

First the good news: going into a studio usually will result in sound quality that is acceptable for demo submission. But time at a professional studio is expensive, no two ways about it. And the sad reality is that booking studio time to record your demo, if you have no prior studio knowledge or experience, often does not guarantee you a clear and effective representation of your music. It does guarantee that you will spend significant dough in the process, regardless of the result. The process is also fraught with other potential pitfalls.

Issues of Recording in a Studio

Recording at a studio requires you to contend with the nerves that occur while attempting to perform your music in an unfamiliar environment, and in front of an engineer whom you most likely don't know. Also, most artists forget that this engineer is not a producer. He is there to get the sounds of the music down on tape as efficiently as possible—not to help you arrange your songs, or even critique them. While you would like his approval or comments regarding your music, this is not his job. Even if it were, these poor souls are often so fried from recording demos twenty-four hours a day that they have most likely lost control of the muscles in their mouth that enable speaking and are therefore unable to let you know what—if anything— they think of your music. As positive feedback is one of the most important elements to successful recording, the lack of it can create a difficult and unproductive dynamic. It is nearly impossible to perform at a high level if you are not confident. If you feel the engineer doesn't like your music, it can create issues of confidence that can result in poor performance.

Another large problem you face when you enter a studio to record a demo is the stress of knowing that the clock is always running, and the process is costing you money that you most likely don't have to spend. Having to ask yourself, "Why, oh why, is it taking so long to find out where the hiss is coming from," and "Am I really paying for the time it is taking while the engineer takes the board apart (again) to try and find the hiss?" and knowing that the answer is, "Yes, I am," makes it more difficult for you to focus on what you are there to do: record a great demo.

Lastly, and most importantly, most artists focus on the act of writing or performing great songs, not on the technical aspects related to capturing those songs on recordable media. They often don't know what all those pretty little machines with the flashing lights do. (Quick, tell me what the Blonder Tongue Audio Baton does.) In short, you are largely at the mercy of the engineer when it comes to the actual "sound" of your demo. Don't like your vocals drenched in reverb? Too bad, brother man, that's the engineer's "signature" style.

I don't mean to generalize. Of course, not all—or even most—demo studios are bad. In fact, for the most part, engineers like making music and like helping artists get the sound they want. Above is a worst-case scenario, which lists things that *might* go wrong. But virtually every band I have ever worked with has at least one (and usually more) horror stories about recording their demo in a studio. Sadly, it often only takes one bad experience to destroy a band's momentum, and often the band. This is not usually the fault of the studio or the engineer. More often than not, a band with no prior studio experience will leave with a CD that is something less than they had hoped for, going in.

A Schedule for Making the Most of Your Studio Experience

The largest issue at professional studios will be the cost. Booking studio time can become real expensive real fast. There are ways in which to maximize your dollars and leave the studio with a very effective demo. Below, I outline what I believe to be a good template for recording an effective demo.

This schedule doesn't cover all types of music. If you are a singer-songwriter hoping to get a good recording of your vocals and guitar, it will be overkill. Conversely, if your recording requires many outside session players, with complex orchestral passages that require rehearsal before the session, the method below will most likely not provide you with enough time. However, there are certain aspects that are typical of all demo sessions. Following this six-day schedule will greatly increase your chances of leaving the studio with a three- or four-song demo suitable for submission to a record company.

Before you come in to the studio, rehearse with a click track (drum machine) for tempo. A drummer who can't play with a click can't play. It means that they're not listening and who wants to play with a musician who only listens to himself. This doesn't mean you have to record with the click but at least hear what your song sounds like with a steady groove. You might have been slowing the chorus down and never known it. Rehearse at low volumes so you can hear your pitch, chords, and arrangements. It's always great hearing two guitar players hitting major and minor chords at the same time. Or record the songs on a handheld cassette or camcorder. They don't lie.

—David Henry, Producer and Studio Owner

Day 1. Setting Up

Setting up instruments and microphones usually takes a full day. This first day of the recording session is the most regimented, as there is a clear progression in which things should happen. The timing on the other days will be more flexible, from hour to hour, but on the first day, everything should be carefully planned out, in order to make the best use of everybody's time. Here's a schedule that will help you make sure that you get set up and achieve good sound levels in a single day.

A note on who exactly needs to be present at the studio: as you will see, there is a lot of time in the studio spent sitting around waiting to play. Because of this, a certain studio fatigue can set in, which can really affect the performance. I understand that most artists want to be there the whole time, whether they are recording or not, but try to pace yourself. For instance, it's a good idea, if you are a band, for everyone to visit the studio and meet the engineer prior to the recording session beginning. This way, everyone knows what the place is like, and won't feel the need to necessarily hang around while drum sounds are being gotten. Really, for a large part of this time, only the drummer needs to be there. Every band and artist are different, and some will perform better when the entire band is there—even during bass overdubs. But frequently, it's helpful to the overall project not to have the entire band hanging around the studio when they're not working.

Getting away from it can give you perspective so that when you return you will have a clearer viewpoint.

Load In: 12 P.M. to 1 P.M. Try to start your session as early as possible, though your studio may be reluctant to start much before noon. It's a late-night type of existence, after all. So, assuming you are able to either take off work or get the studio for a weekend (weekend and day rates are almost always more expensive than weekday and night rates), you will probably begin loading your gear into the studio at around noon. So, you pull up the van and start setting up your drums, amps, guitars, and so on in the studio. Of course, this is not a cardinal rule, and different artists (and studios) prefer to work differently. My advice would be to start no later than noon if possible.

Setup—Not Lunch: 1 P.M. to 2 P.M. If you are starting your session around lunchtime (or dinnertime), eat beforehand, rather than at the studio. Remember, you are being billed for all of the time that you have reserved the studio, whether you use it or not. While a seven-layer burrito is truly something to savor and not rush through, enjoy it before you get to the studio. Trust me, eating breaks can eat up a ton of studio time.

Instead, take this time to begin organizing yourself. Make sure all of your gear is in proper working order. Cords and batteries for effects boxes are notorious for crapping out at exactly the wrong time. Now is the time to do yet another test on things like this. (The first test should have occurred the night before the session.) It's not a bad idea to get your guitars and basses in tune at this point. Certainly, you will need to do this prior to every performance you record, but this is also a time when strings seem to break. Better to have them break now, while you still have time to change them and stretch them out a bit before you must perform, than to be dealing with it while recording.

Generally, take this time to get organized both physically and mentally. You are here (and are paying a pretty penny) for one specific purpose—to create an effective demo in the shortest time period possible. Being focused is critical.

Drum Sounds: 2 P.M. to 6 P.M. In my experience, it is impossible to get drums set up and sounding decent in less than three hours, and it usually takes longer. One way to expedite the process is to make sure that your drums are tuned before you go into the studio. And while you will probably need to make minor tuning adjustments, due to the jostling or temperature changes during the load in, the drums should be pretty close to the way you want them before you arrive. Why pay for the studio time when you could have done it at home for free? Of course, drums sounds are not something to rush through, being that they are the foundation. Getting good drum sounds is essential to a good recording. There are infinite variables to getting drum sounds. It's an art. At a certain point, you will realize that you have found a decent sound, though it might not be the exact kick sound that Lars got on Metallica's black album. You should, however, work with the engineer to get it where you want. This may take longer than you think.

Bass Sounds: 7 P.M. to 8 P.M. The bass setup will move much more quickly. However, it does take time. It can become complicated if you decide that the studio gear is superior to your own bass rig. You may be tempted to try for a good tone by experimenting with the studio's different heads and cabinets, and so on. All of this takes time. Avoid this temptation. You know your gear, and while different gear (especially of a good quality) will often sound great at first, you will often find that it loses its luster on repeated listening, and you will regret not having stuck with what you knew. That said, one time-saving trick I've used repeatedly for recording an electric bass is to run it through a device called a SansAmp (which most studios have) and plug directly into the mixing board. This will get you a great sound, and you won't have to worry about miking a bass cabinet.

Guitar Sounds: 8 P.M. to 10 P.M. Guitarists with options are very dangerous. Unfortunately, most demo studios have guitars and amps in abundance. I say "unfortunately" not because it's a bad thing that they have them, but because they are impossible for guitarists to resist. No rock guitar player can refrain from at least trying out the Flying V through the Vox AC 30. Now, there are few better sounds than this combination, for certain types of music, but like all gear, they really only start to perform for you once you know their idiosyncrasies. This takes time—far more time than you have in the demo studio. Also, as with the case of the bass gear, just because it's new to your ears, it will necessarily sound cool while in the studio, but this does not mean it will hold up after you are out of the studio.

My advice is to record with your own gear: the gear you know and use to practice with.

Whatever gear you choose to use, it will take some time for you to get your tone right and the amps properly miked.

Dinner: 10 P.M. to 11 P.M. Again, be very careful with your meal breaks. Sometimes, they are just what you need to clear you heads, and will let you return to recording to get a great performance. More often they are time sucks. Of course, you need to eat. But stage your meals and breaks so that once the drummer's sounds are together, he can eat; then the guitar player, etc. This may mean that you do not eat at exactly the time above. Do buy dinner for the engineer and any assistants.

Miscellaneous Other Instrument Setup: 11 P.M. to 12 P.M. This could be a keyboard, harmonica, autoharp or whatever. It will take you an hour. Remember the cardinal rule when recording a demo: It's just a demonstration, so don't go overboard with the "colorings." A well-placed coloring instrument will go a long way to making your demo stand out, but given your time limitations, you need to really prepare in advance—prior to going into the studio—to make sure you know just how you will accomplish this. Studios frequently have many cool and exotic instruments kicking around. Don't be seduced by them. If you don't know how to play a dulcimer, the demo studio is the wrong place to learn.

Scratch Vocals/Headphone Mix: 12 A.M. to 1 A.M. Hearing vocals while you play helps everyone to get the right feel for the songs. Also, you will all want to hear and see each other. This requires a headphone mix and a scratch-vocal mic setup. The headphone mix is different than the final mix. Everyone will want to hear the bass, drums, and themselves most prominently. Achieving this can be a pain, and it often takes longer than you would think to get a mix that will please all band members. Even when everyone is happy, it is very unnatural to play with headphones, at first. Most musicians need time to get used to playing with headphones so that they can give a good performance. But you must really work to get a good headphone mix.

At 1 A.M., my advice is to stop and start fresh the next day. However, most artists will not want to work this long and hard and not record something. Most likely, everyone will be tired, and you won't get much of a performance, but if you must, bang through a song. Better to start the next day.

Day 2. Basic Tracks

Recording the basic tracks is a really fun time. Try to get basics (drums, bass, rhythm guitar, and scratch vocal, but no overdubs) done for four songs during this session. Remember, three or four songs are all you need for your demo. Prior to entering the studio, you will, of course, have rehearsed and re-rehearsed these four songs. I advise having a well-rehearsed fifth song too, so that if you can't quite get one to sound right, you will be prepared with a backup.

As you record the basics, take breaks, listen to playback, and try and keep the energy up. Avoid a prolonged dinner break, but some sort of break is a good idea.

The key with basic tracks is to try to get a real solid drum sound and performance. Everything else can be overdubbed, but the drums need to be solid. Be prepared to work for hours on each song. Try to not lose the spirit of the song in favor of perfection. Remember, no A&R person is going to be sitting there with a metronome checking to see if you sped up during the chorus.

Recording should be thorough but not laborious. Otherwise, everybody gets tired, frustrated, and bored. It's hard to get a drummer to give you a fresh exciting track if you made them pound on the snare for three hours while the engineer tries out fifteen different compression ratios. You should find an engineer/producer who works quickly and keeps the sessions fun. If the band is having a great time in the studio, the tracks will sound that way. You should have a song finished in a day or day and a half. Usually, if it takes much longer than that, then you weren't ready to come in.

—David Henry, Producer and Studio Owner

Recording Media. On day 2, you will actually be recording. Before you arrived at the studio, you will have decided which recording medium you will use. Most likely, you will have three options: tape (expensive), ADATs (cheaper, but often unreliable), or—best—Pro Tools. If you're using Pro Tools, you won't have to worry about tape costs (though the studio might make you buy a hard drive for a couple of hundred bucks). I recommend that you avoid tape. Each reel only holds about twenty minutes of music. That's three or four takes of any given song. You will run up a huge bill if you insist on tape, or if the studio provides no other option. ADATs are digital media that look like VHS tapes. They hold more music, but are limited to eight tracks, unless they are synched together. Unfortunately, they don't always play nicely with each other, and you can spend a lot of time trying to get the buggers to sync up. Go with Pro Tools, if you can.

You should aspire to finish the night with at least two—if not all—of the basic tracks done. Then you will go home, and no matter how late it is, you will try to wake up your significant other and listen obsessively to the rough tracks. You will not be able to sleep because a thirty second snippet from one of the songs will be lodged so deeply in your cranium that it will stick out the back of your head and not allow you to lay flat against the pillow.

Day 3. Basic Tracks, Overdubs

Count on half of this day spent re-recording some of the basic tracks—the ones you thought were perfect yesterday but drove you crazy last night. You will also most likely struggle mightily with one particular song and not be able to get it quite right. Know when to cut bait, in these situations. After struggling for a while, you should either scrap it completely and just focus on the songs that went well, or try recording your backup song. If you keep working on a song that just won't come together, you risk jeopardizing the whole session.

The second half of this day should be spent beginning the overdub process, cleaning up the bass and rhythm guitar parts. Complete these overdubs on day 3, and you will be doing great.

Day 4. Overdubs

You should now start overdubbing the lead guitar tracks, and other instruments that bring dynamic to the songs, be they organs, strings, percussion, or whatever. Don't go overboard here. Use this time to really accentuate the strong points of the song. Remember that there will be setup involved for each of these instruments, which takes time.

Try to get some vocal takes done on the fourth day. It's not a good idea to save all of the vocals for one day. Doing so puts a lot of pressure on the vocalists. Not only do they have to get a good performance, but their voices have to hold up over numerous takes. Try to begin on day 4.

Day 5. Vocals, Vocals, Vocals.

Take the time necessary to nail the vocals—lead, harmony, and background. If you were able to record some on day 4, you should be in good shape. Try to set the mood—whatever that may be—to allow the vocalist to give a great performance. It's a tough and awkward thing to sing in a studio environment, and there's a lot of pressure. Do what you can to alleviate this. This may mean staying out of the control room while the vocalist is tracking. Of course, it may also mean sitting in the iso booth with a vocalist. It's different for every situation. Try to figure out what will work best for you and your vocalist(s), and then keep doing it until all the vocals are done. If you get on a roll, keep moving. Don't even listen to playback. Just keep rolling.

After day 5, you should have completed the vocals and rough mixes for three or four songs.

Day 6. Mixing

Try to take a couple days off before you start mixing, if this is possible. Most studios don't want to divide the time up, but if you can, do this. This time will help you to get a little space from the songs and approach them with a fresher set of ears when you come back. Of course, taking too much time (more than a couple of days) can be a very bad move, as you will start wanting to re-track (or rewrite) songs. Can't do that in a studio setting.

The way it will most likely work is that the engineer will get a good rough mix together on his own. Often, they will mix without the artist in the studio so that they don't have to listen to all the annoying comments. Once they've gotten a "rough" mix together, you will be invited back in to listen and make comments. It is very reasonable to mix three or four songs in one day. Take your time, try making subtle changes for different mixes. One trick I've learned is that if you're really struggling with a mix, have the engineer start taking things away (mute the rhythm guitar, for example), and try to get to the essence of the song. Then start adding stuff back in.

Once you have a mix, listen to it in the studio, but also bring a boom box or Walkman. A good place to listen is on a car stereo. Studio monitors should not be the only thing you listen to your mixes on.

You should leave this session with your songs mixed and burned onto a CD. Take your tapes or ADATs or Pro Tools disk. Tip the engineer. Then sleep for a week.

Having produced many records and overseen a ton of demo sessions, I've lived variations of this schedule many times. You may be able to do it in four days, or it could take you two weeks to accomplish what I've outlined, but expect six days. The key to making it work is to not be overambitious, either with the number of songs you try to record or the amount of sounds you try to put on those sings. Just remember that what you're recording is only a demonstration. It is geared to get you a deal that will allow you the time and resources to really show your stuff.

Costs Associated with Studios

The cost of this type of session would be around $4,000. That's figuring six days of studio time at $500 a day, and then tacking on $500 for a drive or tape (add $500 to $1,000 more if you use reel-to-reel tape as opposed to Pro Tools or ADATs), and some miscellaneous stuff like food and beer, hiring your friend to play cello, busting the studio's mandolin, and so on.

As I said before, this scenario applies to a fairly traditional band. If you're a singer-songwriter who is just recording vocals and guitar, it will be very different (and faster and cheaper) for you. If you are a rapper using samples that you've already programmed at home, you too will have a far different experience. But if you are a "band," in any sense of the word, be it a jazz combo or a salsa band, your experience will be similar to the one outlined above.

The real challenge of recording in a studio is largely time management. Much of the time you spend in the studio will be spent sitting around, waiting. It is during these times that you should eat. For example, while the drummer is getting his sounds together, the vocalist can grab lunch. Also, when you're sitting idle in the studio, schedule things out. Maybe just the guitarist and the engineer can show up at the beginning of the first overdub day. They can set up (miking the amps, getting the tones, locating the parts of the songs for the overdubs, etc.) while the other band members get some needed rest. Then, when the rest of the band arrives, they will be refreshed and able to contribute their opinions and be productive, rather than sitting idly by, waiting. Time management is the key to a successful recording session.

The real danger in recording at a professional studio is that there is very little room for error. If something doesn't go right—be it a bad engineer, a band member getting sick or being unable to get a part right, just general malaise, or whatever—you're out of luck. It's common for things to go wrong because the band isn't familiar with the studio dynamic. Bands that are new to the studio environment will not have the experience or ability to communicate in order to get things right.

Happily, there are other options.

You've got to start at home-based recording. It's really helpful for when you go into a professional studio to have home-based experience recording. I taught myself recording by starting at home.

—Paul Q. Kolderie, Producer/Engineer

Home Recording

Before I fill you in, I want you to get down on your hands and knees and begin supplicating and thanking whoever it is you thank when an astonishing twist of good fate befalls you. You should stay in this position until your knees hurt and you are faint from hunger. Then you should stay there for another day or two as a gesture of respect to all of us who came before you and didn't enjoy the technological revolution that is making you so lucky.

You are, of course, giving thanks for... computer-based home recording.

The advent of digital recording started taking hold in the mid 1990s. It is now so prevalent that it's hard to imagine that it ever wasn't there—and it is getting cheaper every minute. It will cost you roughly the same $4,000 as you would have spent in the studio as it does to buy your own recording gear. And having your own gear allows you to record whenever you want, for however long you want, until you get the desired track. In the studio, you had a short, fixed period of time where you "got what you got," once the money was gone.

If you feel that you have talent that makes you undeniably great, and you really aspire to be a professional musician who has a career writing, recording, performing, and releasing records over a significant part of your life, then consider putting together a home studio. Consider how this route is a much better idea than just handing over your money—and a large degree of your artistic control—to some studio owner. Of course, if you simply want to record some songs you've written to give to your friends and then move on to being an accountant or whatever, then, by all means, rent some studio time, take your chances, and get what you get. Or, if you just genuinely disdain computers, and don't have friends who are good with them, the demo studio may be for you.

The first and most important thing that occurs when you begin working in your own computer-based system is that you begin to understand the process of recording. As obvious as this sounds, it simply cannot be emphasized enough. As with every aspect of this business, the more you understand, the less likely you are to get taken advantage of, and the more likely you are to succeed. Buying your own recording equipment forces you to figure out how to use it. I can tell you, as a producer, it is a life-long quest to find the perfect combination of gear that will give you that perfect sound. The more you do it, the closer you get to understanding what tools will best translate the sound you hear in your head to the sound that you hear on your CD.

Then, when you ultimately do find yourself in a "real" studio, your home recording experience (and the lines between "home" and "studio" recording are becoming more and more blurry) will prepare you for your entry into the "real" studio. You will understand what is going on. You will have the vocabulary to explain how you want to get the sound that is in your head on to the tape. You will know what a compressor does. Being a recording artist today requires that you understand how sound is recorded. If you do not understand, you will have your sound manipulated in a manner that will—most likely—not be the way you would have done it yourself. No two ways about it.

Studio "Language"

As an artist, you do not want your creative output controlled by other people. Therefore you must be able to communicate—in an understandable, common language—with those people (engineers, producers, etc.) that have an effect on your music. If you can't speak the same language, you are left with few options to articulate how you feel about the sound other than saying things such as, "Yeah, I like that," or "No, that sounds like crap."

If you feel something sounds like crap, and the producer or engineer asks if you might articulate for them what you mean, you are left to try to describe it using words that don't really work at describing music. For example, you might hear too much reverb, but not knowing what reverb is, you are reduced to saying, "It sounds too squishy." After you got over the embarrassment of being a rocker who has been forced to use the word "squishy," chances are you are no closer to getting the problem fixed. Or you might say that the track sounds "too brittle," but rather than knowing that this was most likely caused by too much emphasis on the high-end EQ, you are forced to just say that it's "brittle." After you do this a few times, you realize that your initial statement of it sounding like crap is probably as articulate as you are going to get. In short, one of the benefits of learning how to record your own music is that it teaches you the language and vocabulary that allows you to effectively communicate when something sounds good or bad.

Having your own equipment also gives you the luxury of time. You will be hard pressed to find a studio worth its salt that charges less than $500 a day. (And that doesn't include the cost of tape, ADAT, or hard drives, which can easily tack on an additional couple of hundred of dollars). With that kind of money at stake, you really don't have time to try that backwards guitar solo that you just know will make this song a hit. You just can't do it. You also can't take twenty attempts to do a vocal, even though it may be that you need twenty takes to get warmed up properly, and take twenty-one is the keeper.

If you have your own gear, you can record when you want, for however long you need to get the job done. Additionally, you can try things out that you might not have had the time to try in the studio, or that you might have been reluctant to try because you didn't want the engineer looking sideways at you when you ask if you could mic up that trash can to use as a kick drum. (Ask Tom Waits about the relative merits of using non-standard percussion sometime. Or better yet, buy his Grammy-winning record *Bone Machine.*) And you do not want to be writing bridges to songs in the studio. Not only is it not cost effective, it is not a place conducive to creativity; there is just too much pressure. Having your own setup where you can get arrangements right before you go into the studio is a huge hedge against the vagaries of recording a demo in the studio.

Once you have this knowledge and vocabulary, you can use the engineer to really help you get what you are looking for, and you can then use the studio effectively. Most engineers are very good, and will be able to help you get the sound you want, but only once you can articulate it to them in a language they can understand. Until you can do that, there is no real way to communicate your vision. And no matter how much pot the engineer smoked that morning, he cannot read your mind (though, as Bill Hicks says, depending on what other drugs he's taken, he may be able to see through you).

Pro Tools

If you ask ten producers what their favorite home recording setup is, you'll probably get twelve answers. But if you push them on it, one name will come up over and over again: Pro Tools.

Pro Tools is a computer program made by a company called Digidesign. It was written for (and works best) on Macs, but more and more, it is able to run on PCs, as well. The main reason that producers or other experts in the field will tell you that Pro Tools is the way to go is because nearly everyone uses it. Most decent studios, in addition to an analog (i.e., tape) setup, will also have a Pro Tools setup.

This is important because it means that if you start something at home on your Pro Tools rig, and you need or want to go to a "real" studio (because they have better mics, or a grand piano, or whatever), you will be able to use the tracks that you started at home, rather than having to start from scratch. This is huge.

Think about it. This means that you can use your home setup to do all of the time-consuming things like creating loops, getting the perfect vocal, and working on arrangements. Then you can go into the "real" studio to use their more high-end gear. It really changes the dynamic. Of course, with Pro Tools, you may never need to leave your bedroom and go to these "real" studios. It is

> *I use Pro Tools every day.*
> *It's extremely powerful,*
> *cost effective, and still seems to be*
> *the industry standard.*
> *It's a real pain when you're using*
> *an alien format that no one else has.*
>
> **—David Henry, Producer and Studio Owner**

becoming more and more commonplace for even the most highfalutin of recording artists to forgo large parts of the recording process that previously involved the studio and record instead in their home studio. This is clearly the wave of the future (and largely the wave of the present).

It is far better for you to get in this mindset now. Don't piss away your advance money on poorly used studio time, when you could have done much of the recording at your house for a tenth of the cost. Instead, piss it away on flying in your significant other from Paris to solicit his or her opinions about your guitar solos.

Advantages of the Pro Tools Interface

Another reason that most producers and engineers will recommend Pro Tools is because its interface is very similar to that of an analog setup, with which most of them are already familiar. In other words, Pro Tools looks like a virtual recording studio. The interface is laid out the same way a recording console is, with faders and busses, channels, and more. And there are countless plug-ins developed to resemble outboard gear, such as EQs and compressors.

This kind of layout is wildly helpful because as you are learning to record on Pro Tools, you are also learning your way around a recording console and familiarizing yourself with outboard gear. While they're not exactly the same (familiarity with Pro Tools won't allow you to just walk in and use an SSL board), knowing the Pro Tools interface will greatly increase your understanding of more traditional recording consoles. This will help demystify the studio for you, and you will realize that you should not be intimidated when you go into one. This confidence level will improve your music, guaranteed.

Pro Tools Portability

An additional huge advantage to Pro Tools is its portability. As I write this on an airplane, as I fly from L.A. to Seattle, I could plug a mic into the Pro Tools interface (I'm using an Mbox—about as big as a paperback), boot up the Pro Tools software, and begin recording the adenoidal snoring of the fine gentleman next to me. Utilizing a plug-in, I could then make his snores huge-sounding by drenching them in reverb, and then slow them down to resemble the bass line of a huge pipe organ. Then I could position my mic so that it picked up the sounds of the screaming child seated directly behind me, record a few seconds, roll off the high end, and create a loop so that the child's keening now more closely resembles the sound of a pizzicato violin. Lastly, I could point the mic to my left and capture the thumping of the wailing child's sibling, who is currently kicking directly into my kidneys, and in so-doing, creating a not unpleasant tom-tom like rhythm. A few careful keystrokes later, I've got a "drum" loop. Now, I take all three sounds, and mix them together, and I've got quite the little rock band. If I wanted, I could mix it right up (and master it) in Pro Tools at 30,000 feet, burn a few CDs, and begin distributing my music to my fellow passengers on the plane, who I believe, adequately fit the bill of a captive market.

While recording the found sounds of an airplane may not be your thing (though you may want to consider it), my point is that with a fairly decent laptop, mics, and Pro Tools, you have a portable studio that can compete with what used to require a semi and mountains of equipment.

I'll lay out the approximate costs to create your own airplane symphony using the gear I mentioned:

High-end laptop	$ 2500
Pro Tools Mbox (which includes LE software)	500
Good mic	250
Mic cable	35
Headphones	100
Total	**$ 3385**

This is pretty hard to beat. Obviously, you won't use the computer purely for Pro Tools. You'll also use it to keep your mailing list, generate fliers, keep contact lists, write song lyrics, etc. You can certainly spend more money on mics, and other outboard gear (such as mic pre-amps), and I encourage you to do so.

The Right System for You

This is not a book on the art of home recording, nor is it an advertisement for Pro Tools. I happen to use and like Pro Tools, and more importantly, so do the majority of studios out there, but it is not for everyone. Pro Tools—like all recording gear—has limitations. For example, the number of tracks you can record simultaneously at one time is very limited on the entry-level Pro Tools models. Before you plunk down your hard-earned money on any recording system, you need to do the research required to determine if it will suit your needs. Read as much material as you can about recording. There are plenty of magazines and books. Talk to people who have home systems, and try them out. Talk to engineers at studios. Then make your decision based on what works best for you.

Just expose yourself to the art of recording. Simply doing the research will give you experience. There is no better way to learn. As your career develops and you begin using "real" studios and outside producers and engineers, it will be the things that you taught yourself that will be the most valuable and allow you to truly maximize the process.

Home Recording Tips

As you are recording—be it on Pro Tools or some other system—there are some things to keep in mind:

1. Avoid the temptation to make your demo sound more "professional" by drenching it in reverb. It doesn't sound professional. Most producers hate overuse of reverb and use it very sparingly. If a demo comes in slathered in reverb, it usually says to me that the band is trying to hide some weakness.
2. Avoid hissy sounding recordings. If you're using Pro Tools, this won't be an issue. But if you're making your demo on a 4-track or some other cassette-based medium, you really have to work on your recording technique, so that you can get as clear a recording as possible. This means that you will most likely not be able to record the whole band, if that's what you do. The process of bouncing tracks down results in an overly hissy recording that will be perceived as amateur sounding. It is incredibly distracting to listen through the hiss to get at the songs. Most people won't take the time.
3. Avoid wild volume fluctuations between your tracks. Most likely, you'll be "comping" (combining) tracks together from various different recording sessions. Try to make them sound somewhat uniform. While you shouldn't pay to have your demo "mastered" (the final stage in the recording process where lengths between songs are inserted, and volumes are leveled), you should work to get the volumes of the different songs uniform and the spaces between the songs at some reasonably uniform time interval. Anything less is very annoying to the listener, who has to get up and raise and lower the volume for the different songs. There are countless CD burning programs out there that will help solve this problem.
4. Make sure the vocals are high up in the mix. Give the A&R person the chance to determine what is going on with the vocalist. Burying the vocals is never a good idea. If you're not happy with the vocals, work to get them right. Don't equivocate by using a mediocre vocal and then trying to hide it by burying it in the mix. I'd rather hear an accurate representation of the vocalist, even if he hits a couple of off notes.

Wrong notes can be fixed. Better that than for me to be unable to hear the vocalist and have to guess why the vocals are mixed so low. You can probably imagine that my guess is going to be that this person can't sing. Demo listening over.

Other Recording Options

Between the home and professional studio approaches are many intermediate options. They may or may not be able to help you produce a good quality demo, but they certainly will allow you to begin understanding the process, which is ultimately the message of this chapter.

For example, you can download a free (that's right, free) version of the Pro Tools software. This will allow you to get a good sense of what the program is like. This version is obviously limited, but does serve to allow you to try before you buy.

Also, snoop around for friends or studios that are somewhere between the professional studio and a home setup. You may very well find that your neighbor or dorm-mate is a real computer recording genius, and for a six-pack, he will be happy to record you. The barriers of entry are so low (really just a computer, a soundcard, and a microphone) that more and more people are experimenting with recording. Any exposure you get will help you refine your skills and improve your demos. That crazy neighbor who you thought was a disgruntled postal employee may actually be George Martin in the making.

Copyrights and Demos

I'm frequently asked about copyrighting songs for demos. As soon as you commit a song to a "tangible medium of expression," such as writing it down or recording it, you legally hold the copyright.

Registering does give you some added protection and ammunition, should there ever be a dispute regarding a copyright. These disputes can be costly, which is largely why major labels don't accept unsolicited demos: they don't want the aggravation of proving that some guy in Poughkeepsie didn't, in fact, write their mega-million seller's current hit. Therefore, it is a good idea to register you songs officially, but at the early stages, don't get too hung up on it. Rather, spend your time making sure that what your are in point of fact committing to a "tangible medium of expression," is a humdinger of a demo. Then, do register them officially, to give yourself added proof should a dispute ever arise.

Workshop

Contact studios in your area, and ask what there rates are and what is included in those rates (engineer, tape, etc.). (Local music stores may know some good studios near you.) Also, find out if they have a Pro Tools setup.

If you have a computer, download Pro Tools Free, and learn it. This will take some time, but you may as well start now. http://www.digidesign.com/ptfree/

5

Packaging and Presenting Your Demo: All Dressed Up and Everywhere to Go

You've ferreted out the three or four songs that most effectively and quickly represent what your music is all about. You've weighed the various options and recorded them cost effectively and efficiently. Now you're ready to set them free into the big record-getting world.

Well, hold on there, cowboy. As the man said, "Presentation is everything." Before your music is heard, it will be viewed. Before your CD makes it into an A&R person's player, the package it was mailed in has to make it into his office (and into his hands). It has to be opened, the contents removed and viewed, and the CD itself must be taken out of the jewel box or slipcase.

Think about this process and what it really means. Your music is not going to be the first impression. More likely, it will be the third or fourth impression. Each of these little, mini-impressions that precede the listening of the CD are going to have an impact on how the CD is listened to. Sad but true, if those impressions are not favorable, you have much less chance of getting your CD listened to at all, let alone having it listened to with any degree of seriousness.

Elements of a Successful Demo Package

Let's examine the various aspects of the demo presentation, or packaging, one by one.

As an A&R person, every day there are about twenty demo packages in my mailbox. I grab a mail bin, slide them all in, and haul them back to my office. Then I quickly rifle through them, looking at the return addresses, in order to separate the ones I was waiting for from the ones I wasn't. The ones I was waiting for—usually three out of the twenty—go on my desk, while the others stay in the mail bin. As the day progresses, usually while I'm on the phone, I periodically lean down and rifle through the remaining packages in my bin, pulling some out and passing over others.

Demo No-No's

Here are which ones get passed over and put in a separate bin for my assistant to listen to, eventually:

- A crappy looking envelope with no return address on it.
- An envelope, even if it does have a return address on it, that is addressed to "A&R" and doesn't have my name on it. This is not vanity on my part, needing to see my name. Rather, it's a tip-off that the person sending it has not even done the smallest bit of research to determine who is actually going to be listening to their music. This, to me, is irresponsible. It suggests that I am just one on a list of any and all labels for which this person or band could find an address. Therefore, they probably have not attempted to determine whether or not my label would be appropriate for their style of music. Not good. You must do the research required to determine if the music you make has any relevance to the record label you are soliciting. This does not take much more effort than going to a label's Web site.

  How should you find labels in the first place? By looking at the records that you like that resemble your own music and then seeing which labels released them.
- Any package that has an old address of our company on it. Like most companies, we move occasionally, but if someone has sent their package to an address where we have not been for five years, it tells me that this person is just going through a directory (in this case, an outdated one) and doing a blanket mailing. Check the Web or give us a call to get the most up-to-date address.
- I usually pass over a package that has a handwritten address or return address, rather than a printed label. While the record business is a fun and creative one that encourages idiosyncratic behavior, it is also a very real business. I find it hard to believe, in this day and age, that you

cannot gain access to a computer with a label-making program on it.

If you're at this point saying, "Hey, man, I'm an artist, I put all my effort into my music. Why are you hassling me about mailing labels?" My answer would be, I don't expect artists to have highly developed clerical skills (though I find it highly unlikely that someone in your band does not currently work at Kinko's), but I do expect you to know someone who does have clerical skills (hint: girlfriend/boyfriend, successful sibling, etc.). Now is the time to hit them up for some labels. It really will go a long way in making your package look more professional. To that end, avoid any cutesy labels with unicorns or sunsets on them. Simple black and white is best.

- Any envelope that looks like it's being used for the third or fourth time. Look, I'm all for preserving our forests, but in this case, buy a new envelope. And when you are shopping, buy one that has that strip on the back that allows me easy access. (These are also typically padded, which is also a good idea).
- Any envelope that I can't get open. Sounds nuts huh! "Can't get the envelope open, little girly man?" you say. "Perhaps you should spend a few minutes in the gym instead of being computer boy all day." Well, you may have a point, but I defy anyone out there, regardless of their Conan the Destroyer–size biceps, to be able to tear and unravel the reams of duct tape and staples that I've occasionally tried (and failed) to unravel. I promise you that after five or ten minutes of not being able to get a package open because it is so hermetically sealed that it makes the tombs of Egypt look like a screen door shack, you will not want me to get it open. The music inside could be Astral Weeks II. I will not be able to appreciate it, because the exertion (mixed with anger) has caused all of the red blood cells in my ears to temporarily swell, thus blocking any and all aural activity from getting through.

I'm often asked, should I FedEx it or use some other form of more expensive mail so that it stands out? I will admit that I am less likely to just toss a Fed Ex package than I am regular mail. It doesn't mean that that package will get opened faster, but it does mean that it has less of a chance of being immediately tossed. Sorry. Fed Ex third-day is a relatively cheap option, as are some of the UPS and U.S. Postal service options (above regular mail). With this, just make sure that the CD is bubble wrapped, or better yet, placed in a separate padded envelope inside the larger one.

What's Inside the Envelope?

Okay, so your package has made it through the first ranks. Congrats! Really, it's no mean feat. I reach into my bin and pluck your package because it avoided all of the pitfalls above. I notice the nicely printed label addressed to little old me at my current address. I gleefully turn the package over and notice the presence of the dull-red tear strip, and little ripples of excitement pass over me as I daintily peel it back to reveal . . .

What should I see at this point? A severed monkey head? A crisp fifty-dollar bill? Those incriminating photos of me strangling some poor duct-tape-using demo-sender? Well, all of these would be nice (except the monkey head, and don't bother with the bribe—it won't do you any good), but what I really want to see, more than any of the above, is:

1. A CD in a slipcase with the name of the band, the tracks, and contact info clearly printed on the outside of the slipcase *and* on the CD itself.
2. A photo of the band or the artist.
3. A brief one-page bio.
4. A few (no more than two or three) pages of carefully collected and pasted-up clippings about the band.
5. A recent tour itinerary.

Let's go into a bit more detail of each of these items.

CD Packaging

First, the CD in the slipcase is significant. I understand that the visual aspects of a band are wildly important, and that cover art is integral to the success or failure of any album, and expresses visually what the music means to the band. But as an unsigned artist at the beginning of your career, you probably don't have the resources to create this cover art in a way that's going to look anything other than kind of cheesy. If you do have extra money kicking around, I can think of numerous other things to spend it on. Remember those mics I told you to buy in the chapter on recording? Do you have a van to cart yourself around in while touring? How is that acoustic guitar sounding these days? Do you have enough money for postage to get the mailing list out for your next show? All of these, and many other things, should take precedence over you spending the money it takes to develop an elaborate CD package. Because of the price/volume relationship (that is, if you're not pressing many thousands of CDs and booklets, your price will be prohibitively high), you're going to have a hard time putting something together in any sort of economic fashion.

Yes, there are duplication places that offer "packages" that include the CD, booklet, etc. all for reasonable prices. Unfortunately, what they don't offer is an art director, photographer, or designer. So what you typically end up with is something fairly generic that doesn't do justice to what you had in your head.

My advice is to keep it simple and keep it clean. Have the CDs pressed with black type over the metallic of the CD. (Or burn your own, and print out clear labels with black ink.) Include the band or artist name, the track list, and a contact number on the CD itself. Then get plain white slipcases, and just print out stickers (white with black ink) that have this same exact information on them as the CDs.

Why should you put the same information on both pieces? Because I will lose the CD jacket, I promise you. Then, when I'm listening to the CD, liking it, wanting to get in touch, and can't find the slipcase, well, it's a record deal potentially missed.

Not only is this the most effective way to present your CD, it's also one of the more economic ones. With today's technology, you really can do all of this directly from the same computer where your Pro Tools rig is set up. I understand that many bands want to be selling their CDs at gigs, and I absolutely encourage this—in fact, insist upon it. I understand that you probably won't want to hawk some generic looking CD with only three or four songs on it. So, you may be in a situation where you need to press two versions of the CD: one for the demo, one for sale. Do it. Hopefully, you will have enough of a following that this not only pays for the pressing and design costs, but also makes you some money. Nevertheless, I still recommend sending the CDs to A&R people the way I describe. It just makes for a cleaner presentation that allows the music to stand or fall on its own and not be influenced by the packaging. Also, it keeps with the theory that less is more when it comes to sending music to A&R people.

Bar codes only become necessary when your CDs are being sold out of retail stores. They are not necessary on demos. Getting a bar code is expensive (around $750), so be happy that you don't have to worry about it, at this point.

Remember, that package could keep you from getting a record deal, if it's really lame, but it will never, ever get you a record deal—no matter how Picasso it is—if the music isn't there.

FROM THE FIELD **Chris Eselgroth**
Designer

What do you need from an artist to help you design CD artwork most effectively?

Initially, I like to talk to the artist and gather some insight into the band. I want to know about things like title, lyrics, if they have any concepts, band photos, and album packages they like (and don't like). Most importantly, I want to hear their music. I want anything that will help me give the most appropriate visual form to their music.

What are common mistakes musicians make when working with a designer?

Some of the most common issues that come up have to do with supplying images to a designer. Many times, my clients will submit images that are not high enough resolution to be used on a printed piece. Graphics from the Web may look good on a computer screen but cannot be printed because their resolution is too low. Supplied images need to be at least 300 dpi, as opposed to Web images, which are usually 72 dpi. Digital photographs sometime fall into this category, depending on the resolution capacity of the digital camera.

Another issue is the usage of images they don't own. Lots of times, I'll get images clipped out of books or magazines. Unauthorized usage can lead to big problems later. But I do love to see these images, because they might inspire me in a new direction, or I can use them to help find a similar image from an artist, illustrator, or photographer.

That's why I think it is important to talk to a designer early in the process. Even if you don't need help with your concepts, the designer is an expert on getting things printed.

How should an artist go about choosing a designer?

The Web is a great place to start. If a designer doesn't have their work posted, ask to see their portfolio. Also, look at packages you like and see who did the design.

With e-mail and the Web, you don't have to be physically near the designer. Being able to e-mail JPG and PDF files have made it possible to show designs efficiently without a face-to-face meeting.

How should an artist prepare prior to working with a designer?

They should designate someone to be the voice of the band and be the main "art contact." Personally, I like to work with one or two members from the band. My experience dealing with the entire band, management, and label is that it turns into a "design by committee," which can water down some really good concepts. This will keep the dialogue simple, avoiding a pile of e-mail with lots of conflicting ideas.

FROM THE FIELD **Liz Linder**
Photographer

A photo should articulate the feel of the music. An image can have a hook, much like a song can. A photograph can work to introduce or strengthen the musical vibe of an artist in the public eye, thus engaging people who might not have heard the music.

A photo session doesn't have to be a big, drawn out, and costly production, but you should be willing to spend some money to get a solid image that backs the musicians. Make sure the image is clear, sharp, and recognizable, with good contrast. Think about what grabs you when you are flipping through the newspaper or a magazine. It helps to show samples to the photographer so everyone can get on the same visual page. Trying to get too complicated or too high-concept can work against you, if you are not clear with the photographer about the idea and the execution.

I find the best sessions involve a dialogue between artist and photographer. Ask your photographer how they work, and work with them as closely as possible. I tell my subjects to send me their music. Usually, we meet ahead of time to toss around some ideas, so that they can point out images they like and don't like—more particularly, the ones they like. I also ask to see previous shots they have had taken in the past, if any, and we talk about what went right or wrong with those.

One of the best things they can do is give me a few adjectives to describe the vibe they are trying to achieve. Then we consider whether the studio or an outside location would best support that intention.

Photos and Photo Replication

The next item on the list is the photo. Here, we get into a really dodgy and potentially un-PC area. Let's get the tough one out of the way first. I cannot and will not tell you whether you should highlight it if you have an incredibly sexy, good-looking guy or girl in your band. I think the market has made it abundantly clear how much emphasis is placed on the appearance of artists. I hate this, but it's true. I'm also really happy when someone who is not traditionally "beautiful" breaks through. Ultimately, it is a decision that you as an artist or as a band must be comfortable with. I'm not here to speak to the state of marketing or morality or principles governing these things. All I can report is that appearance does make a difference, sadly. Don't think I'm telling you anything new, there.

Happily, I can also report that one person's idea of beauty is not necessarily another person's idea of beauty. Without getting too mushy about it, having a "look" or style (even if that look or style is an intentional lack of style) combined with real talent will go much farther than someone who is traditionally easy on the old eyes but has no talent. It's amazing how appealing people can become—regardless of how they look—if they create great music. There are many examples of this phenomenon—a person who is not traditionally beautiful—being perceived as beautiful or sexy largely due to the music that they make. I'm sure you can think of any number of examples. Of course, if you are that rare breed that is both wildly talented and great to look at (whatever that means), that is not a bad thing, and your photo should—and will—illustrate it.

The key word here is *style*. Style takes precedence over "beauty." Your photo should somehow tie in to the music that you make. Think about the person (or persona) that is singing and writing these songs, and how you would like to be perceived. Think about how you want people to see you when you are walking on to the stage. Think about how you want people to see you when you are answering questions about your music. Take those feelings, and try and convey them in the photo. If the music you make is gritty and honest, then you should appear that way in the photo. How you do that must be determined by yourself and the photographer. If your music is understated and subtle, your photo should express this. Don't agonize over it too much. Find a friend who fancies himself a photographer. Pay for his film, and take some pictures. Live shots work, as well—if they're true to your vision of what you or your band is live.

This also, alas, brings up the difficult "age" question. Again, I think you only need to look at the media and the culture to determine what age group is being perceived as marketable. Record labels are reluctant to sign rock performers after they reach a certain agely appearance. This is sad and unfair, and keeps a lot of really great music from being heard. But, it is the truth. What is the rationale for this? Simply put, pop culture puts a premium on youth. This is ratified via advertising and demographic studies, and trickles down to the gatekeepers of culture. Of course, there are many genres of music where age isn't an issue. It really only seems to be an issue in pop/rock/alternative, and even these categories have exceptions, "Mr. Jagger, do you have your senior citizen card? You can get your movie ticket a buck cheaper with it."

My final word on this touchy subject is that there are always exceptions made when the music is undeniable. Make great music, and present yourself in a manner that reflects it proudly, irrespective of your age, weight, creed, or color. You will be on a path that allows you to enjoy life more, whether that's in the music business or not.

Photo Replication. Once you've taken the photo—and it should be black and white, so you can send it not only to A&R people, but to print medium to promote your shows—you need to get it professionally replicated. This will cost you a few bucks, but it's important to have the band or artist name printed on the photo itself (in the bottom border) along with the band members' names under each of their corresponding photographic likenesses and a contact number. Standard 8" x 10" is fine, but so is 5" x 8"—in fact, I prefer these, just because they're slightly different, and they fit in envelopes more easily.

FROM THE FIELD **John Soares**
Photographer

What advice do you have for artists in order to make a photo shoot as effective as possible?

We all work differently. I like to talk with the subject[s] ahead of time and get a feeling for what they're looking for from me, any ideas about feeling, mood. . . . Be open to all ideas and to what might happen at the shoot. Trust your photographer. Hopefully, you chose this photographer because you are impressed with images he has produced in the past. If you can relax and let him do his job, he will do his best to match the quality of work that drew you to him in the first place.

What are the common mistakes artists make when working with a photographer?

Not being themselves, that's the most common, in my opinion. Relax and don't worry. We all realize it's important to get the shot but . . . it's only a photo. One of many in your career.

How can an artist best prepare for the photo shoot?

Do whatever it takes to come to the shoot in a relaxed and carefree state of mind. Make sure you the photographer has listened to your music, so he can best evoke your style. As unrock 'n' roll as it sounds, try to show up on time and with your stuff, clothes, makeup, props. . . .

Lots of people complain to me before a shoot that they're not photogenic. I love looking at people's face's in photographs, all kind of faces. Be comfortable with who you are and let the camera see that. The most creative and successful sessions I have are when people let themselves be free.

Bios: What to Include

The bio is next. There are many schools of thought on this. Should it be straightforward, should it be creative, should it be funny? If you've read up to this point, you can probably figure out what I'm looking for. You guessed it: something that's straightforward, that tells me what I want to know in a non-hyperbolic manner, and something that is not full of fluff. I like a good joke or story as much as the next guy, but I feel safe in saying that my idea of a good joke is wildly different than yours. Don't risk it. Again, a "clever" bio may very well keep your demo from being listened to, but a clever bio without the musical goods will definitely NOT get you a record deal. Also, avoid the urge to be self-deprecating. You have to fight this as much as you have to fight the urge to be self-aggrandizing. Just state the facts, ma'am. It's very hard to write about yourself, and given the fact that most musicians have a weird combination of huge ego and terrible insecurity (both necessary, by the way), it makes it doubly hard to write about your own music. That said, if you keep it straightforward and informative, things will turn out just fine.

Elements of the Bio. Include, in your bio, where the band is from and how it formed. Have any or all of the members been in bands that the average record label would be aware of? If not—in other words, if you've been in a series of bands that no one's ever heard of—then please don't include the names of these bands. Aside from possibly generating some amusing band name fodder, it does no good. It will just present you like you've been in a long line of bands that no one's ever heard of, and that with this new one, you're trying to keep the streak of anonymity alive.

Give a brief description of the band's sound. It is okay, at this point, to reference other, more well known bands, that you draw inspiration from or that you feel you have stylistic similarities to. This practice really is just a form of shorthand that lets me know where you think of yourself. I may listen to the demo and think you're out of your mind, but it's a start. Also, if you list bands that I like as your influences, that's going to make me more willing to give the CD a listen.

What do I like, you may astutely ask? Well, I'm not telling, but you should basically already know the tastes of your material's recipients. You've done your homework and determined, by the acts that I have on my roster, that your music is compatible before you've sent it to me, right? So list a couple that are sonically similar. Or better yet, if it's the case, let me know who you've toured with or opened for, or been compared to in the press, and let me make the assumption that there must be some similarities. The bio should also let me know where you've toured (and ideally, should direct me to the enclosed tour itinerary). The bio should give me one sentence about how the demo was recorded. Imagine my glee when I see in a letter, "Thanks to your book, Mr. Howard, we set up a Pro Tools rig and recorded this demo in our house in a week." This information—however it was recorded—will give me some sense of what level you are in your musical development.

Press Clippings

Next are the reviews of your demo or your live performance. Obviously, it would be great if these came from *Time* magazine, but chances are, if you had clippings from *Time*, you would already have a record deal, or I would be calling you. This doesn't mean that write-ups in less prominent papers or magazines are not worthwhile. The more national and well known and respected, the better, but it's okay if it's from the local paper. If it's a glowing review, put it in. Paste it up nicely on a piece of paper—with the date of the review—and send it on. If all you have is one review from five years ago, don't send it. It should be current (in the past six months).

If you have many, many reviews, it's perfectly acceptable, and encouraged, to excerpt the most laudatory parts and type them on to a piece of paper. If you do this, you must have enough to at least fill up one side of one page of paper, using a reasonable type size. Again, include the date and the source it was taken from.

Do *not* do the ellipsis trick, where you string sentences of tenuous accolades together with ellipses while carefully excising the derogatory sections. This is transparent and will do you more harm than good.

If you don't have any reviews worth anything, don't grasp and enclose something from some magazine that is clearly your buddy Steve's handiwork and whose sole issue consisted of one gushing review of, surprise, your band. Wait until you do have some actual reviews before you start submitting demos. As you hone your live performance and begin playing out more, you should be getting some decent reviews of either your live show or your demos.

Tour Itinerary

The more dates you can provide me with, the better. If you're touring all over the country, that's very impressive to A&R people. If you're playing big gigs regionally, that too will impress us. However, if you've only played a couple of gigs—or worse—none, it's better just to leave this out. The reality is that selling your music is dependent on live performance. If you're not playing live, you have very little chance of getting a record deal. While it is true that labels can help you get a booking agent and gigs, we would much rather see that we're not starting from scratch. As with the press clippings, don't stretch things. It's transparent, for example, if you've only played in your friend Pete's basement for his birthday. Don't list it, and certainly don't exaggerate it.

Lyric Sheet

If you are a songwriter whose lyrics are the most important aspect of what you do, you might include a lyric sheet. Now, everybody thinks that their lyrics are great. Unless they really are the most important thing about your music—of such crucial import that you can't imagine anyone understanding your music's greatness without reading along—then I would advise against sending a lyric sheet.

Lyric sheets can be dangerous. In some ways, what distinguishes lyrics from poetry is the ability for poetry to stand on its own without music. Before you enclose a lyric sheet, consider that these lyrics are likely to be read while the music is *not* being played. This is because of the vagaries of demo listening, which almost ensure that pieces of the package will get separated from each other. The CD may be playing while the lyric sheet lies unread on a desk, or the lyric sheet may be read while the CD lies unplayed on a player. To my mind, this is dangerous, and a good reason not to include it.

If your demo catches the interest of a label, they may ask you for a lyric sheet. At that point, you'll have already made good progress. Don't take the chance of having a lyric sheet kill your chances. Better to wait and be asked for one, once you're already in the door.

Personal Note

You should enclose another envelope with my name on it, which contains a letter to me, preferably typed, with a brief rationale stating why you are sending this to me, and how you can be contacted (an e-mail address is delightful). Also mention any other really big points. "U2 has asked us to tour with them," or more realistically, "Our song was just added to [insert impressive local radio station here]," or "Please enjoy the recent *New York Times* review that is enclosed," or "We have sold 5,000 copies of our first self-released recording."

Let me know also who, if anyone, is managing you or providing legal counsel (more often than not, if you have a manager or lawyer, the package will come from them), and who, if anyone, is booking you. What you're doing here is not trying to impress me with your connections—though if you have a booking agent, it will impress me. Rather, it shows me where you are in your career, and importantly, directs me to someone I might know, and can then call and suss out the situation. If you don't have a manager, lawyer, or booking agent, don't lie. Just sign the letter and put it in its envelope.

Also, let me know in this letter of any upcoming performances in my relative geographic proximity.

Lastly, this is a good place to inform me of the existence of a Web site, if you have one. There are books written on how to design an effective Web site. For me, the Web site should be an extension of the bio package. It should be a place where I can see some photos, hear some music, get some information about the artist, and find out where the artist is performing. It may have a commercial component too, where the artist's CDs are sold. I like seeing this, as it shows initiative and some cognizance of the commercial aspect of the music business.

Summary

So that's the drill. You need to fill the A&R person in on what's going on with your band. The presentation of your demo needs to be—like the music on your demo—clear and concise. Send a CD with your name, contact number, and track listing, both on the CD itself and on a slipcase. A good photo, some press clippings, tour itinerary, cogent bio, and a personalized letter to the A&R person that shows you've done your homework about the label. All of this should be nicely packaged in an easy-open envelope with a printed label, personally addressed. Do this, and you will be far ahead of the pack.

Workshop

Below is a checklist of all the ingredients that you should included in your demo package. Work on your bio, and get people to read and comment on it, to make it as effective as possible.

- ❑ Bio
- ❑ Photo
- ❑ CD
- ❑ Letter to the recipient
- ❑ Press clippings
- ❑ Tour schedule

PART II

The Team

AGENTS, MANAGERS, AND LAWYERS

If you've made it this far, fi st off, congratulations. Really. Many people stop long before they reach the stage of ever getting a demo recorded, and certainly before taking the needed steps to present it adequately.

By virtue of you making it to this point, it shows a level of seriousness and dedication which, frankly, most artists lack. This seriousness and dedication are precisely the ingredients needed to succeed in this next, more intense level on the ladder to a record contract.

You need these qualities because you are now progressing outside the realm of self-suff -ciency and into the realm of, hopefully, mutually beneficial relationships. You have recorded your demo, you have it packaged well and ready to present, and now, you will begin to use it to weave an ever-growing web of team members who will all play crucial roles in your career.

These people, be they managers, booking agents, or lawyers, will not simply help you to get a record deal—though they may do that. Rather, they will become part of your organization. Now, "organization" is a scary word, which implies a business structure. In fact, that's precisely the stage at which you have arrived, and this is why seriousness and dedication are so key. The people who you will begin to come into contact with at this stage of your career—the managers, booking agents, and lawyers—are, likely, professionals. This business is their livelihood. It is what puts food into their children's mouths. You need to understand this, and recognize the significan e of it. In short, you can't mess around. If you're not ready to step up to this level, you should not enter it. Keep your music as a hobby, and don't risk adversely affecting someone else's livelihood by not being serious.

I'm assuming, of course, that you are serious or else you wouldn't have read this far. That's great, because just as those artists who are not serious are truly detrimental to the managers, booking agents, and lawyers of the industry, those that are serious are their bread and butter. Like record labels, they need you. In fact, they need you more than you need them. And remember, *they work for you.*

So, how do you go about finding these people? What exactly do they do for you? How do you do it for them? What does it cost? Should you get a lawyer or a manager fi st? The mind races. These questions and many more will be answered in the coming chapters.

6

Performances and Booking Agents: The Live Life

You must perform your music live. This doesn't necessarily mean that you must limit yourself to traditional venues, but clearly, playing live is the most immediate and direct way to get your music heard. It is also instrumental in helping you get a record deal—though, perhaps not in the ways you might expect.

The bottom line is that performing is usually the engine that will begin building a community around your music.

If you have completed the workshops in the previous chapters, the package you created for record labels can also be used to advertise your music and get live performances. This is the first step towards getting gigs and building your community. All of the work that you've done picking, recording, and sequencing your songs, as well as putting together a package suitable for submission to record labels (including your bio, photo, CD, etc.) is *exactly* the same package you need to send to the venues where you would like to perform.

If you've done this, pat yourself on the back. Most artists don't take the time to create a package that has any real impact, and by not doing so, they limit their chances of getting gigs. Additionally, if you've created the type of demo and packaging I suggest, your presentation will stand out to those who book the venues. If your music is any good, you will be on the fast track to getting a gig.

Just as you must do research to determine which labels make sense for you to submit your demo to, you must do the same for performance venues. This process is easier because your search should, at first, be limited to clubs in your geographic proximity. If you live in Detroit, you don't need to worry about what the right club for you in Alabama is—at least, not initially. Find venues by using the same technique you used for finding labels: look at which artists perform at which clubs. Where are bands like yours playing? Look at the listings for the clubs, and see who is playing there. Ask yourself if your music could fit compatibly on the same bill. If so, submit your music to that club.

Be realistic in your targets, and understand that most venues are for-profit businesses that rely on ticket sales (and alcohol sales) in order to stay in business. You shouldn't expect to play the Enormo-Dome for your first gig. Rather, look around for places that book new artists. This could mean the smaller clubs, or coffeehouses, or open mics. The important thing is that you try to perform where your music will fit with the venue's aesthetic. This is important, not just because you don't want to be the guy with the acoustic guitar playing between the death metal bands. More practically, it's because your goal, beyond attracting fans, is to expose your music to the people in "the business" who frequent these clubs. These people, be they lawyers, managers, or booking agents, are all potential members of your team.

How Performing Impacts All Facets of Your Career

Understand that a network exists in the music business in which the venues are really on the front line. The people that operate these venues are in constant contact with booking agents, managers, and promoters, as well as record labels. We A&R people have frequent conversations with those who book the venues, and are always curious to hear which bands or artists are drawing big crowds. Additionally, A&R people speak to venue bookers when we want to locally showcase one of our bands. Venue bookers speak most frequently to booking agents, who route their bands into the venue. When a national artist comes through town, the venue may add a local artist as an opening act. In this way, the person who books the venue can potentially expose a local band (that would be you) to the national band's booking agent, the national band itself, and even that band's management.

While it may seem that your local club does not have an impact outside of a small circle, the reality is that it acts like a radio transmitter that can spread the word about you in a very wide and effective manner. This is why it is so important that you choose the right venues in which to try to get gigs, and also that you develop a rapport with the people at these venues. The most effective way to develop this rapport is to play great and get warm bodies in the room.

Putting Bodies in the Room

Get as many people as you can to come see you play. It is your obligation to those who book you and to yourself. At the start of your career, your ability to do this will be somewhat limited. There are some things you should do before you try to get gigs at "professional" venues. First, try to play at "non-professional" venues. These could be parties, church basements, raves, skirmishes, wherever. The goal is two-fold: first, to get your live act together, and second, to build a following in an organic way. If you do this, when you do play in a "professional" venue, you will not only give a better performance, but there may actually be some people there to see you.

Once you feel you have a good enough live show and some sort of following, you should try to book yourself a professional gig. Because you've kept a good mailing list every time you've played, you can invite those people who have seen you at the non-professional performances. Though you may get a gig based on the strength of your demo alone, if you do not bring people into the venue, you will probably not be invited back, no matter how great your show or demo is.

FROM THE FIELD Larry Goldfarb
Promoter, Manager, and Club Booker

What qualities do you look for in an artist when you consider booking them for your club?

Regarding a headline act, it is important to understand what is their marquee appeal, and do they fit the format of the club. This is determined by numerous factors including touring history, retail status, press interest, radio activity, etc. The opening act must complement the headliner, and should be outstanding.

What should be in the package that the potential performer submits to you?

Their CD, a photo, press reviews, and any other information that will enhance their chance to be booked.

What are the mistakes that performers make trying to get a gig at your club?

Not being prepared with their pitch. Know what the room is about, who you might want to open for, and do not waste my time.

What can the performers do prior to the appearance to help make the show successful?

Work to get press, radio, send out their mailer. Although the club will be making the same effort, performers must be part of the promotional effort.

How valuable do you feel performing live is to getting a record deal?

Although I consider it secondary to an artist's recording, it is important to drawing attention from the industry, and will in general improve their artistry.

Maximizing the Gig

Utilize the gig as a way to begin building your community. Much of what you must do to build this community does not show immediate direct results, but it does play an important long-term role in your career. For instance, while the chances are slim that any large scale newspaper is going to write about an upcoming gig for a relatively unknown artist, you should still identify which writers in town seem to have an affinity for your type of music. Send them a package including your CD, photo, bio, and brief letter letting them know when and where you are playing. The package should be similar to your demo to labels and to the venues. Send something similar to any appropriate radio stations. Again, the chances of these actions resulting in big-time publicity for your gig are slim at the early stages. What you are doing is introducing your music to some of the key people in your area who you want to be in the community of your music.

The gig gives you a rationale (and in fact, a responsibility) to send your materials to writers and others. Use your energy in this manner, rather than, say, putting fliers up around town. You will have much more to show for the effort it takes. In this manner, the gig is not a one-time event that occurs in a vacuum, with no relation to growing your career. Rather, the gig is just one piece of an overall community-building effort.

A few words about fliers, because I know you want to put them up. Most artists, for some reason, love making fliers. Resist the temptation, until you have a following. Putting fliers up around town is usually an ineffective way to get people to your gigs. If you're into the whole velvet Elvis-anonymous-art-sold-on-the-highway-thing, and you want to be a part of that rather strange movement; then by all means, post some fliers. But if no one knows who you are yet, it ain't going to get anyone to your gigs. Additionally, in many places, it is illegal. Wait until people might know who you are, before you put fliers up. Even then, make sure you check with the club to make sure fliering is legal. The clubs are the ones that get fined for illegal fliering, and they will not be pleased with you if it happens.

Making the Most of the Actual Performance

A couple of tips once you have the gig. Make sure you are well rehearsed. Make sure you are tuned before you go on stage. Make sure you have another guitar tuned and ready to go in case you break a string. Make sure you adhere to the time constraints of the club by going on stage and—more importantly—getting off stage at the times the venue wants you to. Bring appropriate gear for the size of the club; don't bring huge amps for a small club. Don't be a prima donna with the sound person regarding your monitor mix; get it close, and live with it.

Make sure you mention your name or your band name at the beginning, middle, and end of your set, and make sure people know you have a mailing list to sign.

Thank the sound person (buying him a beer is a good way of doing this) and the booking person. In figuring out your set list, the rules that applied to picking tunes for your demo apply here. The ultimate goal is to get a record deal, so if you treat every show you perform as if there is an A&R person in the audience, bear in mind the notorious ADD issues of A&R people, and present your music in its clearest and most forthright manner. And, most importantly, make sure there is fog in the damn fog machine.

As you move from your first gig to gigging more regularly, try to develop a relationship with a venue that is most appropriate for the music that you make, and grow your crowd there. Loyalty breeds loyalty. This doesn't mean you shouldn't play at different venues around town, but you should try to have a kind of home-base venue. In this way, the venue will be rewarded for their initial belief in you, reaping the financial benefits of the big crowds that will come to their club as your popularity grows. Additionally, this will give you the opportunity to make multiple impressions on the people who work at (and frequent) the venue. It is these people that are in the position to help you with your career—either directly or by spreading the word.

Gigs Outside Your Home Town

As your local popularity grows, you will need to start expanding your base. In this manner, you will go from gigging to touring. The message is that you should start working in ever-expanding circles radiating out from your home-base club. For example, if you are an artist whose home-base is Philly, and you've developed a good following at a couple of venues, start looking for similar type venues that are within driving distance. From Philly, the obvious choices would be New York City or Washington DC, as major cities with venues that cater to the type of music you make. That said, choose the right venue rather than what you believe to be the right city. Yes, if you can make it in NYC, you most likely can make it anywhere, but you will have a better chance succeeding there if you've developed a fan-base and compelling live show before you've arrived. This may mean playing college towns or coffeehouses in the more rural areas, or house parties, or whatever. Follow the music, and follow the same protocol for the out-of-town shows that you did for the home town shows: alerting local media, collecting names for your mailing list, and so on. You will soon be developing a touring circuit.

Booking Agents: How They Work and When You Need Them

You do *not* need a booking agent to do the work we have just outlined for you. Yes, it is in fact work, and work that few people really like to do, but it must be done. When most people are confronted with the idea that they have to do work—and this seems particularly true with musicians—they typically try to find someone else—anyone else—to do the work for them. Well, Tom Sawyer, booking agents are wise to your game, you scamp, you rube. Do you think a booking agent is going to say, "Ah, you've never played in Sacramento before, you have no record out, and no one has ever heard of you... Perfect... I know just the place for you to play?" Of course, not. Booking agents—as we will see with managers, in the next chapter—work on commissions generated from the income the band makes, typically ten percent of the money from the gig. So, even if they could cajole some hapless club owner to put you on a bill in some city where no one has ever heard of you, realistically you will be getting paid in the $50 range, if you're getting paid at all. Ten percent of $50 is $5. The booking agent has now made a whopping $5 for putting his or her reputation on the line. Just think, if the booking agent is able to swing this type of deal in thirty markets, he is looking at making enough money to maybe pay his cable bill for a couple months.

Why agents are reluctant to work with unsigned artists

This is not to say that booking agents never take on artists that have not developed strong markets on their own, They do, but very, very rarely, and usually only if said artist is signed to a label—usually a major. The booking agent knows that if the label is investing massive funds and time into getting this artist known, the label will promote the artist and the performance. Therefore, some people might show up where the artist is booked, and this would generate a commission for the agent. Agents hope that the artist will be able to make real and genuine connections with a live audience, which will grow, geometrically. As the artist's audience grows, so too will the agent's fees.

Few agents are willing to take this gamble. Most feel that an artist must have at least a handful of markets from which they can draw a significant enough crowd that the agent's commission will offset some of the costs endemic to developing new acts. These are essentially the costs that the agent must incur by simply putting the legwork in required to introduce an artist into a market where they are not known. Phone calls must be made, packages must be mailed, and most importantly, time must be spent, which the agent could spend instead on booking gigs for more lucrative artists.

A common fantasy is that an agent will come along and leverage his roster to get you opening slots on tours, and so on. Every new artist wants this to happen. But it is not just unsigned bands who feel that having an agent—and therefore, access to the agent's roster—will facilitate a tour. New artists are in competition with more established artists that are signed to a label. The label, desperate to try to get something happening for this new artist, will be doing everything they can to get them exposure. This means trying to get the artist in front of people. Therefore, frantic calls go out from the labels, as well as the managers and anyone else (mom) who might know a booking agent who will either take the band on or just give them a slot opening for one of their acts. Given the choice, agents will choose an artist backed by a label over one that is unsigned.

If it feels at this point that booking agents are in a more powerful situation than the label, that's because they are. I have often said that it is far easier to get a record deal than it is to get a booking agent.

Building a Following

There really aren't any shortcuts for getting gigs, in the beginning. Being undeniably great will speed this process, as it does all others, but you simply must be willing to do the work yourself, at the beginning. Prepare yourself for the indignities associated with meekly handing some jaded club owner your CD. Prepare yourself for playing in front of your brother and his latest idiotic girlfriend who talks through your whole set and then tells you how great you are. Prepare yourself for driving seven hours to play for twenty people, having your guitar stolen, the club stiffing you on your $50 guarantee, and the van/car breaking down in the rain at three in the morning. You think I'm exaggerating? Go ahead, and ask anyone who has played more than twenty or thirty gigs if they've had any horrible experiences playing live. And then, grab a soft chair, an ottoman, your slippers, perhaps some tea. You're going to be there for a while.

This isn't meant to discourage you. As I said, I don't know any way around this. I'm telling you this so that you don't get discouraged when some or all of these things happen to you along the way. It's just part of beginning a career in this business.

Remember that the gigs are just one part of the pie when it comes to career development. You must get out and do them, because they provide you opportunity to get the word of your music and talent out via other media. For instance, even if a gig doesn't go well, if you made contact with the local paper, and the paper reviews your CD, many more people than those at the gig itself will become at least passingly familiar with your music. This often leads to good things. Chances are that local paper never would have reviewed your demo CD had you not been playing the gig.

Summary

The gig is really ground zero for community in the industry. The following chapters will go into far more detail on the different components of the community, but the gig is where it starts. Additionally, playing live allows you to start building a community of fans.

There are few things more impressive to A&R people than an artist with a large and active fan base.

I mentioned earlier the importance of keeping a mailing list sign-up sheet at your gigs. Have a space for people to include their e-mail addresses. This will save you time and money when you are alerting people to upcoming gigs, as you won't have to pay for postage or printing postcards.

Also, more and more, A&R people will ask you how big your e-mail list is. It has become a real barometer for a band's popularity, and it also shows that you have some organizational savvy, which is very important to A&R people. While you're building your e-mail list, you'll also be building your network and connections that will become your team and community as you move forward.

Workshop

List the clubs in your area that would embrace your music.

List the writers in your area that write live reviews and gig previews in the local papers. Which writers like music similar to yours?

List the radio stations that have artists perform on air to promote gigs. Which stations play music similar to yours?

Create a mailing list sign-up sheet that you will have available at all your gigs. Include a space for e-mail addresses.

7

Management: Finding It and Making It Work for You

What do artists and bands want just about as much as a record deal? That's right, a manager. This is because good managers are worth their weight in gold and can have tremendous impact on your career. Unfortunately, good management is rare as an emu. The manager is perhaps the most important member of your team. Therefore, it is essential that you define exactly what your expectations of a manager are, and then choose wisely among any candidates that meet these expectations.

Managers and other members of your team each have a specific role. You don't want to build an infrastructure if you have no use for it, and therefore, no means to support it. In simpler terms, you don't want "dude" hanging around the rehearsal space being "managerial" by drinking your beer and telling you to work on the second verse of the song, while he hits on your girlfriend. Instead, the manager must be actively engaged in furthering your career.

In order for the manager to do this, he needs tools to work with. The first tool is the demo. The second tool is some kind of fan base, which is typically built by playing live. Certainly, there is no absolute order to the progression, and many bands have management that helps guide the band long before they have demos or play gigs. But for the most part, you're going to have a hard time attracting a manager and keeping him busy if you don't have some groundwork already laid.

There are as many types of managers and styles of management as there are types of bands and styles of music. This chapter presents some of the more common ways in which bands connect with management, and what role management plays in the artist's career. It is not a set of absolute rules.

The Three "Must Have's" of Management

However you and your manager come together, and whatever role the manager finally ends up playing in your career, there are three characteristics that a manager *must* have in order to help your career effectively—both before and after you get a record deal. Those characteristics are passion, connections, and funding. If your manager has passion, he *may* be able to succeed without the others. However, if your manager is without passion for your music, your chances of long-term success will be reduced. The best-case scenario is, of course, having all three.

Beginning-Level Managers

At a certain point—after you've made a demo, played some gigs, and started to develop a following—you may be approached by someone who is interested in managing you. Most likely, the people approaching you at this early stage of your career will be friends, family, fans, or people who work at the venues where you perform. Some of the most successful managers in the business originally came from this pool. Bertis Downs, for example, began working with REM when he and members of the band were college students together in Athens, GA. Brian Epstein worked in his family's furniture store that had a little music division in it when he was asked to go see a band. That band was the Beatles, and he became their manager. Rusty Harmon was a college student and an intern at a management firm, who showed a young band around when they came through town. You may have heard of this band, since they've sold about a gazillion records and won two Grammys under Rusty's management: Hootie and the Blowfish.

Why Passion is Important

Friends, fans, and families who become managers typically have one massively important thing in common: they all are extremely passionate about the artist they work for. Typically, they feel that the artist is great, and while they often don't have a surplus of connections or capital, they believe they can make up for this through sheer force of will fueled by their passion, which they have in abundance. As mentioned above, this can and does happen. Passion, combined with energy (often youthful) is a very potent mix that often knocks down many barriers and allows an artist to experience real career growth. Managers in this type of situation often believe that lacking the experience, knowledge, connections, or money actually allowed/forced them to try things that other more "experienced" managers would have dismissed. In so doing, they create innovative strategies that further the idea of career development. Necessity is the mother of invention, and I would add, it is also the stepmother of innovation. The beautiful thing about the record business is that there are very few rules. When a manager is passionate enough to make the artist succeed—no matter what rules they have to ignore, break, or rewrite—that is often the best type of manager to have.

Such relationships force the band and management to work much more closely than they would in a more traditional management/artist role. This can create an open and honest relationship from day one. In other words, because a beginning-level manager is not going to be able to say, "I'm going to get you touring with this other artist I also manage, and I'm going to set up a showcase for you to perform in front of my A&R friend from Sony," he or she must involve you—the artist—in the decision/planning. Instead, they must say, "Listen, let's figure out what our resources are and begin building something in an organic fashion." This method, while perhaps being a slower route, is a good one, as it directly and closely involves you, the artist, in the process of your career development. A close relationship often has the positive side effect of being an *honest* relationship. Closeness and honesty are imperative, and will give you a far better chance of avoiding the all-too-common litigating over accused improprieties, resulting from the artist not knowing what the manager is doing, but believing that, whatever they're doing, they ain't doing it honestly.

Professional-Level Management

Passion is the key ingredient to making an artist management relationship work. If you find someone who has real and genuine passion and isn't a complete derelict, you will be better off than many. Ideally, however, your manager will also have the connections and the funding.

The Importance of Connections

While it is fine (and often refreshing) for a manager to have a low-key persona, they *must* be able to sell themselves and, more importantly, the artist. In so doing, they will build connections. The record business is one where you live and die by how connected you are. You can make the greatest music in the world, but unless you can get it heard, it doesn't much matter. Simply put, at all stages in your career—from getting an A&R person to listen to your demo, to getting your video played on MTV, to getting a gig to perform at the Super Bowl Halftime Extravaganza—it is often connections that make the difference.

The reality is that the strength of the connection is frequently as powerful as the strength of the music. There are many examples of someone who makes mediocre music but is well connected getting a record deal before an artist who makes great music but has few connections.

To get a record deal, you often must develop your connections from the ground up. The process can be accelerated if someone on your team, in this case the manager, has connections.

A fundamental role of the manager is to expose his artist to more people. Therefore, managers spend much of their time casting a wide web around all the corners of the industry. In so doing, they develop relationships with booking agents, record labels, radio stations, press, and so on. When you partner up with a manager, you are not only getting this person's individual expertise, energy, and hopefully, passion. You are also gaining access to their connections and relationships. It is this quality that will catapult your demo from the bottom of an A&R person's pile to the top. These connections help in many similar ways, from having your music heard by music supervisors at advertising agencies to introducing you to a music publisher to securing you an opening slot on a coveted tour.

Connections are built over time and must be maintained. You need to carefully examine any potential manager in order to determine just how broad, good, and most importantly, applicable their connections are to the music you are making. Much in the way that you research appropriate labels for your music, you must do the appropriate diligence when you are considering your manager. Understand also that connections can and do come in organic fashions. It is perfectly acceptable for you and your manager to have a symbiotic relationship in which your manager benefits from his association with you, and vice versa. The trick is being able to make connections that have real meaning to your career. If you have a manager who is very well connected but not in any way that is appropriate to helping advance your career, they might as well not have any connections.

If this is the case, make sure they at least have ... money.

The Importance of Money: How Management Gets Paid

This brings me to my last essential management criteria: capital. First, you need to understand a bit about how managers make their money. Typically a manager will receive a commission—usually 15 to 20 percent—of all of the income that you generate (the gross). This includes money from gigs, money paid to you from a record label as a personal advance against royalties (typically, not from money advanced by a label for you to record your record), money from merchandise, income from your music being used in movies or commercials, and any other source of income you generate as an artist. It is therefore in the best interest of the manager to leverage all of those connections I mentioned above to help you generate as much money as you can, which of course, generates more money for them. This is capitalism at its finest, and when it works, it works great for everybody.

The problem is that young or unestablished artists typically take quite a while to generate any revenue. Also, these artists typically don't have any money of their own, so the management is left to spend their own money in order to develop the band before any money comes in. Because of this, you will occasionally see management securing other pieces of the artists' potential income as a kind of collateral against the money and time they are putting up. Sometimes, for example, management will acquire some part of the artist's publishing—in other words, a piece of the equity in the copyrights of the songs.

Managers and Publishing

This means that when these songs begin generating royalties, the manager will be paid a percentage of the money. Managers do this because they often defer their commission while spending their own money. They have no guarantee that they will ever recover their investment. This practice has largely been frowned upon (by both artists and managers), and was seen only occasionally in the past. However, I'm seeing it happen more and more, and I believe it will become even more of a common practice in the future.

As an artist, you must seriously debate whether parting with your publishing, in order to provide a sort of insurance to a manager, is the right thing to do. My opinion is that it is usually the wrong thing to do. As we will see in the publishing chapter, I do not believe that you should hold on to your publishing at all costs. Rather, I feel that giving up some part of your publishing is frequently essential to building a successful career. With one caveat: Whoever you assign any part of your publishing to must be able to do something with it. By this, I mean they must be able to "work" your publishing to generate awareness about you and money for you. If they cannot do this, do not assign any part of your publishing to them. Therefore, if a manager is requiring you to assign some portion of your publishing to them, you should only do this if you feel the manager is going to actively engage in working your songs.

Of course, it may not be this simple for you, especially if you don't have a lot of options. You may feel that the prospective manager can help your career in many ways, and that it would be foolish to miss the opportunity to have him or her represent you by clinging too tightly to your publishing. You may be right.

Your publishing is valuable. Part with it with caution, and only if you're getting something of real tangible value in return.

It's Money that Matters

Money is a significant factor in creating effective artist/manager relationships. The manager is spending money, hoping for a return on investment. Publishing is one way to hedge that bet. Of course, managers who have no money will not be able to offer you much for your publishing.

Managers who have no money have a hard time being effective. There are always expenses involved in getting a band signed: recording costs, gas for the van, fan mailings, travel, guitar strings, and so on. It all adds up. Of course, management doesn't have to pay for any or all of these things. But remember, they can't make any money unless the band is making money, so they usually opt to pay for these things and others so that the band has a better chance of getting signed.

Even after you get signed, management is often the fountain of money. For instance, an artist and manager may determine that they need an independent publicist because they feel the label's publicist (if it has one) can't do an effective job due to workload, the label's priority scheme, or whatever. The label is not obligated to pay for this (though often they do), and so the band and management are left to decide whether or not the potential added exposure they would get from a publicist is worth the out-of-pocket expense. Many times, in a situation such as this one, the band itself is not generating enough income to pay for something like this, so the management foots the bill. Theoretically, management will be reimbursed for these costs once the band does start generating some money. If neither the band nor the management can afford to pay, it really is the band that suffers.

Good managers understand that new and developing artists are much like startup businesses. The first couple of years (or records) typically are money losers. The hope is that after the painful initial period has ended, there will be a financial reward that will recoup all the early losses and then some. This is why managers will fund an artist's career at the early stages—and, in fact, sometimes well into an artist's career.

Finding the Right Manager

As you can see, the roles of the manager are varied. The manager needs to be a cheerleader, a liaison, and a bank. Often, managers also take on the role of creative consultant, accountant, babysitter, driver, and on and on. Clearly, it is a good thing to have someone like this on your team. While you may have people approaching you and offering their services, of course, you may also need to do some legwork of your own in order to find a manager. Again, do all of the things you would do to find a compatible record label. Identify who is managing artists that you admire creatively and whose careers are going in a direction you would like yours to go in. Solicit opinions from others in your community. For instance, ask the person who books the club you play at which managers they would recommend you speak to. People who book clubs, as well as journalists, DJs, and others in the industry typically have extensive contact with managers, and may have a very pragmatic opinion on their efficacy.

Labels and Artist Managers

The last point to be made about managers is just how crucial they are to your chances of getting a record deal. Simply put, an artist who has strong management is often going to be signed before an artist who doesn't, all other things being equal. Labels rely on managers to help them create and execute marketing strategy. Additionally, labels often need a buffer between themselves and the artist. The manager plays this role. Of course, there are many artists who prefer to deal directly with the label, whether they have management or not. In most cases, though, the manager allows the artist to focus on being creative, while the manager works out the more nuts-and-bolts aspects of releasing records with the label. This is not to say that the manager should not be keeping the artist informed of all that is going on. They should. But the label relies on the manager to communicate details to the artist in the right manner, and at the right time.

Getting Good Management *Before* the Deal

Labels also prefer artists with good management because they know that once the artist is signed to the label, unless the artist decides to part ways with the manager, they're stuck with the manager for the duration. It is illegal for a record company to meddle with artist/manager relations. Doing so would fall loosely under the term "tortious interference"—a fancy lawyer-boy term for, "Keep your stinking nose out of my business, you jackass." So, if you come to a label with a manager who is a bozo, the label is going to know that they are going to have to work with said bozo until he either gets his act together or the artist wakes up and fires him. Artists are usually reluctant to take this step, out of loyalty, and so, yes, the label gets stuck with the bozo. Of course, the label doesn't have to choose this option. It can just not sign the band. This happens more than you might think. One of the first questions record execs ask when presented with a possible signing, is, "Who is the manager?" If it's a manager who has a bad reputation or is inordinately difficult to work with, or just plain ineffective, the label will frequently pass on the artist.

Summary

In my opinion, it is better to have a manager who is passionate—and not a bozo—than one who is connected or financed but lacks passion, vision, or understanding of what your goals are as an artist. You will be working very closely with this person, and you need to be able to communicate easily and effectively together. Additionally, you need to trust that they will represent your artistic vision in a way that you are comfortable with. They will be your mouthpiece in many situations. Lastly, you need to really understand what your objectives are and choose a manager who will help you get there, and then set new objectives with you and help you achieve those. Good managers aren't easy to find, so you must look long and hard and carefully. In many ways, the manager becomes another member of the band.

FROM THE FIELD **Mike Kappus**
President/Owner, The Rosebud Agency
(Management/Booking)

What does an artist need for you to consider adding them to your roster (as an agent or manager)?

As an agency, we have always tried to limit the number of artists we represent in order to give the best service to each, so we are very particular about adding artists and hope that each relationship will be a long-term one. We want to be moved by the artist and feel that they are offering something special to the audience. We also want to be confident that the artist and/or manager will be reasonable to work with, that they ideally understand the business, are realistic about what can be achieved on their behalf at any given time in their career, and will work with us in a cooperative effort to reach mutual goals. And, we need to feel that it makes good business sense for us to invest the time and money necessary into promoting their careers—that they can at some point achieve a sufficient degree of success that will enable us to cover our costs and make a reasonable return on our investment in their careers.

As a manager, the above holds true even more so. Management involves a much broader role in being responsible for every aspect of an artist's career. This will result in a much greater time investment and the need for a much closer working relationship. Therefore, we have to be even more confident that we are prepared to invest ourselves, time-wise and emotionally, into an artist's career.

Do you work with unsigned artists?

I have worked with unsigned artists in the past and have helped artists get deals, but, especially as a booking agency, the money we can secure for an artist is based primarily on how many people they can draw in any given situation. Without some sort of national or international awareness (usually gained via a nationally distributed CD with reviews and airplay), an artist has little hope of drawing a crowd, and is not likely to get paid enough to cover the cost of touring. That makes working with unsigned acts a difficult situation for anyone but a local agency or a manager who is confident that they can establish an artist from the ground up. Of course, everyone started out as being unsigned, so this is a simple reality, not an impossible vicious circle.

What is the best way for an artist to get your attention?

We listen to every CD that is sent to us, but every additional factor that comes to our attention, like it does for everyone else in the industry, adds to the likelihood that we will look more closely. Again, music that grabs us emotionally or impresses us as being truly special is the primary factor. When an artist begins drawing significant crowds or selling large numbers of CDs or getting on the radio, though, everyone starts to pay attention.

I always suggest that artists do everything they can to build a following. If they are good and stick to it, they should be able to develop an audience. It just may take a lot longer than one would like.

At what point should an unsigned artist seek out an agent or manager?

Artists should be trying to connect with anyone that can help their career as soon as they are prepared to put on a solid performance. Unfortunately, in most cases, an agent who will be interested in picking up a new, unsigned artist may not have the contacts and experience to properly represent that artist if they later procure major national attention, but everything is possible. Most importantly, the artist should make sure that any representative not only believes in them but has the time to devote to them. I once represented an artist whose manager was one of the most powerful in the business, but because he was so engrossed in work on his more famous artists, this artist actually did worse in that situation than he might have by handling his own business. So, don't get just any representative. Try to get the right representative for you—someone who understands what you do and has the time and belief and ability to make things happen for you. And be aware that finding a good manager is one of the hardest things to do. Most of the good ones already have too much to do.

What are the mistakes that artists make with their managers or agents?

The relationship should not begin until each side has a good feel for and trust for the other. An artist should not assume that an agency or manager with more successful artists will automatically be the agency that is best for them. Artists should also learn as much as they can about the business, regardless of how experienced their representative is. When artists have questions or concerns, they should ask them as open questions rather than assuming a negative. With regard to touring, for example, the simple key is that the artist's value is greater than their costs. But many artists have a hard time recognizing that promoters don't pay artists based on the artist's costs but on their value. So, artists need to have a good idea about each of these elements and plan accordingly. I have had the pleasure of working with a number of artists who have had a clear idea of what they want, and they communicated it well. We could still add our own ideas or advice, if we thought any of the ideas should be reconsidered in any way.

Knowing about the business, being realistic about goals, and working together in a trusting and cooperative manner is crucial for an artist.

What is the key for a successful artist/manager/agent relationship?

Trust is probably the most essential factor in any relationship between an artist and their representative. That one word incorporates many other elements, though. That trust should be built upon the artist's confidence that they have chosen someone they believe to be honest, devoted to helping the artist, and experienced enough to do the job. The agent or manager needs to believe in the artist as every career has challenges and that belief is essential to keep the manager involved and dedicated to getting through tough times. The representative should also have experience in the realm in which the artist will work and in the areas in which the artist will need help. Many managers learn as they go. As long as they are conscientious and good learners, and the artist understands the circumstances, that can work too.

The representative also needs to be prepared to invest the necessary time in the artist. If someone worked a 9-to-5 job and then was given other job opportunities, they would perhaps add one other part-time job. But there is a limit to how many additional jobs they could accept before determining that adding another job would mean dropping one of their existing ones. Unfortunately, in the music industry, there are many record labels, agencies, and managers who are driven by a need to pay their bills, greed, or just a desire to make sure they don't miss a great opportunity, and they frequently keep adding the responsibility of representing new artists—even as their current artists are in need of more of their help.

Some artists look forward to getting a record deal as a goal in their career. While that is an essential goal early on, they will soon learn that the challenges never end, and even the most successful artists cannot rest on their laurels.

FROM THE FIELD **Jason Rio**
Manager

What are the qualities you look for in an artist in order to consider working with them?

Generally speaking, besides the obvious answer (talent), a great attitude and a relentless work ethic are a must. I've heard people talk about the "It" factor as the governing rule whether they work with an artist or not. "It" being that indescribable quality that an artist naturally has or does not have. That quality which allows the artist to be larger than life.

A perfect example of the "It" quality is Bono. He has the ability to command the attention of thousands and thousands of people at any given concert or event. One man being greater than an entire crowd.

When I started off in management, I tried to use this as a barometer; however, I found it tough to gauge. The "It" factor does not take into consideration the development and nurturing of an artist's talent. An example of that is Chris Martin, lead singer of Coldplay. I saw interviews and concerts when they first started, and he was quiet and shy. Years later, he has turned out to be one of the more charming front men out there.

Do you work with unsigned artists?

Yes, but there has to be a desire to get that artist from an unsigned artist to a signed artist. I like to work with artists that want to conquer the world. See the above answer about work ethic and attitude. This is why those qualities are paramount to an artist's career. There is absolutely no problem with wanting to remain an unsigned artist. It really all comes down to what everyone wants out of the relationship.

What is the best way for an artist to get your attention?

Not to over simplify things, but if an artist creates great music, that is the best way to get my attention. Some people say to tour and do the DIY thing, and that is the best way. I agree to a certain extent. However, not all artists have the ability to get in the van, Henry Rollins'-style, and hammer it out in clubs, coffee shops, and VFW halls across the country. Some have school or a day job that prevents them from doing all the things they want to do. If I am talking to one of those artists, I say to them okay, but there is no excuse not to try and maximize your potential in your hometown. If an artist creates a profile in their hometown, they will show up on people's radars. Just because I am in Chicago does not mean I do not know what is going on in Boston. People talk to people and those people talk to other people, and word spreads quickly about things of higher quality.

What are the mistakes that artists make with their managers?

Either giving up too much responsibility to the manager or trying to keep too close of a grip on the day-to-day dealings. I have seen some artists secure management, and then they do not allow their manager to manage. Management is direction. If an artist does not want direction, then they should remain self-managed. That said, just because you have a manager does not mean you should give up all control over your career. There has to be that perfect give and take. This establishes itself over a course of time.

I think sometimes managers (as well as labels, agents, promoters, etc.) forget that they are dealing with not only their artists music, but with their lives as well. They become so caught up in the chaos that is the music industry, that they forget that all the decisions made not only directly affect the artists' professional life, but their personal life as well. I think this is a mistake managers make with their artists.

What is the key for a successful artist/manager relationship?

Trust and communication. A manager is an extension of the artist, and an artist is an extension of the manager. The way one handles their business directly reflects on the other. An inner circle has to exist that consists of the artist and manager. Through the thick and thin, an artist has to be able to rely on their manager and the manager has to be able to rely on the artist.

This trust is established through communication. Whether it be feelings on the artwork for the full-length record or deciding on whether or not to tour Europe after a UK tour, it is imperative that artists communicate their thoughts with their manager.

When it comes down to it, the manager is not out there on stage, night after night. The manager's image is not the one that the record label will base their marketing plan around. When an artist can clearly communicate to his manager what he does or does not want, and after the manager has had a chance to communicate to the artist why he should or should not go down certain roads, decisions will be made. Because there was clear communication, the inner circle can trust that the right decision was made.

At what point should an unsigned artist seek out a manager?

If things begin to pick up momentum, it is usually good to have someone in place to advise and liaison. Sometimes, this person is a lawyer. I don't have a problem with a lawyer being involved before the manager.

However, when it comes down to the record label deal, I think it is a must to have a manager in place. Here is why. After a lawyer is done with the deal, they are out of the picture. They are not in the label's marketing meetings or trying to implement the deal points that were negotiated. They are not the ones that the artists will be calling when they run out of money and need an advance on the next royalty check. A manager is the one who deals with the day-to-day, and therefore should be involved with negotiating the paperwork that will guide they day-to-day for the next several years.

Also, too many times I have seen the manager be the last piece of the puzzle put in place. When it comes down to it, an artist is surrounded by a team (label, publisher, agent, etc.). The manager is captain of this team. He needs to have a say in who the other members are. It is very difficult for a manager to come into a situation and be told, "Here are the people you need to work with, now deal with it."

Workshop

What goals do you want your manager to help you accomplish?

Who can you ask for management recommendations?

Who are your five favorite artists' managers?

List three people that you feel would make a good manager for you. Why?

8

Lawyers: Protecting and Serving

The Role of Lawyers

In the chapters on playing live and on management, there was talk of people being paid by commissions and percentages. What is implied is that by signing, you are, in effect, entering into a form of agreement: a contract. Contracts are necessary anytime a significant amount of money changes hands for either a service you perform (e.g., playing at a club) or a service someone performs for you (e.g., booking a tour). While it may or may not be a sign of the apocalypse, we do live in an intensely litigious time. Whether lawyers are the cause or the antidote to this is an argument for another day. But as you begin generating income from your music, you will necessarily be confronted with agreements or contracts. Enter the lawyers. Additionally, a lawyer's role is not always limited to negotiating contracts for an artist. In fact, they often play an important role in an artist's career before the artist has an agent or a manager, much less a contract to negotiate. So what distinguishes the role of the lawyer versus the manager? Well, for these and other answers, read on.

A Protocol Preamble

Know this straight away: in today's society, lawyers are necessary and will save your neck at various times during your career. Just please, please, remember one thing: your lawyer works for you. While you may be the lawyer's client, you are also the lawyer's boss. You can fire him, and more importantly, you can instruct him on how you would like a situation to transpire. At the end of the day, if a deal falls apart because the lawyers can't work out the details, the lawyers will move on to other deals. It may not, however, be as easy (or even possible) for you to do the same.

No deals are perfect. Especially at the beginning stages of your career, it is often far more important to compromise in order to get a deal done, than to take too hard a stance and risk it falling apart. However ironclad a contract might appear, deals are open to re-negotiation. But if you walk away from a deal, it's hard—and frequently impossible—to get the negotiation process going again.

No record company wants to be seen as having some sort of draconian contractual stance. If you are forced to make compromises in order to get a deal done, but end up making money for the record company (or seem likely to do so in the near future), you will be able to go to them and say, "Let's have another look at this piece-of-crap contract you've forced me to sign." This is not to say that they will rush to change things, but there will potentially be room for negotiation. And even if you have the best contract in the world, if you aren't selling any records, it won't matter much, because there won't be any money to be divided up anyway.

So, as a new artist, get the best deal you can, and then concentrate on selling records. Don't lose the opportunity to sell records by over-negotiating a contract and having the deal fall apart.

How Lawyers Get Paid

Let's discuss the role lawyers will play in your career. Lawyers are able to spread the word about your music. In this, they are similar to managers, club bookers, booking agents, writers, and DJs. The more successfully your lawyer can do this, the greater chance he has to make more money from you. In other words, if a lawyer feels like you really have the ability to make money, either from selling tickets or records or whatever, he will take a much more acute interest in your career.

Like managers and booking agents, lawyers must get paid. But they are smarter than booking agents and managers, and therefore generally get paid in the form of billable hours, rather than as a percentage of your income. (Lawyers will say that managers and booking agents are smarter, since they are commissioned, because they don't have to chase artists around to get them to pay their bills.... Probably, neither is smarter than the other.) Expect to pay anywhere from $150 to $500 (this high end is really only found at the elite firms) an hour for their services. Some lawyers *will* work on a percentage basis, and typically take 5 to 10 percent of the income generated from a deal. This includes personal advances paid to an artist from a label. (This payment *is* recoupable against your artist royalties.) Additionally, there is a hybrid arrangement, where the lawyers will charge a low hourly fee with the understanding that, at the end of the deal, they will receive a percentage of the net money that the artist receives from the label. In this scenario, insist that any hourly fees billed to the artist be deducted from the attorney's take. Lastly, some lawyers will take a fee based on the size of the deal once it is concluded. This is referred to as "value billing." In this type of relationship, you pay a fee based on the ultimate "value" of the deal. The more value the lawyer helped you get, the more he gets paid.

In all of these cases, it is important to stress that lawyers should only draw their percentage from the net artist share and not the gross money received.

Lawyers can become incredibly creative when it comes to fees. There is simply no way to cover all the possible permutations out there. The above examples are meant to give you an overview of how the process works.

Whatever your fee agreement, one thing is for certain: the more money you are making, the more you will be paying to your lawyer. Therefore, just like managers and agents, lawyers want you to succeed. They are going to try to use their contacts—be they with record companies, managers, booking agents, advertising houses, or anywhere else potential money might be found—to aid you in growing your career and income.

When to Get a Lawyer

Many artists ask whether or not they should get a lawyer or a manager first. It really is a moot point. Believe me, when you need a lawyer—whether you even know that you need one or not—they will find you.

We A&R people get pitched on new artists by lawyers at least as often as by managers. At the early stage of your career, it is not unusual to have a lawyer, rather than a manager, representing you. As your career grows, you will need both.

A lawyer and a manager provide very different services, once an artist has a record deal. The manager is involved in the day-to-day strategizing and planning aspects related to developing an artist, as well as interfacing directly with the artist's label about all aspects of promoting and releasing the artist's records. The lawyer, on the other hand, takes a back seat in terms of day-to-day artist/label relations, once the deal is negotiated. Unless some contractual issue comes up or a deal needs to be renegotiated, the lawyer will largely stay in the back seat. The lawyer may also be active with other issues involving the business workings of an artist: publishing, foreign rights, and so on.

In effect, the only time that managers and lawyers do the same job is when they are pitching a band to a label. To me, there really is no distinction between getting a package from a lawyer or a manager. If I'm interested in the artist, I will ultimately ask the question to the manager, "Who is the lawyer?" And conversely, to the lawyer, "Who is the manager?"

On rare occasions, I will negotiate a deal with an artist who has a lawyer and no manager (only if a manager is imminent), but I will not make a deal with an artist who has a manager and no lawyer. I just do not think it is ethically right for an artist to enter into a binding contract without getting the expertise that lawyers provide.

Of course, this is an easily solved dilemma. At the point that I'm ready to enter into a deal with an artist, if that artist doesn't have a lawyer, I tell them to go get one. As I said before, lawyers aren't hard to find. In fact, I have recommended lawyers to artists who I am about to sign. As a rule, try and find yourself a lawyer who does not come referred by the record label. Understand that the A&R person's goal is to get the contract signed and put away—hopefully, never to be looked at again. So, the lawyer that an A&R person would recommend would be one who we know can get the deal done quickly, and will avoid a lot of tedious, insubstantive negotiation. These may be different than your own goals.

We A&R people know lawyers who are able to work well with labels, and get deals done quickly, so that we can move on to the more exciting, and ultimately, more important aspects of working together: getting people to hear your music. I personally don't see any problem with this. However, it is impossible for you to know the ethics of the label you are signing with until you have worked with them. So try to find a lawyer who doesn't have too tight a relationship with your label. This is not to say that there is anything wrong with your lawyer knowing the label or the people at the label. In fact, most good lawyers are going to be familiar with employees of the better known labels. Just find someone who is going to put your interests ahead of the label's.

Before you get an offer, a lawyer, like a manager, can help you by using their contacts and reputation to cut through some of the barriers that an unknown artist without representation faces. A&R people are much more apt to open and listen to a package that has been sent by a lawyer—even if it's not a lawyer they know. Once the package is opened and listened to, all of the other rules that we have discussed will apply. The lawyer's representation may get you in the door faster, but if you don't come bearing wonderful party gifts, you won't be asked to stay.

Finding The Right Lawyer

A logical question is, "How do I get myself one of these lawyers with door-opening powers?" As in the case of club bookers, managers, booking agents, and labels, you will have a far easier time attracting a lawyer if you have already done some work on your own.

At this point, you should know very well what I'm talking about. You must have developed aspects of your career, beyond just being a talented artist, that will give the lawyer some hope that he will be able to pique the interest of a record company. Good lawyers will not risk damaging their reputation by submitting a demo to a record company if they don't feel that there is some chance that the record company will be interested. The reason that they will not do this, once again, has to do with professional courtesy. Most good lawyers know that A&R people will open a package from a lawyer they don't know once. If the enclosed demo is appropriately prepared and targeted, the lawyer will be perceived as understanding the process. His future packages will also be opened, business may be referred to him, and a holiday card will likely be forthcoming.

Lawyers also know that the inverse is also true. If, out of professional courtesy, an A&R person opens a package from a lawyer whom they don't know, and the demo within satisfies few or none of the requirements that it should, then there is little likelihood of future packages from that lawyer being opened. This is why lawyers, like everyone else in the biz, are going to be very selective about who they represent. They know their reputation and ability to generate revenue for themselves is contingent upon the artists they choose to work with.

You will have a far easier chance of securing a lawyer to shop your demo if you can present a good package. Once you have your demo package, submit it to lawyers in the same way you submit it to prospective managers, labels, and booking agents. Some lawyers may sign on early in your career and help you develop yourself, in order to give you a better chance to get signed. Just don't expect a lawyer to come in and simply, by his connections, allow you to leapfrog all the steps that artists must go through to get signed. In fact, if a lawyer contends that he can help you skip any of these steps, I would be very leery of him.

How Lawyers Differ from Managers

Once you have secured a lawyer, he will likely work with you to find management, if you don't have it in place already. They will do this for two reasons. First, they know that most labels are going to be more likely to sign you if you have a manager, and second, because they don't want to be your manager themselves. Managing you would keep them from doing what they are genetically predisposed to do: make deals.

Given this genetic predisposition, your lawyer will become incredibly important, once you are presented with a contract. We will take an in-depth look at the types of contracts you might be presented with later in the book. For now, understand that a lawyer can play a very important role in your career prior to deals needing to be negotiated. In fact, they can frequently be the catalyst to getting these deals presented to you in the first place. Like managers, lawyers work closely with labels and others in the industry who can play a role in helping your career. Think of them as being another member of your team who can give you more exposure and connections. They come with the added advantage of being versed in contracts and negotiating, which is always useful. Additionally, they can frequently aid you in setting your business affairs in order early on in your career and thereby help you avoid pitfalls that could come back to haunt you later. Like all the members of your team, lawyers must be chosen carefully.

Summary

Try to develop a relationship with a lawyer so that he can serve your various needs throughout your career, rather than having to hire new ones as you develop. Ideally, the same lawyer who helps you expose your music to record labels and performs other more managerial functions at the early stages of your career will also be the one who negotiates your record deals, publishing deals, and so on. This means assessing the landscape and ascertaining what possibilities are out there. How do you do this? It can be done by talking to other bands about who represents them, looking on CD sleeves for people with "Esq." behind their names in the credits, asking promoters, and other kinds of similar research. Additionally, there is a legal directory available both in libraries and online called *Martindale-Hubbell Law Directory*, which lists lawyers by state and the field in which they practice. (Focus on those who practice in the entertainment field.)

Remember, loyalty breeds loyalty, in this business. You will need a lawyer at some point, so it is in your best interest to find someone who you trust and feel can represent your needs as your career grows.

FROM THE FIELD **David Wykoff**
Attorney

What is the role of a lawyer vis-à-vis an unsigned artist?

An attorney can be of assistance in helping the artist with networking, actual solicitation of deals, or just general education about what the record or music publishing companies are used to doing or the kinds of agreements that may be offered. Some lawyers will go so far as actually soliciting artists to potential record companies or music publishers. Other lawyers will help artists with networking that might lead to recording or publishing deals (i.e., point the artist towards people who might me interested in the artist's music but leaving the artist to do the follow-through). Other lawyers, on an initial consultation, are willing to provide some education on what potential recording and music publishing deals might involve.

Do you work with unsigned artists?

Yes, in several ways. First, many of my clients used to have record or publishing deals that have ended, and they are looking for new deals. Others come to me through my clients. I prefer not to get into the actual solicitation process for a couple of reasons. First, if it is going to be done right, it is very, very time-consuming (and I am very, very busy as it is). Second, I am often in an adverse position with record companies and music publishers for my clients, and it doesn't always make sense to be going back to those companies to try to get them to sign other clients.

There are, however, attorneys who do solicit deals for artists and a number of them who are pretty good at doing that. It is my general feeling that the artists should be doing everything that they can to be getting their careers ahead themselves (such as making strong demo recordings, getting better at writing songs and performing them live, developing a live audience, and meeting potential booking agents and managers), and not relying upon an attorney to create everything to create income or a career for them.

What is the best way for an artist to get your attention?

Get a reference from another client I like and work with regularly. If that client can vouch for the artist, then I am certainly willing to sit down and talk for a few minutes.

What are the mistakes that artists make with their lawyers?

The biggest is not communicating well enough to make sure that everyone is working together as a team and each team member understands his or her place in the team. Another is not going to lawyers when entering into deals or related agreements. The vast majority of time that I spend representing clients who have a problem that needs to be fixed, it concerns an artist signing an agreement that they did not understand or not putting a verbal agreement in written form.

Finally, artists should make sure that their attorneys are experienced in the music business. Just because someone is a lawyer does not mean that they know what they are doing when it comes to music business agreements or copyright or trademark issues. Find out who the attorney represents in the music business.

On the financial side, the artist and the lawyer should have an understanding of what fees and costs are going to be charged back to the artist when the lawyer renders services. That way, the artist does not get bills that are larger than the value of the deal involved.

What is the key for a successful artist/lawyer relationship?

There are a few keys. The first is to understand that lawyers are very, very busy, and they generally don't have the time to talk on the phone every time that the artist wants to talk about things. (A corollary of this is that sometimes lawyers don't return phone calls as promptly as they should, so if something is very important, you may need to keep calling.) Second is to understand that lawyers need to make a living, too. They cannot spend excessive periods of time on work that they are not going to get paid for. Third, and most important, all members of the artist's team need to understand what are their particular responsibilities, and it takes good communication for everyone to come to this understanding.

At what point should an artist consider hiring a lawyer?

Artists can, if they want, go out and read any number of books on how to understand the difference between a standard exclusive term songwriter's agreement and an exclusive term co-publishing agreement, or just about any other kind of music business agreement. However, at the point that a contract is to be signed that involves a grant of exclusivity or ownership, an attorney should be consulted—and maybe hired to negotiate such an agreement.

FROM THE FIELD **Loren Chodosh**
Attorney

What is the role of a lawyer vis-à-vis an unsigned artist?

In the U.S., lawyers have taken on the role of being the professionals who introduce new artists to record companies and publishing companies. This probably came about because there are not agents, as in the film industry, who work with actors to "get jobs." Managers, when successful and well-known, are well-placed to help introduce new artists to the record industry, but it is not easy to find a successful manager with the time to put in the effort. Because lawyers have developed relationships among A&R executives, they are sometimes seen as adjuncts to the A&R search.

If a lawyer is not actively "shopping" the artist (a term that I loathe), then a lawyer might help the unsigned artist to field offers among interested labels and/or publishers, and strategize to help maximize the artist's exposure to the industry.

Do you work with unsigned artists?

I work with unsigned artists when I feel that I can accomplish for them what it is that they want and need under their particular circumstances. If an artist comes to me to be "shopped" (there's that term again), I have to think long and hard about whether the situation is right. I try to minimize the number of unsigned artists that I represent who are looking to me to spearhead the effort to get signed. If there is a manager involved who is leading the way, my role becomes easier, and I can be involved without as much concern about whether I am the right lawyer at the right time for the job. I also give preference to those clients of mine who *were* signed, and who find themselves "between deals" (an unfortunately common occurrence in the last ten years).

What is the best way for an artist to get your attention?

When an artist is referred by a client or a close colleague, I tend to be the most attentive.

What are the mistakes that artists make with their lawyers?

Lawyers can only facilitate getting a deal. They (no matter how important they seem) cannot *make* a deal happen. Artists sometimes mistake the lawyer's apparent "power" for something more magical than it is. It is good to have a lawyer who is well known, well respected, and well liked, but a lawyer is really only as powerful as his clients.

Artists also sometimes fail to ensure that they understand what their lawyer is doing for them in a negotiation, and what has been accomplished. An artist does not have to micromanage the lawyer's activities, but the artist must be aware of what is being negotiated on his behalf.

What is the key for a successful artist/lawyer relationship?

As in any relationship, grace under pressure, humor, respect, and communication, above all.

At what point should an artist consider hiring a lawyer?

Certainly, if the interest from one or more record companies gets more serious than "let us know the next time you are playing," or "send us your next batch of demos." If the interest rises to the level of "what kind of deal are you looking for," a lawyer might well be in order.

Workshop

Who are the lawyers working in your area? What are their firms? Find out if they are taking on new clients.

PART III

Additional Players

GIANT STEPS:
Independent Publicity and Promotion, Publishing, Distribution, and Labels

These final chapters will help you most once your career is well underway. The time to act on this information is *after* you have recorded and developed a winner of a demo and package, and have used it to build your team that includes a lawyer, a manager, a booking agent, or even all three. This last section is for artists who might even be asking themselves whether or not they really even need a label.

Artists who are most likely asking this question are those who are generating some income via touring and/or selling their own CDs from the stage, online, or through local retailers. Some artists who find themselves in this enviable position may be content to stay in their situation, making the music that they like in the manner that they like, and building a decent life for themselves. It's kind of the big-fish-in-the-small-pond approach. There are others, however, who will continue to aspire. For psychological or monetary reasons, they need to spread their music beyond their regional confines. In order to do this, this type of artist will need an added layer of infrastructure, beyond the manager, lawyer, and agent trifecta. In fact, you can assemble this additional infrastructure in an *ad hoc* fashion by combining all of the disparate elements, typically found under the roof (or rubric) of the label, in your own manner. In so doing, you become your own label. Remember how we defined "label" way back at the beginning of the book; it must have three elements: (1) An equity stake (partial or otherwise), for some period of time in the artist's copyrights. (2) The ability to market and promote the artist's work. (3) A means to distribute the artist's work. More and more, artists are able to put these pieces together themselves. They work with independent publicists and promoters, and then make themselves a distribution and publishing deal. Guess what they are, once they've put this structure together? You got it, a label.

Interestingly, the ironic catch-22 of the independent approach is that those who delve into these deep waters and succeed on their own terms with a publishing or distribution deal are almost guaranteed offers from record labels. Only the rare artists manage to wrangle themselves a successful distribution or publishing deal. Doing so does not go unnoticed by labels, who want more than anything to avoid starting from scratch with an artist. Labels much prefer to mitigate their risk and increase their chances of success by working with artists who have already—on their own—established a foundation upon which the label can build.

One way or the other, whether you've reached the point where you feel that you no longer need a label, or you really want to stack the odds in your favor to the highest degree, these remaining chapters are for you. You will now have additional challenges:

- Determining when to consider hiring an independent publicist or radio promoter, and how best to maximize these relationships;
- Determining when (and to whom) you should relinquish some of your copyright equity;
- Determining when you should allow someone else to represent your music to retailers;
- Being confronted with a record label contract; and finally,
- Learning what to expect once you've reached your goal and gotten signed.

9

Publicity and Promotion: Getting the Word Out

Once your music begins generating some notice, you are likely to be approached by a "third party," such as a publicist, radio promoter, or other form of marketing consultant, who can be hired to promote your music. They can play a very important role in helping you to get signed, as their sole job is to get more people to know about your music, either by getting it written about in the press, talked about on TV, or played on the radio. If they get enough people talking about your music, word will eventually spread to the record labels. This chapter discusses how publicists and radio promoters (herein, called "promoters" or "promo people") function, and how they can play a role in helping you to get signed.

How Publicists Work

Every artist wants a publicist. Beyond anything else—even money, at the beginning stages of an artist's career—what most want is to see their music written about or to have the opportunity to perform on TV. As these are the primary jobs of publicists in the music business, it's not surprising that artists are so eager to work with them.

Ideally, a publicist has great relationships with a wide range of writers and other gatekeepers at media outlets (magazines, newspapers, TV, online media, and so on). For a fee, they will leverage their connections and utilize their experience in order to get your music noticed by the people who are capable of giving it media exposure. This is not so simple as picking up the phone and telling Jann Wenner to put you on the cover of *Rolling Stone*.

Rather, good publicists work with you to create a long-term plan that will help to define your music and image in the eyes of the media, rather than just making quick, forgettable impressions. In so doing, their services can generate a more long-lasting value that transcends the limited period when they are working for you. Maybe, one day, this *will* ultimately get you that *Rolling Stone* cover.

To craft this plan, your publicist must understand your vision, and be able to help you cleanly and clearly articulate this vision to your audience. Your music should define your vision most clearly. The publicist should use your music as the seed to begin defining the other, non-musical elements. Among other things, the publicist works with you on:

1. Your bio, which they should write in collaboration with you.
2. A press photo, which, with their experience and knowledge (and photographer/stylist contacts), will help you really communicate what it is that you are visually trying to represent.
3. Organizing an event or events to get your music heard, such as a party for the debut of your self-released CD, or a cocktail type party where your music is played for press, radio, retail, bookers, A&R people, and any of their interested contacts.

While all of the above are crucial and should be done well, the publicist's main job is going to be trying to get someone—anyone—to write about your music. This can be your local papers, or better yet, if you are touring, the papers in the areas where you are playing. Additionally, they should also endeavor to get you some realistic national coverage.

The key word here is "realistic." You cannot expect a publicist (or anyone else) to work miracles for your career and enable you to take shortcuts. It isn't in any artist's best interest to begin their process of getting a record deal by simply hiring a publicist and waiting for the accolades (and record deals) to roll in. Such expectations are unrealistic, and this approach simply won't work. Unless you have a fundamental understanding and appreciation of what it takes to get press for your music, you will end up spending a significant amount of money, and most likely, have very little to show for it, after the publicist's tenure is up.

Maximizing Your Publicity Experience

The better, more effective route is to build your career on your own, with the "second party" members of your team (your manager, booking agent, etc.)

to a level where a publicist can really have some sort of tangible effect. If the first thing you do after recording a demo is hire a publicist, that publicist may very well be able to get you a little—most likely, a very little—coverage in some local papers. While it will be nice to read these (if the reviews are good), and it is always helpful to have some clippings to put in your package to send to prospective labels, it really isn't the smart way to spend your money. These small impressions will not add up to much, as once the local papers have given you a bit of cursory ink as a favor to the publicist, they will feel they've fulfilled their obligation, and won't write about you again unless you're really great. Of course, if you're really great, they'll be writing about you whether you have a publicist or not. You will be able to get all of the nice clippings for your press kit in a much more "real" fashion on your own, and build genuine relationships with writers by simply being great and exposing your music.

The lesson for hiring publicists is this: Do not hire anyone to do a job that you can do yourself. At the beginning stages of your career, it will be as easy (or hard) for you to get bits of press coverage as it is for a publicist. Therefore, wait until you have done everything in your power to get coverage for your music, and then hire a publicist. At that point, the publicist will be able to look at what you've done on your own and suggest ways to take it to a higher level. They must be able to do things for you that you cannot do for yourself. If not, don't hire them.

Publicity Costs

You will be paying significant money for a publicist. The range is wide open, but I would be surprised to find even a very new, very local publicist charging less than $500 per month for a campaign that extends beyond just a one-time event. Most publicists who do national campaigns are looking for $3,000 and up per month. Additionally, you will also be responsible for reimbursing the publicist for their expenses: mailing your packages, making phone calls on your behalf, Xeroxing press kits, wining and dining writers, tickets for writers who want to come see your perform, and more. Not to mention the fact that you have to supply the publicist with CDs, bios, and photos to mail out to the media outlets. You can therefore be looking at a significant amount of CDs and other materials that you need to manufacture. If you are staging a national campaign, it will be hard to do it right with fewer than 300 to 500 CDs, all of which, of course, need to be mailed out. If you figure a buck a CD to manufacture (which may be low, depending on the quantity), plus another $1.50 to mail and $1.00 for the bio and photo, you're looking at $3.50 a package. Multiply that by 500 media targets, and you're going to be tacking on $1,750 in expenses, on top of the monthly charge.

Also bear in mind that publicists typically want to be retained for more than one month. Four or five months is not uncommon, but two or three is really the minimum. By the time the CDs are mailed out, it can take a month just to get a writer to find the CD, and longer to get him to listen to it, let alone commit to writing about it. You do not want to be in a position that by the time the CDs have landed and writers are starting to get around to listening to them, the publicist is off the case. Without the not-so-gentle prodding of a publicist, the CDs have very little chance of getting reviewed, because the writers are certainly being not-so-gently prodded by other publicists about other records. This is why it's important to hire a publicist for a significant amount of time in order to give them enough chance to do some real good.

FROM THE FIELD **Sheryl Northrop**
Founding Partner of the Baker/Northrop Media Group

A manager with whom we had a great rapport had been telling me for a few weeks about this new artist he had just signed. I went to the artist's Web site and thought the photos looked good, and the sound clips sounded really good. I anxiously awaited the CD the manager was sending out. A couple days later, it came and I popped it in. It absolutely blew me away. This kid had an amazing voice, soulful and weather-beaten well beyond his years. It sounded as if he had been born on the Bayou and was channeling the spirits of Motown's greatest.

I immediately called management and told him we had to work this record. I made him an unbelievable deal, one in which we certainly weren't making money, but one in which our expenses were covered and we were getting paid a token amount. I just wanted to be a part of the project. I had that feeling like this artist was going to wind up being a real marquis name for us down the line.

We were able to generate major buzz in the tour markets and start to make significant inroads at national media outlets. After being fought over by a number of labels, he eventually signed with a major. The record will not come out until next year, and by then, I think he will already be well on his way to becoming a household name.

Publicists can and will cater their services to your needs. If you have an important show that you want to make sure gets lots of coverage—say a record release party or an opening slot for a national artist in a major market—then it might be a good idea to hire a publicist for that specific purpose. You can then target your goals, manage your expectations, and hopefully, get some bang for your buck. Additionally, you can set specific targets of publications where you want to get your music reviewed. You should do this. It doesn't make any sense to spend the money and time it takes to get your CD reviewed in the Oxnard, CA daily paper if you're an artist from Mississippi who has no records in any stores in California, let alone Oxnard, and no plans to play there in the foreseeable future. Rather, work with your publicist to set reasonable regional goals that will augment your other efforts (touring, radio, etc.) and add in a couple long-shot national targets as well, such as *Rolling Stone, Spin, Vibe,* and *The Wire.*

It really does come down to having realistic expectations. Additionally, it is of paramount importance that you not think of publicity as something that exists on its own, exclusive of all of the other elements involved in getting signed and having a successful career. Having a great publicist on your side can help you to put people in the rooms at the clubs you play, it can help you get your records stocked in stores, and can even help you get some radio airplay.

FROM THE FIELD **Sheryl Northrop**
Founding Partner of The Baker/Northrop Media Group

Do you work with unsigned artists?

In choosing to rep or not rep an unsigned artist, we focus on a couple of major points. First and foremost, do we like the music?

Is this something we can feel confident in getting behind and talking about? Second, what other elements in the music or the artist's personal story seems newsworthy and/or interesting? The competition for space is incredible. Sometimes, having really good music isn't enough. The story or newsworthiness has to be a part of it.

Third, what is the artist's image like? Looks and overall vibe and personality also can play a role in catching our attention.

What is the role of a publicist vis-à-vis an unsigned artist?

We can help create local awareness, we can generate press for tour dates, and help the artists put together a press kit with bio, photo, clips, and other materials. We can help them learn to do interviews, and we can work with them to help hone their interviewing skills. We can help artists refine their image.

Occasionally, we will help artists find management, agents, and/or labels, though that isn't really our primary function.

How deeply we get involved with an artist, whether signed or unsigned, depends on many things, including how well we "click" with the artist, what our work load is like, and what the parameters are that are set forth at the outset of our working relationship.

What is the best way for an artist to get your attention?

An artist can start by calling or e-mailing us. It's that simple. It's best and we always appreciate it when artists do their homework before contacting us. They should look at our Web site and see the types of projects we do and the artists we represent. They should read our company philosophy and bios so they know whom they are contacting.

It's always good if they can direct us to their own Web site, so we can go there to see photos and/or hear sound clips. They should be prepared to follow up the initial contact with music and whatever press materials they already have.

What is the key for a successful artist/publicist relationship?

The key for a successful artist/publicist relationship is the same as for any other relationship: The relationship is built on honesty and trust. The publicist is there to take the artist's message to the media. If the artist isn't straight up with us, it's hard to maintain our integrity and credibility with the media. I think it's very important for publicists to develop a level of trust with their artists, as that is the best way to maintain a good working relationship. For us, it is important to know our artists. We try to spend time with them in person, if possible, or by phone. Knowing artists beyond their music is always helpful. It helps us understand where they are and where they are coming from. Knowing about the artist's lifestyle and/or hobbies and other interests helps us make an overall better pitch. It's important for our artists to communicate with us and to treat us like we are part of the team working toward broadening their scope and their reach in the media.

With new artists especially, it is important to choose a publicist based on several factors: Does the publicist "get" the music? Does he seem genuinely interested in the artist and the art? What kind of plan does the PR person have to take the artist's music to the press? As an artist, do you feel a connection with the person you are hiring to take your message to the media? Do you have faith and confidence in the PR professional you are hiring? These are all very important points to consider. I think, for the most part, we get along very well with our artists. Many of them have become friends even beyond the working relationship.

At what point should an unsigned artist consider hiring a publicist?

Expenses typically include (but certainly are not limited to) the costs of phone calls, faxes, copies, postage, overnight delivery services, and supplies, such as labels and envelopes. Artists just starting out should do their own photos and try to create their own press materials. There are a few books available. They should read as much as possible about PR to familiarize themselves with the basics. Artists should work to contact local media and make them aware of themselves and their music. Artists should be very serious that this is their intended career path.

Artists looking to hire an independent PR person have many options. They can choose to hire someone locally who will concentrate on local and regional press as the artist continues to build his profile. A band just starting out might even want to consider contacting the local university, since many schools now offer public relations courses where students often earn credit through hands-on training. An artist who already has established a regional following and has a bigger budget might want to contact a bigger PR firm (such as ours) where they will likely pay a higher monthly retainer plus expenses. An artist coming to a firm like ours should be at a point where they are at least somewhat established and are seeking a national profile.

FROM THE FIELD Carla Sacks
Publicist

Do you work with unsigned artists?

On occasion, I have had the opportunity to work with unsigned artists and/or artists with a distribution deal who then go on to sign label deals. These connections usually come from booking agents, publishers, and managers. It makes very little sense to have a company like ours employed without some other avenue of support.

What is the role of a publicist vis-à-vis an unsigned artist?

A publicist can help with establishing the artist in their hometown, which in most cases is the best place to start, and then support their touring with a PR campaign in each market. An independent publicist (not affiliated with one label) will have many direct label contacts and can be very helpful in passing along music.

What is the best way for an artist to get your attention?

Through the mail, with photos and a bio included, and via industry colleagues.

What is the key for a successful artist/publicist relationship?

The artist and the publicist must agree on an overall perspective—musically and visually—for their publicity plan, and most importantly, be in agreement on their expectations.

At what point should an unsigned artist consider hiring a publicist?

When there is suitable news: a record to be released, tour dates to announce, a signing to be announced....

Radio Promotion

Some unsigned artists out there will determine that in order to further their career and increase their odds of getting signed, they should hire an indie radio promoter. There are some ways in which indie promo, like publicity, can be tailored to the specific needs of an unsigned artist, which can not only help them get signed, but also help their career.

Promo people work in much the same way that publicists do, the difference being that while a publicist's milieu is press, a promo person's is radio. Promo people work with radio stations to get songs "added" to the playlist of the station. There are promo people for every genre of music, from Americana to metal to rap. Each of them develops relationships with stations in their format and work to get their artists' music added and then played.

It's hard to say this delicately, but let's put it this way: It's not the songs with the most artistic merit that get played on the radio. Additionally, commercial radio stations—those that run commercials, as opposed to public radio or college radio stations—rarely, rarely add records by unsigned bands to their playlists. There are many reasons why they don't, but a key reason is that if they are going to use their valuable and expensive airtime to play your song, they need to know that their listeners are going to have some chance of finding the record in the stores. If you are unsigned, the station will assume you don't have distribution, and therefore no records in the stores.

When Unsigned Artists Should Consider Indie Promotion

So why would an unsigned band hire an indie radio promoter? Well, as I said, they probably wouldn't. But there are times when a band has reached a level on their own, via gigging, touring, etc., where radio play can really push them over the edge and allow them to increase their chances of getting signed, or allow their careers to flourish without a record label. At this point, they will need to hire a radio promo person to start working the phones and getting their songs added to the stations' playlists, and then spun with some regularity during hours when people other than insomniacs and long-haul truckers might be awake and listening to the radio. Much like publicists have with journalists, promo people have relationships with radio stations. They speak to the stations' program and music directors several times a week and understand what makes those stations add songs to their playlist. This leverage, access, and expertise are all why artists cannot just do this job themselves.

How Promotion Can Help You Get a Deal

If you do hire an indie to handle radio for you, and they have some success, it will be a very powerful arrow in your quiver to shoot at record labels, just like having a song placed in a movie.

It is very impressive to see an unsigned band getting radio play. It means that not only is the band's music of a commercial enough quality that it can get played, but also that some of the long, hard, and expensive introductory groundwork has been laid. In other words, a radio station or two might have heard of you. When a label sees an unsigned artist getting airplay, they will feel that they can build off the base and have success much more quickly than if they were starting from scratch.

The Costs of Indie Promo

Here's the rub. Radio promotion is mucho expensivo. Retaining the services of an indie radio promoter for three months or so is going to run you at least $6,000 and probably a lot more. For commercial radio, on the low end of the dial, you can spend $30,000 to $100,000 in order to get a song played (or not) on the radio, and as for the high end, pick a number and add a zero or two to the end. Being added to a playlist doesn't mean that the record will get spun very often. More times than I'd like think about, I've seen a song get added to a station only to watch it get played two or three times a week. At that rate, it is impossible to judge whether or not the song has the potential to connect with the listeners or not. It just isn't getting played enough.

This is where the promoters must really earn their keep. They must get the rotations up, and if they don't, you should pull them off the job. The problem is that sometimes a station can add a record, and it can take weeks or months before the promoter is able to convince them that they should be spinning it with some regularity.

Frequently, after these months of waiting, the station will decide to drop the song from the playlist without ever spinning it frequently. Whatever the ultimate result, during this time, you are shelling money out.

How to Get and Keep Radio Play

If you do start to get airplay, you better darn well make sure you:

1. Have records in the stores.
2. Will soon be performing in the area where the station broadcasts.
3. Are getting some press coverage.

Radio does not and will not push a record in a vacuum. They may add a song, but if they don't see other action outside of radio going on around the song/artist, they're going to drop it fast. Additionally, radio stations look to other radio stations to gauge what their playlists should be. There are charts kept by trade magazines (such as *Billboard*, *Hits*, and *R&R*) for every format of radio. These charts are created by combining the playlists of the individual stations. (Stations send their playlists to the trade magazines that keep the charts.) Therefore, if a song is getting played a lot on twenty of the stations that make up the chart, that activity will appear on the chart. Other stations will take note, and not wanting to be left behind, they will often add the song to their own playlist, causing the song to attain an even higher spot on the chart. Of course, the inverse is also true. If a station adds a song and then sees from the charts that no one else added it, they will quickly drop it.

The Catch-22 of Radio

This is why it is very hard for a new artist to get radio play. Few radio stations are willing to be the first to take a chance on a song from an unknown artist.

This is where the weight and connections of an indie promo person can make a difference: by getting a couple of stations to go out on a limb and try a song. Even with an indie on the case, it's still very hard to get a station to be the first to try a song out. This is partly why you hear the same songs played on the radio over and over again.

Of course, if you are signed to a label with a track record of delivering songs from artists that work for a specific format, the stations will feel more secure that other stations will add the song, and therefore the process is far easier.

All of this is actually meant to discourage you from wasting your money and hiring an indie promo person to go after commercial radio too early in your career. Maybe one unsigned band in a thousand should consider it. That said, radio of some type should be part of your plan. Even commercial stations have specialty shows that play unsigned bands. Certainly, there are formats that are more open to unsigned bands—college, for example. There are indie promo people that specifically work these types of outlets, and you should consider them, at a certain point.

When to Hire an Indie Promoter

So, when should you hire a radio promoter? If your music has gotten good response on the college stations in your area, it may be wise to think about hiring an indie radio person who specifically handles college radio to work your CD. College indie promoters cost far less than those who work to commercial formats. Additionally, you can have them focus on certain geographic areas, in order to get the most bang for your buck.

Similarly, you can hire promo people to work specific genres of music. As they are somewhat niche oriented, they will also be less expensive. If, for example, you are a blues musician, there are indie promoters who know the blues radio landscape well. They will be a great asset when it comes to making sure your music gets to the right places.

As we have seen, in all aspects of trying to get a record deal, being smart and targeting what you are trying to accomplish is essential. When it comes to indie promo, being strategic is crucial. There is no other place in the music business where you can spend so much and potentially receive so little in return. Be very careful.

Working Radio into Your Game Plan

Lastly, it is important to be cognizant of radio even at the early stages of your career. There is still a certain step system in radio. If your music has broad enough appeal, you can rise up through the format ranks. For example, if you have tremendous success at college radio and can begin to get some of the bigger college stations to support you, you may start to appear on the radar of the AAA (Adult Album Alternative) programmers. This might lead to some recognition and play on the Hot AC (Adult Contemporary) stations, and perhaps onto the CHR stations (Contemporary Hit Radio), which used to be known as Top 40, and is the ultimate in terms of exposure and sales.

This progression will only happen once you get signed. Think about it earlier on, though, and think about your career trajectory in stages. Laying some groundwork at the college level can have a broader impact than you might imagine. It will also help you with your immediate concerns: getting exposure for your music, and giving prospective labels a sense that they are not starting from scratch.

FROM THE FIELD **Sean Coakley**
Founder of Songlines, Ltd.

Do you work with unsigned artists?

We base our decision to work records solely upon the quality of the music. We have to be moved by it and feel that our enthusiasm will translate into quantifiable airplay at Triple-A and/or Americana radio. The ability to play well live is very important, as it is the surest way to connect with an audience who might buy the CD and return to see you again.

What is the role of a promo person vis-à-vis an unsigned artist?

To give an honest read on the music's ability to connect with radio programmers and listeners.

What is the best way for an artist to get your attention?

Send a package with a short descriptive note. Is any station playing it? Has the artist made progress locally or regionally to gain an audience? How is that manifested? Does their CD sell after shows? All these things help paint a picture we can understand and will affect our decision whether to be involved.

At what point should an artist consider hiring a promo person?

Once there is a real story developing, as described above. We like to work with people who have a vision, both in their music and in the careers. We can help if they are ready.

FROM THE FIELD **Matt Kleinschmidt**
The Music Syndicate

Do you work with unsigned artists?

Yes, we do. We have worked with and will continue to work with unsigned artists. We never just work with them in one capacity, either. What we do before we even begin a campaign is find out what their goals are—what do they want out of the promotion. Then, we determine the steps we can go on from there. Some artists want to gain profile in order to get signed to a label. Others want feedback on their record (who likes it, tracks to focus on, etc.). Others are interested in starting a tour, and they are interested in where they have the best chance to land shows as they travel across the country.

The best thing to remember is that every artist has different goals, and every goal usually has a different path that needs to be taken for a campaign to be a success. There is no real answer for them, no business model they can take home and study that states, "To get from point A to C, follow path B." If it were, every band in the world would have a record deal and be famous. I do know that it takes hard work from an artist, who must be willing to work as hard as us, and more. They need to be self-promoting and willing to sacrifice a lot personally, socially, and sometimes financially.

What is the role of a promo person vis-à-vis an unsigned artist?

My own strength is that I can be flexible and liquid when it comes to catering to an artist's needs. I can act as a liaison between them and a radio station, a record label, a booking agent, a manager, or a club promoter. Since my job is not a defined position, I get to wear many hats and learn about more then one aspect of how the industry works. This also helps me answer questions for smaller/unsigned acts without having them to search far and wide for answers.

Ultimately, my job is to help the artist get to the next level, whatever that level may be: getting a manager, increasing awareness at radio, helping them get signed to a label, or moving to a larger label. I get no bigger enjoyment in taking an artist that is not well known, opening some doors, and getting them a career of some sort where being a musician is their only job, and they can quit the 9-to-5 they had been working until they "made" it.

What is the best way for an artist to get your attention?

That is the easiest question yet. PUT OUT A GOOD RECORD. I do not need a gimmick, a fancy press sheet, or names of people they worked with. Some of my favorite artists I discovered were from simply playing their record and hearing what they were all about.

Once that is done, you better be able to deliver it live! I cannot stress how important it is to a new/unknown band to tour. Get in front of anyone, no matter how small a crowd. Some artists expect their great single to go to radio, catch on, and then they are famous! That way of thinking never lasts.

The artists I respect most earned every fan they have, played in front of crowds who had no idea who they were for a long time. Career artists are the ones who have a fan base that grows with them, buy each new record (which might not have as much hype), and continue to see an artist live.

What is the key for a successful artist/promo person relationship?

I often tell potential clients to go for the person that is most enthusiastic about your work. That is who will go to bat for a record when no one else may be able to. When I am interested in working with an artist, I try to know as much about them as possible. I listen to their goals and ask a ton of questions—sometimes ones they never thought of. The reason I do this is to see where their head is at and what they are looking to get out of a promotional campaign. I turn down clients daily because they think they are ready to commit to the process but I find out they have nothing in place to accommodate the amount of work we are going to give them.

Most unsigned artists come to us with a record, and say "I want to take it to radio. How much does it cost?" I always answer with "Send me the record, I want to hear what I am dealing with," as well as try to find out if they are able to tour, do interviews with stations, and other promotional-type things. All this conversation takes place before I even tell them what it would cost them. Most of the time, they end up rethinking their status, they realize that they are not able to fire on all cylinders, and it would be a waste of their time and money to perform a campaign at that time. Yes, I turn away money all the time! Basically, it's because our reputation is everything, and the last thing I want is someone feeling that they did not get everything out of a campaign they can, and then feel cheated by the experience.

Honesty is also important to me. I think we work in an industry where this person is out to screw that person. If people were more upfront and honest about things, we could get stuff done a lot better and quicker. I think someone's word is invaluable. The type of position I have fortifies that idea even more, because the last thing I want to happen is to have someone unsatisfied with my work.

At what point should an artist consider hiring a promo person?

Most people come to me asking to have their record promoted without really knowing what else they need to have in order to have a successful campaign. The best way to look at promotion is as a part of a larger picture. Artists need to have some sort of idea what they want to do with the information and support they are getting from radio. It is too often the case they come in and expect the radio promotion to be the factor that 'breaks' them. This is almost never the case.

The best time for an artist to get promotion is around the release, after they have started a press campaign of some sort, and right before a tour. This way, every possible aspect of their promotional campaign is effectively helping the other. These are all very necessary pieces of the puzzle and should not be overlooked. Radio promotion is not the end-all-be-all of a campaign and should not be viewed as such.

How important is college radio for the unsigned artist?

It is probably the best way to get your music heard by people who are open to the idea of listening to new music and are the most prone to embrace it. Unfortunately, it also, at the same time, acts as artist development for artists on labels as well. Most labels have some sort of financial backing (the label, previous album sales) to help them tie all the parts of the puzzle together more easily.

College radio cannot support every artist the same. There are constantly heritage artists at the format that sometimes eclipse the importance of an unsigned artist. The CMJ charts are chock full of them. Unsigned artists should not despair, though. They should rather focus their efforts in gathering more information about stations, supporting and looking for exposure (like playing campus shows, showcases), rather then for a chart position.

Ultimately, working hard to convert the support into tangible goals is what is going to help most. A chart number looks great for a press sheet, but if it cannot be transformed into album sales or concert tickets, the entire process may feel unfulfilling to some artists.

FROM THE FIELD **Sean O'Connell**
President of Music Allies

What is the role of a promo person vis-à-vis an unsigned artist?

When an unsigned artist spends money on indie promotion, it is almost always guaranteed to have little effect on their CD sales or tour sales. Be very cautious when going down this path. There is an entire industry of indie promoters who make a living taking money from countless unsigned artists. These indie promoters have absolutely *no* clout or solid relationships with radio. Without a roster of solid, signed bands who are touring, have good distribution, and are receiving great press nationwide, an indie promoter is nothing more than an annoying telemarketer to radio stations. Working with telemarketers will get you nowhere.

What is the best way for an artist to get an indie's attention?

Grow your career and let them discover you. Indies are connected to labels and managers. (Some indies have their own management company or label). An indie promoter may be more valuable connecting you to the right industry people then getting you radio airplay, while you're unsigned. This is a great scenario, since often, that indie will be contracted by the label you sign with to you, and they will feel vested in your career.

What is the key for a successful artist/promo person relationship?

Look at their roster of bands they work. Only work with indies where unsigned bands are the exception on their roster, not the rule. If the indie has a solid lineup of well-known bands, then consider what your game plan is. Most likely, an unsigned band can't reinforce their music through other marketing channels (let alone have decent national distribution).

At what point should an artist consider hiring a promo person?

If an artist is committed to developing a long career (which takes money, perseverance, patience, and talent), then promoting to college radio may not sell you a ton of records, but it may be a good career builder. It may get your name out. If you want a shot at doing well, wait until you can get records in stores (that means a few thousand nationwide), you are touring, and you have someone on your team to talk to radio in addition to the indie. (Indies aren't good at setting up promotions, contests, interviews, etc.)

Summary

Usually, it is not in the best interest of unsigned artists to hire an indie publicist or promo person until they really have many other things going for them, such as consistent touring, some regional press, or some local airplay. Once you are generating some income, you may want to think about reinvesting in your career and dipping your toe into the world of indie marketing. When you have reached that point, look for a publicist (or publicity firm) and/or a promo person (or firm) that have expertise in your type of music. They should also have a successful track record with artists that are at a similar stage in their career as you are in yours.

Be wary of publicists or promo people who can only point to one or two artists with whom they have had success. These artists may have had some sort of wind behind them—other things going on that are driving media or radio action, beyond the work of the publicist or promo people. In these cases, the publicists or promo people are along for the ride, rather than driving the ship. Instead, focus on firms who are able to do good, quality work for artists that are similar to you.

Find them the same way you find any other member of your team: speak to other artists, look in the credits of records under the thank-you's, and speak to managers, club bookers, and others.

The temptation will be there for you to hire a publicist or promo person. It seems so pleasing to allow someone else to swoop in, *a la* Batman, and solve your problems. Hopefully, this chapter has shown you that the chances of Batman having any effect are slim, and also that Batman don't work cheap—unless you're Catwoman.

Workshop

Plot out the course towards when you should expect to consider a publicist. What can you do on your own? What can't you do?

What local media outlets might be interested in your music? What college radio stations might play it? What local papers might review a local performance? Can you perform live on your local access cable channel?

What publications are in the next level up from these media outlets, where you would need better contacts to get your music featured?

Take a calendar and schedule when you should try to gain some of this media exposure for yourself. Determine how long these local mechanisms can keep you busy, and then mark that point to explore the possibility of hiring indie marketing people.

10

Publishing: Rights and Wrongs

Ah, publishing. Such mystery and taboo surrounding such a simple word. Given the misinformation about what publishing is, you would think the Knights Templar were involved. It is, in fact, a complicated subject that lifetimes can be devoted to understanding. This chapter will give you an overview of the basics of publishing, specifically focusing on what it means to you, the hungry record-label-deal striver. In short, publishing can be broken down into three pieces: registration, collection, and exploitation.

After you write a song, it must be *registered,* so that you, the writer, can track when it is used (released on a CD, played on the radio, used in a movie, etc.). Once it's registered, it can be tracked, but then the money must be *collected* from the record labels who commercially release the song, the radio stations that play the song over the airwaves, or the movie producers who use it in a film. Lastly, the song that you've written needs to be *exploited* to reach its full potential. This exploitation, among other things, entails attempting to get the song recorded ("covered") by other artists, as well as getting the song used in movies, TV, or ads.

In order for these three things to take place most effectively, the song must be recorded and released by a record company. Because of this, publishing is important to the songwriter who is looking for a record deal. For the most part, record labels are looking for the songwriter to also be a performer of the songs. However, if you are a great songwriter who doesn't perform, there are still ways to work with labels—and more frequently, publishers—who will pitch your songs to artists who do perform.

Mechanicals

At its core, publishing is concerned with making sure the writer of the song is compensated whenever his song is used for a commercial purpose. Note, that's the *writer* of the song, and not its *performer*.

There was a time when the performer of the song was rarely the writer. Someone had to pitch the songs to performers.

Enter the publisher. The publishers matched songs with performers. The song would be performed live and transcribed and sold as sheet music. The music publisher would simply print up the songs that the writers had written in the form of sheet music. They would then pay the writer some percentage of the profits from the sale of this music. Additionally, the songwriter would be compensated when the song was played in a public area, such as over the radio.

Everything went along fairly with this system until piano rolls came into existence. Once someone figured out an entirely new way in which music could be distributed, the publishers had to figure out a way to make sure the writers (and the publishers themselves) got paid, now that music was being mechanically reproduced in this new form. So they invented the "mechanical royalty," which states that for any music "mechanically" reproduced and sold—initially as piano rolls, but later as acetates, then vinyl and cassette, and continuing today as CDs—a royalty must be paid to the songwriter. We're currently wrestling with online distribution. When there is money being made from this means of distribution, the writer of the song will be compensated via a mechanical license agreement.

Songwriters could, in theory, place their songs with performers and collect their money themselves. But, being the creative types that they tend to be, they quickly realized they would not be able to administer all the aspects that would be required, in order to place songs and collect the money, and still have time to write songs. They therefore turned to publishers for help. The writer signed over his song's copyright to the publisher, and the publisher went out and tried to generate interest and revenue from the song, and then split the revenue of the money collected with the writer on a 50/50 basis.

This type of relationship continues today. One of the most basic specific services publishers provide for songwriters is to make sure that their mechanical royalties are being paid by those who use the writer's songs. Today, the main use for songs is for release on records. As more and more songwriters today are also performers, mechanical income becomes very important for anyone looking for a record deal.

Why Publishers Want You to Get a Record Deal

Publishers want their songwriters to have record deals so that they will have some money to collect. It doesn't do your publisher any good if your songs are never mechanically reproduced, as there is no one to collect from. Therefore, while you are trying to get signed to a label, if you get a publishing deal, the publisher will become another member of your team. Again, their goal is to help you to land a record deal so that they can start collecting mechanical royalties for you based on your record sales.

How Lucrative Are Mechanical Royalties?

"Just how much can you expect to make from these mechanical royalties?" you are no doubt greedily asking, at this point. The mechanical rate has gone through an evolutionary process since its inception in the 1909 Copyright Law. The mechanical license law was instated to not only make sure that writers get paid when their songs are used, but also to force copyright holders to allow others to record the songs and not set the price too high for anyone to afford the license. In effect, it set a fixed price at which the copyright holders *must* grant a license to those who desire to mechanically reproduce the holder's songs. The term for this license is a "compulsory license."

One of the catches of this compulsory license is that it only applies once the work has been recorded and released commercially. Prior to the "first use" of a song, a publisher may charge whatever they can get from someone who wants to record it—effectively determining who has the privilege of recording and releasing it first. After the first use, the *most* they can charge for the use of the song is this compulsory license rate. So, once a song has been recorded and commercially released, if you want to record it you can, as long as you do so under the terms of the compulsory license. These terms state that for each record manufactured and distributed that contains the song, the statutory rate (so called because it refers back to the Copyright Statute that decreed it) must be paid. That rate has evolved over the years and is periodically re-examined by a Copyright Royalty Tribunal.

The rate currently is $.08 per song. If the song is over five minutes in length, the rate is the song length (number of minutes) multiplied by $.0155. This rate will change, and in fact, according to the schedule from the Copyright Royalty Tribunal, by the year 2006, the statutory rate will be $.091, or $.0175 per minute, if the song is over five minutes.

This evolution is a good thing for the songwriter. Historically, the mechanical rate has never gone down.

The "Controlled-Composition Clause"

When you sign to a label, the label will have to pay you (or your publisher, if you have one) a mechanical royalty for your songs that are mechanically reproduced on your record.

Now, before you think, "Great, I'm going to record myself a fifty-song record and make $4 a pop on each record sold," realize that record labels have already thought this through. There is a clause in all record label contracts called the "controlled composition clause." This clause limits the amount of mechanical royalty liability that the labels have—that is, it reduces the obligations that they would have if they were issued compulsory licenses from the publisher. Your contract will state that if you, the performer, wrote any part of the song that is being released on the record, it is a "controlled composition." This limits how much they will have to pay. Here is how they typically limit their exposure:

1. No matter how long the song is—even if it's over five minutes—the labels will only pay the minimum rate. That is, even if you record a ten-minute song, which for a non-controlled composition would earn you ten minutes multiplied by $.0155, they are going to pay you as if the song was less than five minutes. That is $.08 (in reality, only $.06, as explained below). In that ten-minute song, this would result in you getting paid less than half of what you would, were they not paying on the "minimum statutory rate."

2. They will only pay 75 percent of the statutory rate. Why? I don't know. It occurred after the 1976 Copyright Law cleaned up some issues that lingered from the prior law, and it's been in place, and become accepted, ever since. So even though the statutory rate today is $.08 per song, the labels will only pay you $.06 per song for controlled compositions.

3. They will only pay royalties for up to ten songs on a record. Sometimes, you can squeak it to eleven, but don't count on it.

4. They will fix the statutory rate at the time of either when the song was recorded, delivered to the label, or released. You will want it at the latest possible date, in case the rate goes up, and they will want it at the earliest, for the same reason. In fact, labels know the rate has always gone up, so they set it in stone that no matter how high the rate goes, you will be paid on the rate at the time the record was recorded, delivered to the label, or released—whatever you are contractually bound to.

5. The controlled composition clause also limits your mechanical income to records that are sold (not distributed, which is what a compulsory license must be paid on). Therefore, free goods (records given to retailers for free as an incentive to order more records, but which are still sold) and promo copies do not generate any mechanical royalties for a controlled composition.

There are additional issues, such as if you have cover songs on your record (i.e., non-controlled compositions), which force the label to pay more than what they would pay for a record full of controlled compositions. Guess where the extra needed money is coming from? You got it, your pocket, in the form of reductions from your mechanical income. There is very little wiggle room in the above terms. Sometimes, you can get a label to move on some of these, but not often, and only after you've had some real success.

The Importance of the Mechanical

Even with all of these reductions, your prime source of income early (and sometimes always) in your career will be your mechanical royalties. Learn to understand them, learn to love them. Know that your publisher understands and loves them and that your publisher wants you to get a record deal so that they can start making money off you via the mechanicals. Very few artists ever recoup their advances and costs that the labels pay out. Therefore, they never see record royalties. The only money they generally see is in the form of mechanical royalties. This is why it makes sense to think of the label as the engine that drives the publishing revenue.

Administration Deals

There are publishers who limit their roles to collecting mechanical royalties on behalf of their writers. In this case, the publisher is said to be "administering your publishing." The publisher, in the role of an administrator, has no ownership equity in your songs, but is only acting as a sort of agent for you: collecting the money and taking a cut. Typically, a publisher acting as an administrator will take 10 to 15 percent of the mechanical income they collect. This is not a bad deal, considering that it's not easy getting money out of record labels. These types of "admin" deals, as they are called, are usually term deals (meaning that they are for a limited period of time), with little to no advances, which renew automatically unless you decide to break the agreement. For instance, you may sign on with an administrator and grant them the rights to be the exclusive administrator for your songs for two years. Then, if no notice is given by you to terminate, the contract will automatically renew for another year.

Once you have a record deal, align yourself with a publisher at the very least to serve as the administrator that collects your mechanical royalties. But remember that the publisher can play an important role in helping you get a record deal, even if it is acting only as an administrator. They will use whatever contacts they have to find a label to record songs in their catalog.

Co-Publishing Deals

Should you choose to not limit the role of a publisher to simply administering your mechanical licenses, the next step up would be to do a publishing or co-publishing deal. A publishing deal basically means that you are signing over all of your copyrights (in the form of songs) that you write during a term to a publisher, who pays you an advance and then "works" (exploits) the copyrights and splits any income with you 50/50 after recouping the advance.

A co-publishing deal means essentially the same thing, except that the rights for the copyrights are split between two or more publishers—one of whom may be you. That is, if you maintain any ownership of your copyright, but assign some portion of it to a publisher, there are in effect two publishers, and hence, a co-publishing deal. In these types of deals, the splits will be different than the typical 50/50 usually occurring between a publisher and a writer.

Not all publishers are willing to make these types of deals where you retain some ownership. When they do, the advances will be smaller.

Syncs and Placements: Your Music in Movies and TV

Once you enter into a publishing or co-publishing deal, the publisher will perform functions beyond simply registering your songs and collecting your mechanicals. Crucially, they will help place your music in movies, TV shows, advertisements, and so on. This is referred to as a "sync," because your music is being synchronized in time to a visual image in a movie, ad, or TV show.

I am absolutely amazed at the way views have recently changed. What not many years ago was considered to be the height of "selling out" is now deemed not only acceptable, but almost a *de rigueur* part of any record's marketing plan. I personally have very mixed emotions when it comes to using music to sell things like appliances and beer, but its impact on record sales is undeniable. The greater, long-term career implications of using your music in advertisements may be trickier to pin down, but at this point, there seems to be little concern for this.

Whatever the case, publishers can and do work on behalf of the artist to secure placements or synchronizations. When the publisher takes on this role, they are no longer simply collecting mechanical royalties, and therefore are no longer seen as simply administrators. Rather, they are actively working the copyrights for the songs of the artist to various outlets, which transcends the typical artist/administrator relationship. In point of fact, they are really performing the service that publishers originally did, trying to get a songwriter's songs heard by as many people as possible. In this manner, they work with music supervisors to get a song synched in a movie. They pitch ad agencies in the hopes that the song will be placed in an ad. They approach other artists about potentially recording ("covering") one of the songs they represent on that artists' album. In the first two cases, synching to movies or commercials, the publisher will negotiate a deal with the film producer, music supervisor, or ad agency for the use of the music. Additionally, the publisher can refuse a request from a movie or ad agency, and not allow the music to be used in the film, if they don't feel the money is good enough or if they have an issue with the content. If the music has been released on an album, the film producer or music supervisor must work out a deal with the record company for the rights to use a song that has been released on a record that the label released. (This is called the "master use.")

When a song gets performed ("covered") by another artist, the publisher simply negotiates whether or not the record company who releases the cover version of the song must pay the full mechanical rate or a reduced rate, and then collects the money. The publisher cannot keep another artist from covering a song, after it has been commercially released. However, if it has not been commercially released, the publisher does not have to grant the rights for the song to be covered.

Publishing Deals Can Lead To Record Deals

"This is all great," you say, "but how does it help me get signed?" Well, if your publisher is able to get your music placed in a film or an ad, and said film or ad has any commercial impact whatsoever, you will really have something to say to a potential label that will undoubtedly pique their interest. There are few more powerful trump cards when trying to get a record deal then telling a label that you have a song in an upcoming movie or ad. Given the consolidation at radio that has narrowed the playlists, and the generally difficult market for alerting consumers to the release of records by new artists (and established artists as well), more and more labels consider placements of music in films, TV, or ads as a very key marketing component. It is often easier to get a song placed than it is to get it played on the radio. Therefore, if you come to a label as an unsigned artist with as powerful a piece of ammunition as a sync in an upcoming movie, the label will often see that as a way to leapfrog much of the arduous work, alerting the marketplace to the existence of a new artist. They will use the placement as a catalyst to allow more traditional marketing (radio, press, touring) to really begin to take hold.

In this way, the publisher is doubly incentivized to get your songs placed. First, they reap some of the financial rewards from the income paid for the placement (anywhere from 20 to 50 percent of the money paid for the usage). Second, they realize that such a usage will often lead to a record deal, which then leads to the publisher's ability to collect mechanical royalties from the sales of those records.

> *Most of the artists that attract my attention do so when I catch a glimpse of them from the corner of my eye. That is to say, the artists are out doing their thing, making music, getting it out there. Someone takes notice, a magazine or fanzine I respect writes a small piece, someone on a cyberlist drops a link to a song they like. Or in an interview with an artist I like, a few names I don't know are dropped, and my curiosity is sparked. . . .*
>
> **—Nathaniel Krenkel**
>
> **Sony/ATV Music Publishing**

When to Get a Publishing Deal

Though a publishing deal can help you get a record deal, my advice is to hesitate before you give up any portion of your publishing. Wait until you are certain that your publisher will help you from both a monetary standpoint and from a career development standpoint—which may both be solved by helping you get a record deal. If and when you find this person, you should consider making a deal.

Almost as bad as making a publishing deal with the wrong person is holding onto your publishing and not doing anything with it. One hundred percent of squat is squat. If you are an unsigned artist and a publisher with a track record shows interest in working your songs, you should seriously consider making a deal with that publisher. It could lead to income and to a record deal. If someone comes waving a bunch of empty promises at you and wants any portion of your copyright, run—don't walk—away. Further, consider carefully people that want pieces of your publishing in return for services that don't have anything to do with publishing—for example, managers or lawyers who, rather than taking payment in a more traditional manner of fees or commissions, want a piece of your publishing. As we saw in the management chapter, you must really be careful about who you grant your publishing to. You should only grant it to people who are in the business of actively working the publishing and not just using it as a way to hedge their bets against the odds of your career taking off and the publishing then becoming valuable.

Types of Publishing Deals

The types of deals you can make with publishers are all over the map. Advances on publishing deals (as opposed to admin deals) do get paid, and as a rule of thumb, a publisher will base their advance on roughly a dollar per record they believe you can sell. So if a publisher thinks it's reasonable that you can sell 15,000 copies of your first record, they may offer you an advance of $15,000. The logic behind this is that they will be collecting roughly a dollar a disc in mechanicals from the record label, and will therefore recoup their advance off the mechanicals. Should a sync or placement come about, that's gravy. Should you sell 30,000 records instead of 15,000, great, you will recoup your advance, and both you and the publisher will start making money. This is a very crude formula, and certainly other factors go into determining how much of an advance should be paid. Additionally, as you saw above regarding the breakdown of mechanical income, it doesn't quite add up to a dollar a record. That said, I've seen this logic used with frequency.

Understand that in these types of deals, the publisher has the exclusive rights to administer and exploit the copyrights in perpetuity. Therefore, you will not be able to go out and make another deal with another publisher for any of the songs that are on the album. And often, any songs at all that you write during the term of your publishing deal fall under the auspices of this deal. Like a record label, a publisher will sign you on for a term. It could be anything from one to five (or more) albums. The publisher will pay an advance to you for each album that is released by a label. If the contractual advances due to you are sizeable, the publisher will typically put a clause in the contract stating that, in order for you to receive your advance and have the record you release be considered a "contract fulfilling album" for your publishing obligation, your record must be released on a major label (or be distributed by a major). In this way, the publisher is protected from the risk of you deciding to put your record out on Jimbo's record label and just pocketing the huge publishing advance while Jim struggles to sell 300 records—let alone pay a publisher mechanicals.

Publishing Pitfalls

While this protects the publisher, it can also trap you. For instance, if you sign a record deal and a publishing deal, and after the first record, the label either drops you or goes out of business, you are going to have to find another label that will release your record that fits the criteria of the publisher, in order for you to get your publishing advance on the next record. If you can't, you will not be receiving any more sweet publishing money, and you will also not be able to write songs for any other publishers, as you are exclusively signed to your publisher. This means that unless placements come from your publisher, they won't be coming at all. Obviously, it is in the best interest of a publisher who has paid a sizeable advance to you on your first record to do everything they can to recoup that money. In theory, they will continue to work on your behalf.

There is, however, a very real phenomenon that occurs if you release a record that stiffs: people tend to want to distance themselves from a failure, chalk it up to a bad idea, and move on. They often would prefer to write off the advance money and move on to the next happening artist than try to figure out a way to resuscitate your career, which in their eyes, is damaged goods.

This sounds harsh, but it happens a lot. My advice is, should you find yourself in a situation where either a publisher or a label is throwing big money around, determine if it is, in fact, big enough money for you to never need money again, ever in your life, because it may very well be the last money you see from a publisher or record label. If it is, you should probably take the money and roll the dice. If it's not, try to structure a deal that gives you the best chance to have a career. For example, you can get the record label to agree to a "two- or three-firm deal," which means that they guarantee to release at least two or three of your records before they can drop you. This would also trigger the publishing advances. This type of deal may give you enough of a chance to really build a following and not be as reliant on the label or publisher.

Performance Rights Organizations (ASCAP, BMI, SESAC)

The last piece of the publishing puzzle is the performance rights organization. When it comes to these organizations, you don't have complicated decisions to confront, such as choosing between an admin deal and a publishing deal. You simply must choose between one of the three societies: ASCAP, BMI, or SESAC. Whichever you choose, you should immediately register with one of these.

How Performance Rights Organizations Work

All three do basically the same thing. They issue "blanket licenses" to venues where music is either performed (concert halls, arenas) or broadcast (be it over radio, satellite, or CD). These venues pay a fee proportionate to the number of people who hear the music in the places where music is used. In other words, a small club pays far less than a TV station for a blanket license. The money generated from the blanket licenses is divvied up based on what music is used the most and distributed to the writer and the publisher (often the same person, at the beginning of a career). How do they know what music is used the most? They require that radio stations submit logs that list what was played. Additionally, they require "cue" sheets to be sent to them from TV stations, which list what music was used and in what capacity (theme, background, etc). Lastly, they monitor the live performances of the top-two-hundred-grossing touring artists, according to the touring trade magazine *Pollstar,* to find out who is playing what and to how many people. If you are not one of these top-two-hundred-grossing performers, you have to jump through some hoops (submitting tour schedules and set lists, for instance) to collect money from your live performances.

In order for these organizations to collect this money, you need to register any CDs you release, on which you must also list your affiliation. This is why artists list song titles followed by the songwriter's name, publishing company, and performance rights organization (usually in parentheses) on the backs of CDs. For example, you might see "North of the Moon" written by George Howard, Kill Devil Music (BMI), were you to scour the record stores for a song I wrote.

It is fairly simple to register with one of these societies. Call them and request the number of forms you need for each song you've written, or go to the Web site and download them. Fill them out, mail them in, and wait for your songs to get played on the radio and start receiving checks.

Unlike every other form of publishing revenue that comes your way, the societies pay directly to you, the writer, as opposed to paying the publisher and letting them pay you. When you fill out your performance rights forms, you will be asked to inform them of both who the writer is and who the publisher is. They will then divide the money that comes in and send you your share directly and the publisher their share. Be wary of publishers who ask you to sign over your share of the performance rights income. Most of the time, they won't do this, as the performance rights societies will refuse to pay them, but just double-check that it doesn't happen. As a musician, you will need as many separate streams of income as you can possibly have. Getting your performance rights money directly is a good one of these streams.

How Performance Rights Organizations Can Help You Get a Deal

Of course, if you don't have a record deal, you're not likely to get a whole lot of radio play. But, like the publishers we've talked about, these performance rights organizations have a vested interest in getting your music publicly performed. It justifies their existence, and therefore, they want you to get a record deal. I have relationships with people at all of the performance rights organizations, and they are constantly alerting me to artists that they believe have merit and should have a record deal. Additionally, these organizations actively work to promote their artists and will often set up events in which their artists perform for labels, music supervisors, or publishers. It really is up to you, how active you want to be with your performance rights society. If you simply register and wait for the radio play to begin generating airplay, they will certainly let you do that. However, if you work to build relationships with these people in the same way you do with booking agents, managers, and so on, they can become an important part of your team.

Summary

Learn as much as you can about publishing. Appendix B suggests some good books on the subject. Figure out exactly how publishing fits in your overall plans, and ask yourself if you are comfortable with your songs being used in movies or ads. Do the legwork required to find out which publishers are doing good work for their writers, and start submitting materials to them in the same way that you submit demos to record labels. Register each and every song you write with a performance rights society, and find out what type of services they provide that will help you reach your goal of getting signed.

If you are a performer who writes your own songs, you will soon realize that your publisher will be as important as your record label, and potentially the source of far more revenue. Do not underestimate the importance of the publisher.

Beyond all else, do not hold on to the old misinformation that exists out there that publishers are bad and you must never part with any portion your songs. In reality, you must part with some percentage of your songs in order to maximize their value.

The trick is to make sure that the publisher you choose is really working on your behalf. If you can manage this, you will have a real symbiotic relationship that can give you economic security long after your performing days are over.

FROM THE FIELD **Nathaniel Krenkel**
Sony/ATV Music Publishing

In 1997, I stumble into the Living Room on Stanton to get out of rain. I end up seeing an artist named Jesse Harris. I like his songs, sign his mailing list, go to see him perform more, and generally get to know him. In 1998, I sign him to a developmental deal at Sony Publishing. The deal gives him enough money to continue moving forward in his career—not enough to buy a house or a new riding pony, but enough to press some records to sell at shows, and buy some new gear.

For years, Jesse and I talk daily. We pitch his songs to established artists, we try to break into Nashville, we push his original recordings towards film and TV. Frustratingly, execs tell us they cannot imagine their female singers doing a song of Jesse's because his demos are sung by a guy.

Around 2000, Jesse encourages his pal Norah Jones to move to NYC. We bring Norah up to Sony's Demo Studio (which Jesse has access to via his deal) and cut a stack of Jesse's tunes with Norah's *female* vocal. These demos circulate and eventually Norah lands a deal, and Jesse's tunes stay in the mix and make it on the record.

Spring 2003, Jesse wins a Grammy for Song of the Year and signs to Verve, who will put out his record in May.

Main point of this story: In 1999, we were discouraged. In 2000, we were pretty bummed out. In 2001, things weren't really going anywhere. Yet the songs were great, and getting better. People were coming down to shows and came back again and again. We all felt it wasn't a matter of "what the hell?" so much as "when the hell...."

Patience, persistence, and luck.

FROM THE FIELD **Sue Devine**
ASCAP

Do you work with unsigned songwriter/artists?

ASCAP works with both signed and unsigned songwriters and composers. We help writers join ASCAP as both writers and publishing companies. We also nurture and help develop our songwriter/composer members at all stages of their careers.

ASCAP presents valuable workshops in pop, country, r&b, gospel, Latin, jazz, film scoring, musical theatre, concert music, and other areas to help songwriters and composers refine their craft. ASCAP also sponsors showcases, seminars, and networking events and offers many types of support such as scholarships, commissions, and cash awards to writer members who qualify.

What is the role of the Performing Rights Organization (PRO) vis a vis an unsigned songwriter/artist?

Our main function is to represent our members by licensing and distributing royalties for non-dramatic public performances of their copyrighted works. These royalties are paid to members based on surveys of performances of the works in our repertory that they wrote or published. Our licensees include radio, television, cable, live concerts, orchestras, shopping malls, bars, clubs, Web sites, ring tones—all types of customers that use music.

In addition to career development opportunities described above, we have a wide array of member benefits geared towards working music professionals. These benefits include MusicPro Insurance offering health, life, long-term care, instrument, equipment, studio and tour liability insurance; a credit union; an investment program; Guitar Center benefits; and discounts on musical instruments and accessories, CD manufacturing, promotional merchandise, and much more.

At what point should an unsigned songwriter/artist consider registering with a PRO?

Composers/songwriters join ASCAP at all stages of their development. It is imperative to join if your works are having public performances, so that you can collect your performance royalties. Writers should consider joining sooner and participating in all of our artist development programs. See the above.

In what ways can the PRO help an unsigned artist?

ASCAP provides a community for our members to network, learn the business, and make important creative and business contacts through our Web site and through our many career development programs, including showcases, workshops, seminars, awards, grants, commissions, and other types of support. Our Member Card benefits, exclusive to ASCAP members, are geared toward making the life of the working music professional easier. As the only member-owned performing rights organization in the U.S., ASCAP is the leading advocate for our members' rights and there is never a conflict of interest when we negotiate on our members' behalf. These are just some of the many ways in which ASCAP can help our members.

Workshop

Determine which performance rights society is right for you and register.

Make a list of potential publishers.

Determine which publishers are looking to work with unsigned bands.

11

Distribution: Moving Product

Understanding distribution channels will give you some insight into how labels work, which is always helpful in terms of you getting a deal with them. In a similar manner to indie marketing, there are a tremendous number of unsigned artists who feel that getting a distribution deal will solve all their problems. This is rarely true. Therefore, it's important that you understand what is really involved with distribution so that you can avoid the many potential pitfalls, as well as develop strategies to use it to your advantage—both in helping you get a deal and in forwarding your career.

Distribution follows marketing. You must appreciate this fully. Few people do—even those at major labels. Thus, many artists are constantly disappointed by their distribution company and blame them for things that are not their fault. Understanding that distribution follows marketing will clarify why distribution is not relevant to very many unsigned artists. Put simply, most unsigned artists simply do not have the infrastructure or cash required to do the marketing that would justify a distribution deal.

If you manage to secure a distribution deal for yourself, you are, at that point, a label. Remember the "label" criteria: you have an equity stake in the copyright of your music; because distribution follows marketing, you must be doing some promotion; and now, you have a means to disseminate your music—your distribution deal. The largest responsibility that you will have is trying to effect a good working relationship with your distributor. How do you do this? Marketing, marketing, marketing. Therefore, in order to fully understand distribution, you need to understand a bit about marketing. This information will prove useful in many ways vis-à-vis getting a deal, as it will allow you to better focus your own energies onto things that will have real appeal both to potential distributors and labels.

How Distribution Works

Just like labels, there are distributors of all different sizes and specialties. The major labels all have their own distribution networks. In fact, part of what makes a major label a major is that the label is distributed by one of the five major distribution companies: Sony (which distributes Columbia, Epic, and others), CEMA (which distributes, among others, Capitol and EMI and their affiliated labels), WEA (Warner Bros., Elektra, and Atlantic), Universal (MCA, Island/Def Jam, and others), and BMG (RCA, Arista). Outside of these major distributors, there are a handful of distributors who are wholly owned by the majors but act as kind of quasi-independents. These include RED (owned by Sony), Caroline (owned by Virgin, which is owned by EMI), and ADA (owned by WEA). Then there are the many, many true independent distributors, some of which are national in scope and some regional. All of them—indies, quasi-indies, and majors—function in basically the same way.

Reserves aside, distribution is pretty simple. A distributor acts as a wholesaler and buys records from a label (or an artist who is acting as a label) and then sells them to retailers. In exchange for this service, the distributor takes a fee from the label of between 20 and 30 percent (give or take a point or two on either end) of the wholesale price. For example, if the label's wholesale price of the records to the distributor is $10, and the distributor charges the label a 20 percent distribution fee, the distributor pays the label $8 per record and pockets the remaining $2.

Co-op

Distributors typically pay labels on a monthly basis for the records that they have purchased. They subtract from this payment any deductions for records returned by the retailer. They also deduct any "co-op" charges. (Co-op is shorthand for cooperative, in that the label/distributor and retailer work together, cooperating on a promotion.) Co-op charges are the expenses involved in getting the records in the store in the first place, and sometimes, paying for prominent display in the store. It can also include ads in the paper or other marketing. Expect at least $1.50 per record for co-op, though it is often more. Additionally, the distributor will typically offer a "deal" once a month where retailers can get 7 to 10 percent off any records they order during that time. That will also be considered a deductible co-op expense.

After all these deductions, a label is looking at around $6 per record as their net payment from the distributor.

Distribution Follows Marketing

So you figure, "Okay, $6 per record ain't a bad take—far better than my piddling $1 or $2 royalty, if I got signed. So, George, why are you so adamant about me not just hooking up with a distributor?"

Well, here's why. From that $6, you have to pay for everything else involved in releasing the record. First, you have to pay roughly $1.50 to manufacture each CD, and around $1 mechanical to the publisher for each one sold. (Of course, if you are both the artist and the writer, that money flows back to you.) Then you have to market them—at the low end, it's around $3.50 per unit to market the suckers.

The Record Business is a "Pull-Through" Business

This $3.50 for marketing is necessary for the distribution process to work. When it comes to marketing, you must understand that the traditional record business is "pull-through" and not "push-through." The label or the artist must create a demand so that the consumer literally walks into a store and pulls the records off the shelves. Labels try to make it a push-through business by shipping tons of records, paying for low sale pricing and great positioning in the stores, but boy, are they taking a gamble in doing so. If the CDs don't get successfully "pushed" down the consumers' throats so that they purchase them—and they rarely do—the label is on the hook for all the records coming back in the form of "returns." Record retailers can return unsold records to the distributor for a full credit. Overestimate the market and ship too many out, and they're coming back.

More importantly, an artist who is the victim of over-shipping can be perceived as damaged goods—unable to sell—in the industry, both at the retail level and at the label level. Often, their careers end.

Marketing Breakdown

This all gets back to my original point that distribution follows marketing. The necessary $3.50 per unit for marketing will at least give you the chance to have an effective relationship with your distributor, rather than a nightmarish one. In short, it may give you a chance to have some records pulled through by consumers, rather than vainly hoping that simply having distribution will push them through. Should you disagree and decide that you want to keep the $3.50 rather than use it to market the records, you will end up out of a distribution deal so fast you won't believe it. Sadly, the flipside is that even if you do what you must and spend the money, you often end up not making a dime. This is because you must spend this $3.50 per unit to:

1. Make promo copies for press and radio
2. Manufacture singles
3. Hire independent publicists and promo people
4. Make postcards and fliers
5. Pay for a Web site
6. Buy ads in magazines
7. Pay for tour support
8. Pay for some sort of staff—preferably, a sales person to augment the distributor's effort (a position which all full-service labels have)

As you might guess, $3.50 per unit ain't going to go very far with all of these costs. In reality, it is not uncommon for labels to spend $10 and even $20 a unit in order to market new bands, in the hopes that the records will be pulled through by consumers. A label might spend $200,000 or more to sell 10,000 records. That, my friend, is $20 per unit sold. Yes, it would have been more economic for the label to go out and buy every record they put in the stores themselves than to spend $20 per unit to market them.

Why Labels Pay the High Cost

Why would labels spend this egregious amount of money? They do it for the same reason that you as an artist would do it. They hope that at a certain point, a record (or artist) will make it into the public's consciousness and begin to sell in significant numbers. You see, some of the costs that are associated with developing a new artist are not "per unit," meaning they occur only once, rather than every time a record is sold. Costs incurred in making the master recordings, shooting a video, taking press photos, and so on—because they are one-time-only costs—don't factor into a "per unit" cost. The label figures that if they can get over the very expensive initial costs, the future expenditures will be less.

Of course, some costs are always "per unit." Manufacture, mechanical royalties, and co-op must be paid for every record. But even these, except mechanicals, come down when a record is really selling in volume.

Therefore, labels understand that the first quantity of records is the most expensive to sell, and once through these, the costs start to come down. Frighteningly, very few records ever sell more than these first, expensive copies, and so their costs per unit never come down.

A similar reason some record labels are willing to spend a lot in order to sell records for a new artist is because they feel that they are building "catalog," or long-term equity. (Though, this seems to be a less and less popular philosophy, these days.) If a label spends $10 or $20 per unit on the artist's first record, it may establish a fan base for that artist.

When the artist releases a second record, because of this base that the label paid so dearly for on the first record, it should be less expensive the next time around. So now, rather than it costing $10 or $20 a unit, this second record may only cost $5 a unit. Still not cheap, but better. Importantly, the first record should continue to sell, as more and more people become aware of the artist due to marketing for the second record. More simply, if a consumer finds out about an artist on their second record and likes it, they may search around to see if the artist has any other music out. If so, they will likely buy the "catalog" record too. At this point, the per-unit cost of the first record (the "catalog" record) is very little—really just the cost of manufacture, co-op, and royalties. In this way, once an artist has a catalog, the per-unit costs begin to amortize.

Unfortunately, this theory requires near saintly patience on the part of the record label. They must have the intestinal fortitude to withstand watching money flow and flow out while little comes in, with no guarantee that the artist will ever make another record—or even if he does, that anyone will care. Few have the type of bankroll required to withstand this. Most go out of business before the amortization process is able to begin.

Starting Your Own Label

I'm going into so much detail on this in order to discourage you from trying to become a "real" label and thereby needing a distributor. I do encourage you to start a label to release your own music. (Do start with your music so that you don't decimate someone else's career and then have to deal with not only the economic toil, but also the guilt and ultimate karmic retribution.) Starting a label is the best way for you to understand how the record business works. But you must do an awful lot of building of your career (and label) before you should enter into a distribution deal.

There are many other ways to get your records out to an audience, besides going the traditional distribution route. This is true now more than ever, with the Internet. Hopefully, after seeing a bit of what it takes to sell records, you realize that you will get eaten alive, if you just distribute some records to the stores, do no marketing, and just wait for them to start selling.

P&D Deals: Distributors as Marketers and Manufacturers

Generally, your distributor should not be your marketer. They are not set up to do it, and they don't want to do it. Yes, some distribution companies provide some marketing services. Be very careful of this. It comes with a price tag, which is taken from your sales, and more importantly, limits your control over the type of marketing you actually get. It's always a bit dodgy to put too many of your eggs in one basket, in the music business. Having your distributor do your marketing is one too many eggs in a small basket, in my opinion.

More frequently than providing marketing, distributors occasionally provide manufacturing to their clients. In the biz, this is called a "P&D" deal: pressing and distribution. Under the terms of these deals, the distributor will manufacture (or, anachronistically, "press") your CDs and then distribute them. On the surface, this seems like a marvelous thing, as you can avoid the upfront costs of manufacturing CDs, as well as the cost of warehousing them and shipping them from the manufacturer to the distributor. However, the downsides are the same as if you have your distributor doing marketing for you. They charge a premium for this service, and they take the control out of your hands.

Often, with both marketing and P&D deals, you can get "upside down" with a distributor. After the records have been sold to the retailers, less the usual deductions, and the distributor's manufacturing and/or marketing fees, you can end up owing the distributor money. Not good. The distributor will soon drop you.

Why Distributors Avoid Unsigned Artists

Distributors know how rarely things turn out positively when they distribute an individual artist rather than a label. That is why it's so hard for an unsigned artist to get a distribution deal. Far too often, distributors get left holding the bag, after they have taken a chance on distributing an unsigned artist. In these scenarios, the distributors often end up losing money and having to deal with a lot of excess inventory that they either haven't been able to sell or has come back in the form of returns. Therefore, they just don't do it very often.

You see, a distributor who handles a label with multiple releases has some leverage and security. If the label puts out a record that stiffs and the distributor gets returns up the wazoo, they can simply deduct those losses against payments for other records that don't stiff. On the other hand, if you're an artist that only puts out a record every two years (and maybe not that often), the distributor has no recourse if your record doesn't succeed.

When to Consider Distribution

The rules are the same for hiring a distributor as for hiring an indie publicist or radio person. Before you go banging on a distributor's door, you need to have laid a very firm foundation that the distributor can build upon. Specifically, that means that you have managed to get some records in some stores, and that these records have consistently sold-through. In other words, they have not just gotten into a store, but actually been purchased by consumers, who are aware of you due to the activity around your music: touring, press, radio, and so on.

You then must replicate this outside your hometown and into a broad regional and then national base. At this point, and not before, you should be thinking about trying to get a distribution deal. Of course, at this point, you may not need a distributor. You will probably have label offers and/or your own system working so efficiently that you wouldn't want to give away any of the profit margin to a distributor or anyone else.

You should be developing your fan base and activity first locally and then regionally. You will be pleased to know that there still are some regional distributors out there. So, if your music is widely known in the Northeast because you have developed a touring circuit and gotten some press and radio, you will be able to find a distributor who specializes in this region. Be careful not to sign an exclusive deal with this distributor. If you do and your fan base begins to grow beyond the geographic area where this distributor has weight, you will have troubles.

Artists and labels commonly have multiple distributors, so there's no reason to sign an exclusive deal until you find a distributor who can truly handle all your needs.

One-Stops and Rackjobbers

Even when you do sign an exclusive distribution deal, you will not just be using a single distributor. Distributors also use distributors; they call them "one-stops." A one-stop is a sort of middleman between the distributor and the retailer. They exist because no distributor can possibly reach all of the tiny indie stores out there. Additionally, most distributors have minimum quantities that a store must buy from them—as well as tough credit checks—in order for the distributor to do business with them. A one-stop comes in and acts like an aggregator. The one-stop will buy from all or many of the distributors and then solicit these smaller retail accounts, giving them the opportunity to buy product from multiple distributors through a single source. In this manner, the smaller retail accounts don't have to worry about whether or not they are buying enough product from a single distributor to justify an order. They can make an *a la carte* selection across the whole range. It is possible as an artist to make a deal with a one-stop to carry your music and bypass the distributor. However, it is no easier than making a deal with a distributor.

The other type of distributor is called a "rackjobber." Rackjobbers rent floor space in the mass merchandise stores (such as Wal Mart), set up their displays (racks), and then stock them with CDs that they have bought from the distributors. Stores like Wal Mart are largely the domain of the mega-hit records, and therefore not really useful to the unsigned artist.

Summary

The goal of this chapter is to explain how distribution works, in order to underscore that distribution follows marketing. Once your marketing is cooking, you'll have distributors nipping at your heels. At that point, you'll benefit from understanding the many complexities of the distribution process. Prior to that, understanding this process really should be an incentive to get that marketing cooking.

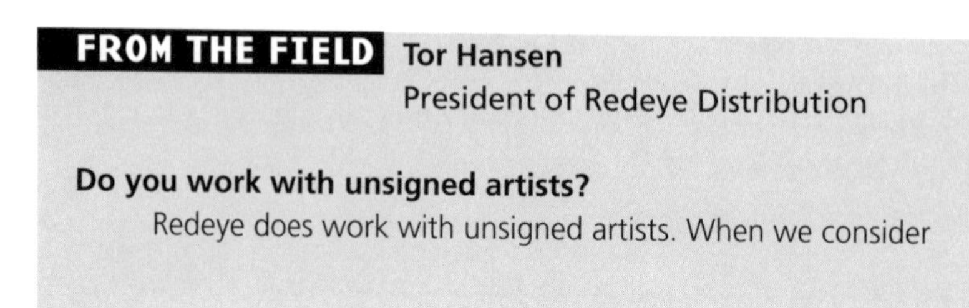
FROM THE FIELD **Tor Hansen**
President of Redeye Distribution

Do you work with unsigned artists?

Redeye does work with unsigned artists. When we consider

bringing on a new label or artist-run label, we scrutinize an unsigned artist label as much as we would a record label with a hundred titles. With each unsigned artist, it requires a new vendor contract, and all of the accounting, marketing, and warehouse attention as any other label vendor. Redeye's distribution business model requires that we analyze the costs of distribution of the vendor with the return on investment. A label needs to be working in our business model; otherwise, we will drop the label. Our initial questions to the label are whether this unsigned artist has a realistic release plan and fan base to "distribute" product and sell through.

What is the key for a successful artist/distributor relationship?

Communication. Proactive promotion and marketing efforts. Realistic expectations.

Our best labels use our departments and communication network to the hilt! A personal relationship always works the best. They learn how to communicate effectively to advance their tour dates, breaking new stories and markets on a regular basis. Our best labels utilize our account base and marketing tools by supporting their ongoing promotion. They also follow up calls and keep track of successes and failures. It is very important that a label understand the retail landscape and what is and is not realistic in terms of sales.

At what point should an unsigned artist consider distribution?

I would say after their first successful record or when the artist feels like it is getting out of control, and they can't keep up with the orders.

Workshop

Go to your local independent record stores (if they still exist in your area), and find out what indie distributors they buy from. Also find out what one-stops they buy from. Lastly, determine whether they will take records on consignment from local bands.

12

Contracts: Getting the Best Deal

Let's look at the types of deals that labels may present. Understanding these deals will help you in your quest to get signed. It's a bit like knowing your enemy in order to best do battle.

When looking for a record deal, put yourself in the shoes of the label and think about what type of artist you would sign if you were them. To do this effectively, you need to know what types of deals the label makes. Unfortunately, there is no "standard deal," but most labels' contracts are simply variations on a couple of similar themes. Understanding these generalities illuminates certain aspects of the signing process—specifically, why it is so darned hard to get signed. Additionally, it will help you see what is really important to labels, beyond the music. After looking at the complexities of these deals, you will see that it is in your best interest to have a lawyer help you navigate the dark waters, once there is an offer. See the chapter on lawyers.

The Royalty Deal

The *royalty deal* is the most common type of deal among record labels. It has been evolving since it was first conceived, and it will continue to change and be refined, but at its core, the conceit is that the artist gets paid a percentage of the money—referred to as "royalties"—received by the record label from album sales, less certain "deductions" and "advances."

Advances and Recoupment

So, a label signs a band and funds the making of a record. This is referred to as the "recording fund." Occasionally, the label also provides some money for the band to live on while they're making and promoting the record.

This money is referred to as a "personal advance." Collectively known as "advances," all this money immediately goes onto a ledger referred to as "recoupable" money. This means that before the artist gets paid royalties for any records that are sold, the label must first pay itself back, or "recoup," any advances. This is why you might have heard an artist say, "Yeah, we've sold a lot of records, but we're so un-recouped that we haven't seen a dime in royalties." If, for example, a record label advances an artist $50,000 to make their record and another $50,000 to live on, before that artist sees any royalties, the label must make back their $100,000 from record sales.

Other Recoupable Costs

It is not just recording advances and personal advances that are recoupable. Typically, labels operating under a royalty deal will also recoup any money they pay out for tour support. This money differs from a personal advance in that it is specifically earmarked for expenses resulting from touring in support of the record: van rentals, hotels, gas, food, crew salaries, "per diems" (money provided by labels to band members for incidental living expenses while on the road), and so on. Additionally, labels often recoup some or all of the costs associated with making a video and "indie radio promotion" (that is, money paid to someone outside the label who works to get your songs played on the radio). Frequently, there is a cap put on the amount of money a label can recoup for indie promo, above which they need the artist's approval to spend more. Some labels are also recouping money paid to "indie publicists." Like indie promoters, indie publicists are hired by the label to get your music written about in the press. As previously mentioned, this is a relatively new development, but one I'm seeing with some frequency.

Non-Recoupable Costs

So, it seems that record labels are just getting all their money back, does it?

Well, even with these recoupable expenses, there are many other expenses that the label has to eat, under the category of the "cost of doing business." Some of these costs—phone and electricity bills, rent for the office, computer upgrades, and so on—are obviously costs that most businesses have to pay just to operate, and therefore should not logically be recouped before royalties are paid to the artist. However, there are things that record labels pay for and don't recoup under the terms of a typical royalty deal that really do have direct impact on your specific career. Things like manufacturing CDs (those to sell, and promotional copies as well);

paying the mechanical royalties to the songwriter (or publisher); paying the staff who sell your records; maintaining a Web site that features you; doing promotional mailings to press, radio, and anywhere else (cafés, hotels, etc.) that might lead to record sales; making posters and other materials used to promote you in stores; paying for the "co-op" ads you see in papers listing your CD as on sale; paying the "co-op" costs associated with getting the CDs prominently displayed in the stores (and, in reality, in the stores, at all); and, among other things, paying for consumer ads (i.e., ads in places like *Rolling Stone*).

Labels aren't spending all of this money out of the goodness of their hearts. Once two things happen—you get recouped, and the label recovers its own expenses—the label stands to make 80 to 90 percent of every dollar that they pay you in royalties, with the balance (the other 10 to 20 percent) going to you. It is this money from sales that allows labels to fund all of the above services (ongoing or otherwise), as well as advance other artists the money they need to record their music.

Now, before you begin feeling like the labels really do have a fine grubstake deal here, realize that very, very few records ever recoup their advances. Advances to artists are deemed *non-returnable*, so labels can't come after you to get the money back they don't recoup. This means that not only are the labels out the money that they advance to the artists to sign the deal and make the record, but also the money spent paying for the promotion of the record, and all the money spent just keeping the lights on while the record was being worked.

Why You Should Strive to Become Recouped

As you can see, it ain't easy being a label. In fact, the costs that labels must incur to simply get records in stores and on the radio has gotten so steep that many seriously question whether the business model can continue to work in its current form. But that is another book.

These devilishly tough economics are why labels desperately cling to those artists that actually do recoup. It is also why savvy labels attempt to develop catalogs that sell consistently over time. The costs for these types of sales is often less than those associated with selling records by new artists, though this too is changing.

What you are hopefully gleaning from this little record label economics lesson is that the more you bring to a record label, the less they can take away. A label can't force you to take recoupable funds. For instance, I advise that you be able to tour self-sufficiently before you sign to a label so you won't need to take any recoupable tour support money. Additionally, if you've heeded my advice about familiarizing yourself with Pro Tools, or some other recording system, you should be able to make your record for a reasonable amount of money, take less of an advance for recording upfront, and not be too far in the hole before your record comes out.

Aspire to get recouped as fast as you can. Until you are recouped, you are really an indentured servant to the label; they are able to call all the shots. For example, want to do a tour that the label doesn't think is wise? Well, if you're unrecouped and need money from the label to finance the tour, it will be the label's call as to whether or not it's going to happen. On the other hand, if you want to do a tour and you are recouped, you will just tell the label that's what you are doing, and if you need money to do it, you tell them to pay you some of the money they owe you. More importantly, when it comes to creative issues, such as hiring a producer for your next record, if you're making money for the label (or at least, not owing the label money), you will be much more likely to make the record the way you want. However, if you're deep in the red with the label, believe me, they are going to be micromanaging your recording like you wouldn't believe. This is often very bad.

What You Bring to the Table Affects Your Ability to Get Signed

It is also important to understand how this applies to getting a record deal. Labels are in the business of making money. If they recognize that you have the potential to make money for them, you will have a better chance of getting signed. Perhaps more relevantly, if you represent a lower risk to the label, you also have a better chance of getting signed.

If you can assure them that you don't need as much recoupable money as they ordinarily have to risk on artists, you also have a better chance of getting signed. To be very specific, if you are an artist that doesn't require a ton of tour support or indie radio promotion, there are many labels that will be keenly interested in you. Of course, different labels have different setups. What may save one label a ton of money, to another label, may be insignificant. Some labels—most of the majors—focus on radio and have the infrastructure and expertise to support this focus. It is, in short, what they do. If you go to one of these labels and tell them they should sign you because you don't need commercial radio play to sell records, it's not going to impress them. In fact, you may have sealed your fate there.

Again, it all comes back to doing the research required to determine what a label's capabilities are and how you can support them. That said, if you can tour self-sufficiently, I can't think of a label who won't see that as a positive.

How Royalties Are Calculated

Let's trace the finances of record sales. In essence, the label makes your records and sells them to a distributor (sometimes, directly to a retailer), and the records end up in the stores. The distributor or retailer pays the label for the records they buy from the label—not for the records that they sell to the consumer. Every six months, the label calculates how many records were sold to the distributor or retailer. Assuming the distributor or retailer has paid the label for these records, the label then subtracts whatever outstanding recoupable costs they have incurred. Then, if what they have brought in from sales recoups any advances, the label pays you your royalty, sixty to ninety days after the close of the period. Everyone is happy.

However, there are factors that complicate this scenario. The first is, what is the royalty payment a percentage of? More importantly to you, what percentage are you getting? And, lastly, what deductions is the label taking? Let's go at these one at a time.

Royalties

First, your royalty is calculated (for 90 percent of labels who operate on a royalty basis) off the suggested retail list price (SRLP). This is the price at which the retailers theoretically sell the records to the consumer. There must be a suggested retail price in order to avoid issues surrounding free trade laws. It is illegal, for instance, to sell the same goods to one retailer at a different price than you sell to another. Of course, this doesn't mean that the retailers have to price the records at the same price. You can, as you know, find records priced all over the map at different retailers. Whatever price the CDs end up being retailed for, you are going to get paid on the SRLP: around $17.98 for front-line (full price) records, $11.98 for mid-line (reduced price) records, and under $10.00 for budget-line records.

Second, the percentage that you can expect to be paid ranges from 10 to 12 percent of SRLP on the low end or 17 to 22 percent on the high end. If you hear someone refer to "points," it's simply an abbreviated way of saying "percentage points." In other words, someone who says they have a 15-point deal means that they are getting 15 percent of SLRP. New artists will receive a lower royalty, more established artists with a track record and demand will get more, and only superstars get the highest rates.

Royalty Deductions

Lastly, deductions affect your actual percentage take. These deductions reduce the percentages you will be paid. To give you a sense of how your royalty rate can change, here are some deductions that labels typically take:

1. Packaging charges, instituted to pay the artist only on the income generated from his music, and not the money associated with the package. In other words, the labels feel that you should only be paid for the music, not for the value that the consumers associate with the package.
2. Free goods and promo records, used to either incentivize retailers to stock the record by giving them some free recordings, or in the case of promo records, records used to generate press or radio play for an artist. Some labels claim to not take deductions for free goods, but they will then pay you on only 85 percent of sales, which is the same amount reduced by labels who do take a free goods deduction.
3. Reserves (discussed below)
4. Deductions for sales outside your home territory. If, for instance, you are a U.S.-based artist, your royalty for your European sales will be, typically, 65 to 75 (and frequently less) percent of what your US royalty rate is.

Labels will only pay you using this royalty type of formula (with these deductions) if your records are sold through what is called in the USNRC, which stands for United States Normal Retail Channels. These are places like record stores, where you typically buy CDs. If your CDs are sold via record clubs, online, at discounters, or outside the US, the royalty you are paid on these records will be reduced.

All this speaks directly to why it's difficult to get a record deal these days. Put simply, there are too many records released, and neither the labels, the distributors, nor the retailers can keep up with them all. The way in which they have decided to try to combat the ridiculous amount of records being released—many of which never sell more than a few hundred copies—has been to institute a 100 percent return policy. This means that a retailer can return the CDs to the distributor and receive reimbursement for the full price they paid. Typically, this comes in the form of a credit issued by the distributor to the retailer, who can use it for future purchases from that same distributor.

Returns and Reserves

Labels must therefore be very careful of what they sell to the distributor (who then sells to the retailers) because they can get all of those records back, if they choose the wrong records or the wrong amount to put in the store.

There was a time not that long ago, before the glut at retail, where new records where somewhat of an event. This didn't mean that every record succeeded, but it did allow records more time to find their audience, who could also find the records.

That time is gone. Now, labels must be more cautious than ever about what they sign, and will demand that artists have things going for them (such as touring, press, radio) beyond great songs. These artists, they figure, are more likely to sell records than have them returned. Seems obvious, I know, but if people really paid attention to this, and didn't release records unless the artist had more going for them than good songs, we would have far, far fewer records released and far, far fewer problems associated with records being returned. Of course, you are now aware of all of the things that you must do to not only give yourself a better chance of getting signed, and of avoiding having your records returned when you do get signed. But sadly, others aren't, and so problems persist, and they affect you and every other person who releases records.

Here's how their behavior affects you. Labels have to make concessions for the records that get returned. If they didn't, they would be paying you for records that were sold and then returned. Labels know that they can't go back to the artist and ask them for their money back, so instead, they have come up with a way to hedge their bets. This is called "holding reserves." Typically, a label will only pay you on about 50 to 60 percent of the records sold to the distributor in the first royalty payment. That is the time from when the record was released to when they calculate sales. They will "hold in reserve" the other 40 to 50 percent of the money because they know that some—often, a lot—of the records that they shipped out will be returned by the stores. The distributor pays the label based on records sold to the stores. As records are returned, the distributors pass their economic loss on to the label in the form of deductions against other records.

Here's an example.

1. Label sells 10,000 records from Artist A to their distributor at $8 per record and invoices the distributor $80,000. Distributor pays the label monthly, and therefore writes the label a check for $80,000 at the end of the month.

2. Distributor sells 10,000 records from Artist A to their retailers at $10 per record and invoices various stores $100,000. Stores usually pay distributor in thirty days.

3. Three months later, label sells 10,000 records from Artist B to the distributor. Again, the label invoices the distributor $80,000. . . . But!
4. During this time, 3,000 records from Artist A have been returned by the retailers to the distributor, and the distributor must now issue the retailers a credit of $30,000. The distributor has already paid the label $80,000 for the sale of the 10,000 records from Artist A, and can't ask the label to reimburse them. Instead, the distributor deducts $24,000 (the $8 per unit for the 3,000 returned records) from the money they owe the label for the sale of the 10,000 records of Artist B. Instead of paying the label $80,000 for the sale, the distributor pays $56,000.

On and on this goes, and you can imagine how complicated it gets when a label is releasing ten records a month and retailers are returning records that they've had for a year or more. Now, Artist B shouldn't be penalized for the returns taken from Artist A. This is why the label holds reserves rather than just paying Artist A in full as soon as the check from the distributor arrives.

As time goes by, the amount of records coming back reduces, and therefore, so does the amount of reserves the label holds. Typically, it goes down from 50 or 60 percent to 25 percent or so over the first year, and then they just will hold some small percentage—10 to 20 percent. Over time, they "liquidate"—pay you the money they have kept in reserve—if the records don't get returned.

Penny Rates

So with reserves and other deductions, how in the hell do you ever know what you are actually getting paid? My advice, if and when you are presented with a royalty-based contract, is to ask to see a "penny rate." This is basically a real dollar amount that you can count on receiving for royalties. Rather than, for instance, only being told that you are getting a 15 percent royalty, ask also to know what the penny rate is, so that you know, for instance, that for every record sold, after recoupment and allowing for reserves, you will make $1.10 on the record royalty side. The reality is that 15 percent for one label is not 15 percent for another, so it's best just to pin them down to a dollar figure. They won't like it, and probably won't do it, but if you try to make 'em do it, you might get lucky—or more likely, at least get a better understanding of what the percentages mean in actual dollar terms.

Profit Sharing/Joint-Venture Deals

The second most common deal that you will encounter is the "profit-sharing deal," also called a "joint venture" (JV) or a "profit split." The gist of it is that the label keeps track of *all* the expenses that are incurred in the recording, manufacturing, promotion, and selling of your record. It keeps all of the income until those costs are paid and then splits the profits, if any, with you 50/50. These types of deals are typically seen either at the small to mid-size indie labels, and from companies who are new to the record business and feel this is a more equitable system.

Sounds pretty sweet, right? Well, not so fast there, cowgirl. Remember, there are many costs that labels eat under a percentage deal that you will pay for half of, should you opt for this route. For example, if you are an artist that needs significant press coverage in order to sell records, you are going to fly through money, because of the photo shoots, indie publicists, press mailings, etc., which under a percentage deal, you would most likely not be paying for. Radio too, even if labels are recouping the cost of indie promo. There are many other costs associated (promos, travel, etc.) that labels frequently do not recoup in a traditional royalty deal. Not so in a JV; you share the cost on every expense. Additionally, you're not going to believe the costs associated with getting records in stores. Count on $1.50 to $3 per record. Tah-dah! That too is now 50 percent your financial responsibility. You'll pay for half the manufacturing of the records, the printing of the posters, any stickers, phone calls made on your behalf, postage, consumer ads, and more. Also, before any of that typically non-recoupable stuff gets eaten up, you first have to recoup all the traditionally recoupable costs: recording, tour support, and so on. Additionally, since you're not going to want to deal with this accounting headache, the labels will often tack on an extra 10 percent administration charge. It's a headache for them too.

Issues with JVs

Very few labels will do this kind of deal—at least, in the way I just described. In the first place, calling such a thing a JV is inaccurate. A true JV stipulates that both companies are viewed by the law as one company; if one party in a JV gets sued, for instance, it means that so too does the other. Neither the label nor the artist want this, so they make sure that it's not really a JV except in name. Also, a true JV requires two companies to contribute roughly equal assets at the outset of a venture in order to jointly share the profits. If a label is funding everything, and all the band brings to the party is some tunes, it doesn't add up.

However, paradigms are shifting, and new business models are emerging that are potentially making this a more workable option. For instance, if an artist has funded his own recording and a label is interested in releasing it as is, that recording is "good and valuable" consideration (an asset) that potentially justifies some sort of JV.

Most medium to large labels shy away from these deals, as they are almost impossible to administrate. The artist almost always needs an additional advance, which then puts them deeper in the hole, and puts the label more at risk. I have seen many deals start as JVs only to have the artists want to renegotiate back to a more traditional royalty structure deal after the release of the first JV record.

Term ("Licensing") Deals

It also brings up the important question of ownership. Who owns the master? In all record deals, someone must own (or control) the master. The question is ultimately for how long.

Typically, if a record label takes the risk of putting up all the money required to pay for a recording and promote a band, they insist on owning the master recording in perpetuity. This is called a "copyright ownership deal."

These seem a bit draconian, I'm sure, but understand that so few records ever recoup that the only way that labels can stay in business is to have ownership in long-term assets that generate revenue, which allows them to attempt to develop artists. It's going to be tricky to convince a label that they should fund your record and enter into any record deal if they don't own the master.

When a label agrees to retain the rights to a master for a fixed period of time, rather than own it forever, it is called a "license deal." Under the terms of a license deal, the label has the right to exploit the master under the terms of the deal, but after this period of time (referred to as the "term"), the label no longer has any rights over the master recording. Whoever owns the master—be it the artist, another label, an estate, or a production company—can then make a new deal, extend the old deal, renegotiate, or release the record himself.

Licenses have traditionally been tricky to get unless you are a superstar, with the exception being artists who come to the label with a finished master. Again, the more you bring to a label, the less they can take away. If you have managed to fund your own record and you have a label (or preferably multiple labels) keen to release it as is, you should absolutely push for a license deal rather than a copyright ownership deal. The logic is that the label has much less risk in this scenario because they know precisely what they are getting into.

How Issues of Term Relate to Getting a Record Deal

This too relates directly to strategy concerning getting a record deal. As we saw in the early chapter on recording a demo, it is entirely possible to affordably create high-quality songs using Pro Tools or some other home-based recording setup. If you do this, you will not only be efficiently creating an effective demo, but you also may be positioning yourself to make a more artist-friendly deal, such as a license deal or some sort of JV, rather than a copyright ownership deal.

The point is that there is room for creativity when it comes to the types of deals you make, but only if you (the artist) bring something to the negotiating table. This could be a finished master, a big live draw, or other labels competing to sign you. When you have these things going for you, your lawyer will have an easier time attempting to structure creative deals, such as a JV.

Sales and Mechanicals

A couple of last words on JVs. If you don't sell a significant amount of records relative to the cost of the record, you are probably better off sticking with a typical royalty structure. There are just too many things being recouped for you to see any money going the JV route, if you are not selling a substantial quantity of records. Ballparking this number is difficult, because there are too many variables in the costs related to making the record, what type of promotion the record needs, etc. However, if you are really selling a lot of records, a JV will probably work out better for you. I've A/B'd the two deals many times and this is what I've found. You and your lawyer should do the same, when strategizing about the type of deal that will work best for you.

The other important thing to consider regarding JV-type deals is mechanical royalties. Labels must pay the songwriter for the right to "mechanically" reproduce their song on CD. Importantly, the labels must pay this mechanical royalty from the very first record sold, and this payment should not be recouped from any record royalties—that is, from money owed to the performer of the songs (whether or not that is the same person who writes the songs). This can complicate a JV-type deal, where all money is recouped before any money is paid out.

You cannot let this happen. You must stipulate that you receive your mechanical royalties "outside" the JV, meaning they get paid off the top, and then the JV functions according to contract.

If you decide to do a JV type deal with a label, you must make sure that the mechanicals are paid out off the top, and not recouped with the rest of the expenses. This type of thing often happens with small, inexperienced labels. In an effort to try and make as "fair" a deal as possible with the artist, they are in fact withholding money from the artist that they should not be. Mechanical royalties are largely the life-blood of a musician, and frequently the largest—if not the only—source of income they have. As an artist, you need to understand that these royalties should not be recouped against other expenses, whatever type of deal you enter into.

Demo Deals

The demo or development deal is perhaps the one unsigned artists come upon with the most frequency. In short, a demo (remember, short for "demonstration") deal stipulates that a label will give you some money to go and record some songs. In return, this label usually has certain rights. After you record the songs, you must present them to the label who paid for them before you play them for any other label. The label will then have some exclusive period of time (typically sixty days) to do one of three things:

1. Sign you immediately, under terms to which you may have already agreed in order to get the money to make the demo in the first place;
2. Exclusively negotiate with you to come to terms (called the "right of first negotiation"); or
3. Allow you to play the demo for other companies, with the caveat that if some other label makes you an offer, you must then go back to the label who funded the songs in the first place and give them the opportunity to match this offer (called the "right of first refusal").

Importantly, unlike record advances, which don't have to be paid back to a record label even if you don't recoup them, demo money typically does have to get repaid. If you sign to a different label than the one who funded your demos, that company will typically have to reimburse the company who funded them.

Other than that, demo deals are pretty simple. Just be careful not to let the label who funds the demo have too much time to decide what they want to do. The $5,000 or so that you got out of them may be the most expensive money you've ever received, as it may keep you from making another more lucrative deal elsewhere.

Important Contract Points

A sample artist agreement is included in appendix A. As you can see, it is confusing to read, and really does require the services of a lawyer. Hire one rather than trying to negotiate for yourself. While I have said earlier that contracts are always open to renegotiation, it is far better to make yourself a good deal to begin with.

However, if you insist on not using a lawyer, here are the key things that need to be outlined in any type of contract you enter into with a record company:

1. **Copyright Ownership v. License.** Who owns the master? If the label is funding the recording, they can make a claim that they should have perpetual ownership. If not, for instance, if you have recorded the record on your own dime, you should negotiate a license.

2. **Term.** The duration of the contract. This includes both the number of releases you will owe the record company before you can enter into a deal with another company, and/or how long the record company will have the exclusive rights to exploit the master(s). Typically, record labels want a seven to ten-year license to exclusively exploit the master, if they don't have it in perpetuity. I've seen five-year licenses (and occasionally two- or three-year licenses), but you'll be hard-pressed to get one that short, if you have no track record.

   "Term" also refers to how many "options" the record company has for future records. Note that it is the record company who has the option, not the artist. If you sign a deal where you have a commitment from the label to release one record with an option for four more, the record company (not the artist) will determine whether or not they want to "pick up" or exercise the option. Major labels will try to get as many options as possible. It is not uncommon to see major label deals where the artist grants the label five or six options. The catch is that these options get more and more expensive for the label to pick up. The first option may force the label to pay $50,000 in order to pick it up, but by record six, they may owe you $300,000. This is how labels justify tying an artist up for this period of time.

   My ideal term is a three-record deal. I feel that it's enough time where a label can feel that they are working to build something of value (and therefore, expend the money and energy), but it is not so long that the artist feels they are going to be tied up forever. One- or two-record deals, in my opinion, just don't incentivize the label enough to really do what they need to do to develop an artist. So frequently, the artist won't recoup on the first or second record, and if the label has no future with the artist, they will just cut bait and stop spending. This effectively kills the record, and often the career.

You must strive to have a partnership with your label. You want them to feel that they are part of the process of building your success and that they will share in the reward. Forcing a label to do a one- or two-record deal will make them feel that you are using them as a steppingstone. Conversely, a six- or seven-record deal seems odious to me. By record three, both the label and the artist should be able to determine whether or not things are working or likely to work soon. At that point, they can either renegotiate or part ways. One way or the other, both should have something of value. The artist should have gained exposure, and the label will have built a catalog. If the artist utilizes the exposure that the label was partly responsible for to get another deal with a different company, the first record company will then be able to exploit the catalog pieces, as the new label does the heavy lifting.

3. **Royalty**. As discussed, push for a penny rate. Short of that, figure out what all the deductions are and the bottom-line cost of each one.

4. **Territory**. Where the label has the rights to exploit the master. This can be the universe or a specific territory. The real question here is whether or not the company has any way to exploit the master in any territory other than their native one. In other words, if it's a small label based in the U.S. who has no foreign distribution, you should fight to limit the territory to the U.S. You may ask why a label who has no infrastructure or distribution in foreign territories would fight for worldwide rights. The reason is, because they want to be able to have the opportunity to license these rights to another company, or exploit them on their own, should they set something up in these territories. On the other hand, if the label can do an effective job of promoting and selling your record in many territories, then you are typically better off doing a worldwide deal rather than breaking it out territory by territory. It is very hard to administer foreign sales. Some artists do very well by breaking the territories out and granting the rights to labels in different countries, but be prepared to put in the energy needed to make sure those labels (in those odd time zones) are doing what they say and paying you royalties. Ask yourself if you're willing to get on a plane for 23 hours to chase down some Australian distributor that owes you $400.

5. **Accounting.** When will you be paid or accounted to? Labels typically account to you twice a year. Make them do it.
6. **Controlled Composition Clause/Mechanical Royalty.** Discussed in the publishing chapter.

These are the key ingredients. There are many more, however, and again, I strongly recommend that you not go it alone regarding contracts. Even if you are releasing your record through your well-intentioned friend's label, you should nail down these issues. If you don't, I promise, they will come back to haunt you.

Summary

As you can see, record contracts are complex. I encourage you to familiarize yourself with the key terminology of contracts. *Do not* try to negotiate any contract without the assistance of a lawyer. No matter how friendly a deal may be (and how friendly you may be with the person you are entering into a deal with), it is better, for all parties, if professionals are brought in. Labels always have lawyers looking at their contracts, or at the very least, had lawyers help formulate their contracts at the beginning. Don't skimp here. You can end up getting really hurt by thinking that some small, friendly deal is all hugs and kisses.

So much of the kvetching about how evil the labels are could have been avoided if the artists had had lawyers advise them, before signing the contract. That said, don't let the lawyers "overlawyer" a deal and kill it. Remember that they work for you. At the end of the day, you must determine what is best for your career. This may mean signing a deal that isn't perfectly acceptable to your lawyer. Sometimes, you have to do this. Until you get to the point of signing contracts, knowing their key components will help you strategize about how to best structure your career, and ultimately, will help you get a deal.

Workshop

Talk to artists you know who have record deals. Try to find out how their deals are structured. Do they have JVs? Do they have term deals? Try to understand what their thinking was regarding the deal they made. Was it simply the deal that was presented, or did they work with the label to find a meeting ground that satisfied both of their needs?

13

You've Got a Deal or Did You Know That "Utopia" Means "No Place?"

What Happens When You Get Signed

The Sisyphian travails of learning how to procure a record deal are rewarding in and of themselves. Even if you never get signed, understanding the processes of commercial record development, sales, and distribution will help you in your career, giving you insight into how your music is perceived and how you might sell it on your own. This last chapter will discuss what you can expect once you've managed to get signed, as well as suggest a few pointers about how to best maximize your experience.

Labels come in all shapes and sizes, so there is really no way to describe precisely what it will be like for you, given all the possible variations. If you sign on to a small startup label run by one or two people, you will have a wildly different experience than if you sign to a major, or even a mid-size indie. Regardless of how many people work there, the same jobs must get done. Frequently, the difference between a big label and a small one is that where a big label has a staff of people to do the various jobs that must get done, a smaller label does those same jobs with fewer (sometimes only one or two) people.

Whatever the size of the label, it is imperative that you as an artist (frequently in conjunction with your manager) communicate effectively with a "decision maker" at the label, or at least with someone who can keep you informed about the decision-making process. This sounds obvious, but it is very common for artists to find themselves unable to get answers about what is going on with their career. This is not good, and whether you're dealing with a bedroom operation or a multinational, you must strive to have rapport that enables you to know what is going on. Understanding the process that transpires after you are signed—which is similar across most labels—will help you to best facilitate this communication.

Issues Surrounding Scheduling Your Release

Be it from a demo, a live performance, a great lawyer or manager, or most likely, a combination of all of the above, you have been offered and signed a record deal. Certainly part of any negotiation that led to this record deal would involve discussion of when the record will be created and released. The next step is:

1. If you have a record already, decide when it's coming out.
2. If you don't have a record in the can, start the process of making one.

If your record is done when you sign to a label (a more and more common occurrence), you need to set a release date.

This is never as soon as the artist would like. Often, artists have waited their whole lives to release their first records. They may have funded and completed their own recording, and then sat on it for a whole year or more, during their process of finding and negotiating a deal. Finally, they get signed, but then learn that it must be yet another four or five months before their album can be released. It's always a delightful conversation.

There is a reason for this delay. To understand why, you need to understand a few things about release schedules.

Certainly, other record execs have different philosophies about when to release records, but for me, release date options are severely limited for new artists. I think it is unwise for a new artist to release a record in October, November, or December. This ever-growing holiday season is really the domain of the superstars. All of the majors are putting their big guns out at this time. They know that this is when the vast majority of records are sold. They are doing the full-on media blitz to generate attention for these releases. This means that every media outlet is being pounded to write about these records, and they are therefore even less disposed than usual to give space to a new artist. Additionally, retailers are so frenzied during this time, making sure that the shelves are stocked with the big releases poised to fly out the door, that they do not have the time to pay attention to a release from a new artist.

It is very easy for works by new artists to get lost during the holiday months. You have a short window in which to grab attention for your release. If you put a record out in November and just wait until the holiday season is over before it starts attracting attention, you will most likely be disappointed. This is because, come January, there will be other new releases that are vying for attention. Your record will be viewed as old news by the media and retailers, and therefore, by consumers as well.

So the holiday months are out.

Mid-May to the end of August are also out. If you're a new artist, you will probably need college airplay or college touring in order to start generating some buzz. This means that you don't want to put a record out when colleges aren't in session. Some labels feel September is a rocky month because all of the records from smaller labels come out this month, but at a certain point, you have to just decide to take a stab. I personally have found September to be a good month. Late January through mid-May is also an acceptable time period.

So avoid the holiday season and summer vacation. Labels must also consider what else is being released at the time. If you're low artist on their totem pole, they shouldn't put your record out too close to a bigger name. The label's staff will be focused on the "big" artist's release, and therefore, you will have a hard(er) time getting the attention you need, during this period.

This doesn't mean that you need to have a release date all to yourself. In some cases, you can benefit from sharing a release date with another artist. Many labels cross-promote records and save money by running single ads that feature multiple artists, putting two or more CDs in mailers to send to press, thereby cutting their postage costs. They might even put two artists on the same tour and have them share a van or bus. This can be a good thing, but typically, one artist ends up getting more attention than the other, and the other ends up feeling like Jan Brady. That said, this does happen frequently, and you should try to make it work for you. Of course, if you're Marsha Brady, everything will be groovy anyway.

Finally, there are various other details. For example, records are released on Tuesdays in the U.S. and on Mondays in Europe.

So, you must work with your label and strategize in order to determine what the best release date for your record will be. This can be quite a process. In addition to the other hurdles we have seen above, you must give the label ample time to set up the record's marketing efforts.

You can't have enough setup time, but you must have three months, if your record requires press. Press outlets have long lead times, which means that if you want your record to be reviewed when it comes out in May, you darn well better get it in the hands of media by February. Even if press isn't a big sales driver for you, I would still advise three months. You need the time to get music in the hands of retail. You need to do some form of marketing (be it sending CDs to spas or sniping posters in subways) far enough in advance of street date for people to be aware of the record. In order to do this, your record must be completed—including recording, artwork, press photos, bios, and so on—at least three months prior to street date.

Artwork

And ah, the struggles around artwork. I believe that the music's creator should also be active in generating the album's art. That said, just because you are a great musician does *not* mean you are a great visual artist. So, utilize the label's resources to flesh out your ideas. Even if you are a great visual artist, you should still utilize the label's resources. If the label is small and has no real resources, you still should work together to make sure that your aesthetic vision dovetails with the label's commercial imperatives.

That's a highfalutin way of saying, "Don't generate art that makes the record label's job harder than it already is." This applies to labels of all sizes. There is a very fine line between something that's original enough to be visually grabbing and something that does you more harm than good. Remember, by the sheer nature of signing on to a label and having your record released commercially, you are necessarily accepting that your music, on some level, is "product." Well, product has to sell, and in order for it to sell effectively, it must be packaged effectively. Exactly how is hard to pin down. It's one of those things that you know when you see, and it differs from person to person, and from department to department. Ask a label's sales person, and he might tell you that the ideal cover has the artist's name emblazoned in flashing neon and huge type on the CD cover. Ask the A&R person, and he might say that the band's identity is best summed up visually by a plain white cover with a single tiny dot in the lower right-hand corner. There is no magical solution. Some albums have sold very well without even having the artist's name or album title on the cover. There have also been albums that should be in the advertising hall of fame because of their eye-catching design, but that haven't sold.

FROM THE FIELD **Steve Jurgensmeyer**
Creative Director, Rounder Records

Some Thoughts on Design

You need to articulate your image very clearly. I usually get my clients to put it down on paper: Who are you? This helps us to articulate what a successful design for them should be. Also, at the beginning, establish who is responsible for approving the final design. Avoid a group decision at all costs. Input from too many people, including spouses and friends, often just confuses things.

New bands frequently make the mistake of working with friends simply because, well, they're friends! But you probably wouldn't let a non-musician friend play the lead guitar break on your single. Why would you let friends who aren't designers do your demo package or album?

The art of visual communication is as simple as it is multi-faceted—as intellectually complex as it is a gut reaction. An oxymoron to be sure, but go look at your favorite sleeve designs, and try to put into words what, exactly, it is you like about it. Then this intangibility will become clear.

Determine what kind of image you are seeking. Should the artwork reflect the band, the band's audience, the designer's vision, or a combination? Think of, say, Pink Floyd's *Dark Side of the Moon*. Who does it reflect? *London Calling* by the Clash? The Beatles' *Sergeant Pepper*? These are three very different approaches: one an illustration, one a live photograph, and one a meticulously conceived conceptual shoot/collage. All are definitive visual works, instantly recognizable, and identifiable with the band.

If you are confident that you know what you want and what is right for your music, trust your gut. If not, find a designer whose work you identify and empathize with, and trust this person. Above all, keep your mind and your eyes open to interpretations, both expected and unexpected, that give a visual identity to what lays beneath the covers. To paraphrase one of my favorite musical maxims, "It's not so much what you play as it is what you don't play." It's not so much what you see as it is what you don't see.

There are conflicting interests inherent to the visual presentation of an artist. You must effectively navigate these waters in a manner that pleases you, personally, but also is something that the label feels that they can really get behind and sell. This is not an easy thing to do. The best way to make this process as painless as possible is to give yourself the time needed to fight the fights, hold your ground, give a little, and take a little, in order to reach the best possible *product* with enough time to adequately promote said product. In order to do this, you should begin working on your CD package as early as possible—like the day after you get signed.

Working with Your A&R Person

Once you have been signed to a label, if you don't already have a completed album, you will need to record your music. In other words, you will be signed based on the strength of demos or a live show with the understanding that the label wants you to record a new record, rather than releasing these "demos." If this is the case, you will dive headlong into the A&R world. The person who helped you get signed is probably an A&R person. You will therefore already know him and have discussed how things are going to proceed on the recording. Again, if it's a smaller label, the A&R person may be wearing any number of other hats, in addition to the traditional white A&R toque. One way or the other, you will be dealing with A&R matters. These include choosing the songs to record, the studio, the producer, the budget, and other expenses related to recording your music. You will be very involved with this process, and it's frequently a fun one. Like all label interaction, try to make it feel as collaborative as possible. If you have little or no track record, the label will play a stronger role in guiding your recording. Assume that the label is going to want to be involved in the process, and make them feel a part of it.

Yes, most likely, you will make fun of the label people at regular intervals, when they aren't around (and sometimes when they are around), but you will ultimately have more control if you keep the relationship from being adversarial.

That said, it is your music. You must have the final say. Do bear in mind that you may not have the benefit of experience that people at the label do, and you should at least hear them out. Ideally, you will respect and like your A&R person, and come to look to him or her as an objective set of ears, and a person who can really help you fully develop your music.

Key People at the Labels

At many labels, your A&R person will also perform the function of a product manager (there's that "product" word again). At others, you may be assigned a separate product manager. At the smaller labels, the product manager will be the same person who is doing everything else. In any case, the product manager serves as the day-to-day person who will help you coordinate everything having to do with your release. They are, in effect, the liaison between you and all the various departments at the label. Whoever this person is and whatever their title may be, you must make them your closest friend. This person will most likely be who you speak to the most at the label. In turn, they will be communicating to others at the label (if there are others) what is going on with you the artist. They will also work with you to figure out how to skin the wily cat of selling records. For instance, if you want to run an ad in *Time* magazine for your record, you will run this idea by the product manager (or however you refer to them). He will either make the decision himself, and tell you you're off your rocker, or run the idea by others, and then report back to you that you're off your rocker.

Other key people at labels

There may be other people at the label who you will be interacting with regularly. If the label is large enough that it has an in-house publicist and/or radio person, you (or your manager, or both) will be in regular contact with them. Also establish a good rapport with these people, as they are the ones who try to convince others to play/write about your records.

Similarly, get to know the sales/distribution staff who are actively engaged in selling your records. Few artists work hard enough to ingratiate themselves to these people, but they should. Again, the possibility of this will depend on the size of the label and their relationship with their distributor. But labels frequently arrange for artists to meet their distributors. If the distributor has a field staff, you will want to keep them up-to-date on any performances you have in their areas.

Developing relationships is the key. It's amazing to me how many artists feel that they can just deliver a record and have no further interaction with the label. It just doesn't work well, that way. Every day, the label is going to be talking about your music and trying to get people interested in it. You must give them the tools to do this work effectively. The best tool you can give them is knowledge that transcends your music on the CD. The only way to communicate this is to get to know them.

Like football, the music business is a game of inches. It is the little tiny things that, over time and through repetition, can add up to something very big. Frequently, it comes down to someone making a decision between pushing one artist over another. You want this artist to be you. You are more likely to get that push, especially at the early stages of your career, if you have a personal relationship with those who decide what to push.

Once you've set a release date and completed the record, you will be working on generating some "buzz" so that when those records finally reach the stores, people will look for them. This means working with publicists, radio people, Web people, and other marketers, as well as retail people.

Since you're with a label now, hopefully you will be working with in-house publicists and radio-promo people, as well as potentially with indies. One way or the other, they will be sending out previews of your music. These are frequently called "advance CDs," for publicity, and called "CD pros" or "promos" for radio. Radio promo CDs may be the entire album or a single. They will also send a bio, a photo, and perhaps an electronic press kit (EPK), which is a video profile of you and your music.

You may also be making a video to submit to the likely candidates (MTV, VH1) prior to or just around street date. They may also give it to other outlets that play videos—both traditional and on the Web.

At this time, you will also be trying to get some sort of tour together to coincide with the release of your record. This tour will put you in front of audiences, and it will also provide marketing ammo, as they will be able to talk to regional press and radio about your record by telling them about your appearance. In this way, among other things, on-airs at radio stations and interviews can take place.

This time leading up to the release of your record may be the most exciting time. After all the time spent recording your record, getting a deal, and setting up the marketing, the actual release may be an anticlimax. Hopefully, it will be just the start, and the real excitement will begin once the record has been released.

Sadly, this is not the way it happens for most artists and records. Rather than the record release being the beginning, it is often the end. Unfortunately, many record labels today treat record releases the same way movie studios treat movies. They drive everything for that opening "weekend." (In the music business, that would be the "opening Tuesday," but it doesn't have the same ring.) If that opening is a strong one, they will then mobilize and really drive it home. If not, sadly, they will often move on to the next project. Not all labels are like this. Many realize that it takes a long, LONG time to make the connections necessary between an artist's music and a consumer's attention to cause a record to sell. Many labels simply don't have the money to treat record releases like movie releases, and instead, have to make up what they lack in money with persistence. This can be a very good thing for the right type of band.

Keeping the Label Focused on You

There are ways you can try to keep the label focused on you beyond the initial push around the release. Much of this involves working with the label to plan events spanning six months to a year after the street date. While it would be wonderful if you could just write such a plan and have it be so, typically it will not.

You need to take matters into your own hands, and largely, keep doing all of the things that got you signed—after you get signed. In other words, if you were a touring machine, and that impacted largely on you getting a record deal, by all means, keep touring. Just make sure the record label is maximizing your efforts. If you had a great Web site with your own street team that was effective and helped build the buzz that you got signed, you need to keep that going.

Find ways to integrate the things you were doing well pre-signing into the things you do post-signing. In this way, you will constantly be keeping active, regardless of whether or not the label is. Of course, worst-case scenario, if you are dropped by the label, you won't want to have lost all of the good things that led you to a deal. You are far less likely to get dropped by a label if you have your own activity going on around your music that complements their activity. Labels really don't like feeling that they are doing all the work.

Summary

Throughout this book, I've stressed the importance of team and community and relationships. To be a successful recording artist, you must build and maintain communities and teams of people who support your music. The marketing, recording, distribution, and performing are all means that can enable you to make these connections.

You must also connect with your label. Once the bloom is off the rose, which occurs about ten seconds after you sign the deal, there will necessarily be problems and conflicts of interest regarding your career. The way to handle this is to understand that some compromises will have to be made.

Pick your battles. If you battle with the label over everything, you will either have a miserable and likely unsuccessful experience or you will be dropped. Do not take a stance over every issue. But do take hard stances over things that are very important to you. Only you can determine which ones are worth it. If you compromise on the things you can stand, and hold fast to what you really feel strongly about, you will be viewed as an artist with a vision who is reasonable and a team player.

With all of the talk these days about how labels are evil, you need to know that the majority of the people who work at labels really, really want you to succeed. This is especially true with those who work with artists day-to-day. They take pride in working on your behalf. When artists understand this and find ways to corral this enthusiasm by working with the label instead of against it, records sell.

The more you bring to a record label, the less they can take away from you. More than anything else, this book is designed to allow you to not simply give yourself the best possible chance to get a record deal, but to have developed your career to a point where you will be able to get the most favorable record deal possible.

Again, the more you bring to a record label, the better will be your chances of getting a deal that will truly be an tremendous asset to your career.

Being signed to a label can be a cooperative wonderful experience. It requires a tremendous amount of work. If you apply the same effort into making your relationship with your label a good one, you stand a good chance of having tremendous success.

Workshop

What do you need to do next? Write songs? Get your band together? Get a photo for the package you will send to a prospective label?

Write down every step you need to take. Take a calendar and schedule when you will accomplish each task, down to the date when you will lick the stamps and mail the package.

Then do it!

A

Sample Contract

There are so many different types of contracts that including examples of all types would easily double the size of this book. Contracts can be hundreds of pages long! But I thought it would be helpful for you to see an example, just to get the vibe of what it is that you'll be signing. There are many good sources of contracts available, such as the Internet, books on the music business (like the ones in appendix B), and people you know who have record deals. They vary so much that I hesitated even to include this one, but ultimately, decided that it might be helpful to you.

> The following, when signed by you on behalf of yourself and your production company, if any, and by an authorized signatory of ________________, ("we" or "us"), shall represent a binding agreement whereby you shall perform services and record for us as our exclusive worldwide recording and video artist.
>
> 1. Term
>
> The term of this Agreement shall commence concurrently with the execution hereof and shall continue until the last day of the twelfth (12th) month following said execution or the last day of the ninth (9th) month following our initial United States release of the album embodying your recording commitment for the initial period, whichever is later. We shall have _______ (__) options to renew this Agreement for consecutive periods (the "Option Period[s]"), each of which Option Periods shall commence upon the expiration of the immediately preceding period and shall continue until the last day of the twelfth (12th) month thereafter or the last day of the ninth (9th) month following our initial United States release of the album embodying your recording commitment for the applicable Option Period, whichever is later. Each Option Period shall be exercisable by written notice to you on or before a date thirty (30) days prior to the expiration of the then current period; provided, however, that in the event that we fail to send such notice to you, we shall not lose our right to exercise the applicable option period unless you have notified us in writing and we have failed to send you

written notice [within thirty (30) days after receipt of your written notice] that we intend to exercise the applicable option. The initial period and each individual Option Period of the Term shall each be deemed a "Contract Period." The initial period and each Option Period together shall also be deemed the "Term."

2. Recording Commitment; Ownership of Copyrights and Other Rights

(a) During each Contract Period of the Term you shall record for us one (1) full-length record album ("LP") of newly recorded original material containing, at our election, __________ (___) audio master recordings of approximately ________ (__) minutes' duration, recorded entirely in recording studios (as opposed to live performances). The aforementioned master recordings shall be deemed "Masters" as defined hereinbelow, provided, however, that the term "Masters" as used herein shall not be limited to these particular master recordings. Special projects, including, without limitation Live, Christmas, or children's projects, shall not count toward the recording commitment, and we shall negotiate in good faith with respect to the recording elements therefor in each instance. You shall record the Masters and deliver them to us or our designee promptly after they are completed to our reasonable satisfaction.

(b) We shall own the entire worldwide right, title, and interest, including the worldwide copyright in all Masters hereunder (which term is defined below), and the performances embodied thereon in perpetuity, from the inception of recording. We shall have the perpetual and exclusive right to exploit the Masters in any manner that we may choose, (which right shall include licensing or otherwise permitting any other person, firm or corporation to do or refrain from doing any or all of that which we shall have the right to do herein) through any markets, by any means and in any format now or hereafter known, including but not limited to the right to advertise, sell, synchronize with any medium, or otherwise release the Masters under any trademarks, trade names or labels (whether or not affiliated with us), to perform the Masters publicly, and/or to commit the Masters (regardless of the configuration or manner of transmission) to public performance by radio, television, the Internet or other direct transmission, or by any other media now known or hereafter devised. Our rights herein shall be free from any claims by you, or by any person, firm, or corporation. It is agreed and understood that for purposes of the United States Copyright Act, the results and proceeds of your services hereunder shall be deemed a "work for hire," or as a work specially ordered by us as a contribution to a collective work. Upon our request, you shall cause each person providing personal services on or in connection with the Masters recorded hereunder to execute and deliver to us our then-current "work for hire/power of attorney" form.

(c) Notwithstanding the foregoing, to the extent (if any) that you are deemed the "author" of any Masters hereunder, you hereby grant us the entire worldwide right, title, and interest derived from you, including, without limitation, the copyright in and to the Masters and the performances embodied thereon. You hereby grant to us an irrevocable power of attorney, coupled with an interest, to execute for you and in your name all documents and instruments necessary or desirable to effectuate the intents and purposes of this Paragraph and to accomplish, evidence and perfect the rights granted to us pursuant to this Paragraph, including without limitation, documents to apply for and to obtain all copyright registrations in and to the Masters recorded hereunder, and documents to assign such copyrights to us.

(d) "Masters" or "Recordings" shall be deemed to mean each and every recording of sound created, owned or controlled by you during the Term hereof, including sound accompanied with visual images, by any method, and on any substance now or hereafter known, regardless of the manner and/or market of exploitation, and whether or not "delivered" by you hereunder. It is expressly understood and agreed that we shall not be limited in any manner whatsoever with respect to how (or how many times or in how many different formats) we use or exploit the Masters. As the exclusive owner of the Masters, we shall have the sole discretion to mix, remix, master, remaster, record, rerecord, release, rerelease, compile, recompile, and in any other manner use or exploit the Masters without your consent or approval therefor or over any of the elements thereof, provided that we agree to use reasonable efforts to consult with you concerning same, but we shall not be deemed in breach of this Agreement nor shall you have any recourse if we shall fail to so consult with you with respect thereto. The royalty rate applicable to a particular Master embodied on any projects recorded or released hereunder shall be the basic royalty rate specified herein for the Contract Period in which such Master was recorded. We may also compile up to two (2) "Greatest Hits" LPs, subject only to consulting with you as to the repertoire to be included if such compilation is released during the Term. Any such Greatest Hits LPs compiled during the Term hereof shall, at our election, include up to two (2) newly recorded Masters, specifically recorded for inclusion thereon. Neither any Greatest Hits LPs nor any Masters newly recorded therefor shall count toward the foregoing recording commitment, and the royalty rate applicable to a particular Master embodied on a "Greatest Hits" LP shall be the basic royalty rate specified herein for the Contract Period in which such Master was recorded. You shall diligently, competently, and to the best of your ability perform the services required to be performed by you hereunder as a recording artist.

(e) Each LP shall be recorded and delivered pursuant to a mutually agreed upon time frame, approximately twelve (12) months after delivery to us of the immediately preceding LP. You shall use your best efforts to record and deliver each LP within six (6) months after the beginning of each Contract Period. Any delay in such recording and delivery shall result in an extension of the particular Contract Period and the Term by the same amount of time. You shall not allow another recording company to release Masters recorded for it prior to nine (9) months after the end of the Term. Time is of the essence with respect to the delivery of Masters and LPs.

3. Recording Elements

(a) All elements of the recording process and the creation and production of the Masters shall be mutually approved by you and us, including songs, recording studios, record producers, recording personnel, time of recording, etc. In the event of any disagreement, we shall have final say. Further, once a particular element, issue or set of elements or issues has been mutually approved by you and us, you shall not be entitled to later withhold, change, condition or otherwise limit the previously granted approval. You hereby agree that no "sampling" (as that term is understood in the United States recording industry, i.e., incorporating into the Masters any copyrighted or otherwise proprietary material belonging to a third party other than us) shall be used on or in connection with the Masters hereunder unless and until you have acquired our prior written approval therefor, which written approval may be conditioned upon, among other things, budgetary considerations, your willingness to allow us to recoup from mechanical copyright royalties payable to you hereunder any budget overages arising from the securing of any such "sample" licenses/clearances, and your acquiring from the applicable third party owner of such "sampled" material written verification of our perpetual right to use such "sampled" material on and in connection with the Masters.

(b) We shall be responsible for the payment of all recording costs (as that term is hereinafter defined) pursuant to budgets determined by us, after consultation with you, which budgets shall be inclusive of any producer's advances, artwork, producer fees, and mastering costs. We may, at our sole option, pay to you, at times and in increments determined by us, the recording budget, in which case you shall pay therefrom (and be solely responsible for and indemnify us from) all recording costs. The recording budget for the initial period hereunder shall be determined by us. The recording budget for each option period recording commitment album (if any) shall also be determined by us.

(c) Recording costs shall be deemed to include all union scale payments required to be made in connection with the Masters as well as all payments made to any other individuals rendering services in connection with the recording of the Masters (including producer advances), all other payments which are made pursuant to any applicable law or regulation or the provisions of any applicable collective bargaining agreement between us and any union or guild (including, without limitation, payroll taxes and payments to union pension and welfare funds, except payments to the AF of M or AFTRA, which payments are based on sales of records and are our sole responsibility), all amounts paid or incurred for studio or hall rentals, tape, engineering, mixing (and remixing), editing, "sample" clearances, instrument rental and cartage, mastering, transportation, accommodations, immigration clearances, payments for and costs incurred in regard to trademark and service mark searches and clearances, payments for Internet domain name registrations, so-called "per diems" or any other payments in respect of any individuals (including you) rendering services in connection with the recording of the Masters, together with any and all amounts incurred in connection with the recording of the Masters which are commonly considered recording costs in the United States recording industry. Notwithstanding the foregoing, you shall not incur any costs or expenses with any unions or guilds without our prior written approval thereof. Recording costs shall also include the costs for the design and preparation (including separations) of cover artwork through the print ready stage. Notwithstanding anything to the contrary herein contained, we shall not be obligated to continue or permit the continuation of any recording session, even if previously approved, if we reasonably anticipate that the recording costs will exceed the approved budget, or that the Masters will not be technically and commercially satisfactory. Upon our request, you shall re-record any Master until it is technically and commercially satisfactory to us.

(d) All recording costs shall be deemed advances recoupable from any and all artist (but not mechanical copyright) royalties payable to you under this Agreement or any other recording artist agreement between you and us or our affiliates. In the event that recording costs exceed the relevant recording budgets herein for reasons within your or any producer's control, you shall promptly, upon our demand therefor, pay such costs, reimburse us for all such excess costs if we pay them, or we may, at our election, deduct such excess costs from any and all monies payable by us to you hereunder or under any other recording agreement between you and us or our affiliates. Each and every payment made by us or our affiliates to you or on your behalf or at your request (except the royalties described herein) shall, unless otherwise specifically set forth to the contrary herein, be deemed an advance recoupable from any and all royalties and other sums payable to you hereunder.

(e) We shall have the exclusive right during the Term hereof to create and produce films, videotapes and other audiovisual recordings (regardless of the format) ("Videos") featuring your performances of musical selections. We shall mutually determine all of the recording, creation and production elements for all Videos, and __________ percent (__%) of the production costs therefor shall be deemed additional advances recoupable from any and all artist (but not mechanical copyright) royalties payable to you under this Agreement or any other recording artist agreement between you and us or our affiliates. In the event that we shall commercially exploit the Videos or any of them, all of such video production costs which have not theretofore been recouped from artist record royalties shall be recoupable from artist video royalties, provided that we shall not "double recoup" any part thereof.

4. Delivery Requirements

You shall deliver to us, for each Master, a fully edited and mixed two (2) track stereo tape and all multitrack tapes (including, but not limited to, any twenty-four (24) and forty-eight (48) track tapes) in proper form for the production of parts necessary for the manufacture of technically and commercially satisfactory phonograph records. You shall also deliver to us simultaneously a fully mastered DAT. All original session tapes and any derivatives and reproductions thereof shall also be delivered to us or, at our election, maintained at a recording studio or other location designated by us, in our name and control. Within seventy-two (72) hours after each recording session and in accordance with all rules and regulations of all unions having jurisdiction over the recording process, you shall submit to us all union contract forms and report forms for recording sessions, all bills and invoices pertaining to such recording sessions, and all payroll forms (including, without limitation, all W-4's, I-9's, and other tax withholding forms) pertaining to such recording sessions. You shall also simultaneously deliver to us all label copy, album credits, mechanical licenses, sideman clearances, and other consents necessary to allow us to manufacture and commercially exploit the Masters, including, without limitation, the "work for hire" agreements referenced in Paragraph 2(b), hereof, as well as any so-called "sample clearances" and fully executed agreements with all producers and mix engineers (if any) rendering services in connection with the Masters. Notwithstanding the foregoing, we shall assist you with the acquisition of (but shall not be responsible for any costs beyond the mechanical copyright "caps" set forth herein for) the requisite mechanical licenses, provided that you have timely (i.e., no later than the commencement of recording of the applicable Masters) provided to us all writer and publisher information, including, without limitation, the applicable and accurate song-splits.

5. Biographical Rights; Marketing

(a) You hereby grant to us and our designees the exclusive worldwide right in perpetuity to use and permit others to use, at no cost, your name (including any legal, fictitious or professional name), likeness, photograph and biographical rights for purposes of trade and otherwise without restriction on or in connection with the exploitation of the Masters in any manner or market now or hereafter known, and the advertising in connection therewith, which such right shall be exclusive during the Term and non-exclusive thereafter.

(b) In the event that you disapprove of any such names, likenesses, photographs, or biographical information chosen by us for use hereunder, you shall provide to us an appropriate substitute therefor within two (2) days after our submission to you of such intended disapproved use, provided that we shall not be required to utilize any such substitute if we have not received said substitute from you prior to any previously scheduled mass reproduction of the disapproved use, even if prior to the expiration of the aforementioned two (2) day period. Further, our inadvertent failure to provide you with the opportunity to approve name, likeness, photograph and biographical information shall not be deemed a breach of this Agreement, nor shall you have the right to enjoin us from using any such materials. You shall not be deemed to be in breach of this Agreement solely by failing to provide such substitute(s), but in the event of such failure, we shall have the right to utilize such names, likenesses, photographs, and biographical information as we desire and the same shall be deemed approved by you. Any names, likenesses, photographs or biographical information provided to us by you or once approved by you shall be deemed thereafter approved by you for all purposes set forth in this Agreement. For purposes of example only and without limiting the scope of this provision, if you approve of a particular use of your name, likeness, photograph or biographical information for album cover art, you may not then object to said use (or a substantially similar variation thereof) by us in or on other materials created hereunder in connection with the exploitation of the Masters. The aforementioned approval rights shall apply only to album cover artwork, but shall not pertain to marketing materials and other marketing opportunities which require time-sensitive decisions on our part.

(c) You hereby warrant that you are the sole owner of any legal, fictitious or professional name used by you hereunder, and that no other person has or will have the right to use such name in connection with the exploitation of master recordings or otherwise relating to the music and/or entertainment industry.

You agree to use your best efforts during the Term to be billed as our exclusive recording artist and we shall have the right to refer to you as such.

(d) All packaging, advertising, marketing, sales and distribution decisions shall be made by us. __________ percent (__%) of the costs incurred by us or our affiliates for independent (as opposed to "in-house") marketing, publicity and promotion in connection with the exploitation of the Masters shall be deemed additional advances to you hereunder and shall be recoupable from any and all royalties and other sums (except mechanical copyright royalties) payable to you under this Agreement or any other recording artist agreement between you and us or our affiliates.

6. Artist Royalties

(a) Provided that you have faithfully performed all of the material terms and conditions hereof, on the Masters recorded hereunder, we shall pay you royalties at the rate of __________ percent (__%) of the retail list price of net sales of full price albums sold by us in the United States through normal retail channels of distribution.

(b) Albums shall include LPs, cassettes, accompaniment tracks, compact discs ("CDs"), digital audio tapes ("DATs"), digital compact cassettes ("DCCs"), and any other form of reproduction now or hereafter known (regardless of the manner or market of exploitation), embodying sound alone or sound synchronized with or accompanied by visual images, provided that the suggested retail list price of DATs as initially released shall be deemed the same as the then-current price of the corresponding audiocassette. For the purposes of this Agreement, so-called "CD plus" and "enhanced compact discs" which contain an audio and/or a visual component shall be deemed audio-only CDs. With respect to new technology and new mediums of exploitation (i.e., any other configuration of which we are not in general commercial distribution as of the date hereof, including, without limitation, MDs, DATs, DCCs, CD-ROM, CD-I, 3DO, AVCD, CD Plus, Enhanced CDs, solid state memory devices, DVD, etc.), we shall pay you ___________ percent (___%) of the otherwise applicable royalty rate (with a ________ percent (__%) packaging deduction) for the first ______ (__) years after the introduction of each new medium. Thereafter, you and we shall negotiate in good faith with respect to the applicable royalty rate, but in no event shall we be obligated to pay more than a royalty rate equal to one hundred percent (100%) of the otherwise applicable royalty rate with a ________ percent (__%) packaging deduction. Royalties shall be payable on __________ percent (__%) of net records (i.e., less returns and credits of any nature) sold. Further, in the event that we enter into a distribution, license or other similar relationship regarding the exploitation of Masters with a third party whose policy it is to pay royalties on less than ___________ percent (__%) of net sales, such reduced basis shall be automatically applied to sales of Masters by or through said third party after the effective date of our agreement with said third party.

(c) With respect to singles, maxi-singles or EPs, 7", or other vinyl records (if any) sold by us in the United States, the royalty rates or other compensation therefor (e.g., product trade-out, etc.) shall be negotiated by you and us in good faith, provided that our failure to agree shall not preclude us from making and selling the applicable medium. The term "EP" shall mean a recording embodying five (5) to eight (8) Masters or a recording embodying more than eight (8) Masters which is sold at a retail price commensurate with a standard EP. The term "singles" shall mean a recording embodying two (2) Masters, and the term "maxi-single" shall mean a recording embodying more than two (2), but not more than four (4) Masters. Singles, maxi-singles, and EP's may each be manufactured in vinyl format.

(d) Midline and budget sales shall result in the royalty on United States sales being seventy-five percent (75%) and fifty percent (50%) of the foregoing rate, respectively. The term "midline" or "mid-priced record line" shall mean a record line or label the records of which bear a suggested retail list price in the country in question in excess of sixty-six and two-thirds percent (66 2/3%) and less than eighty percent (80%) of the suggested retail list price in such country of top-line records on which recordings of the majority of our artists are initially released in such country. The term "budget sales" or "budget record line" or "low-priced record line" shall mean a record line or label the records of which bear a suggested retail list price in the country in question which is sixty-six and two-thirds percent (66 2/3%) or less of the suggested retail list price in such country of top-line records on which recordings of the majority of our artists are initially released in such country.

(e) Notwithstanding anything to the contrary herein contained, no royalties (whether artist, producer, or mechanical royalties) shall be payable on free goods, which shall be limited to __________ percent (__%) of sales on trade sales, _________ percent (__%) of sales on trade sales of singles, and _________ percent (__%) of sales on record club sales. Notwithstanding the foregoing, with respect to short-term special promotions or marketing campaigns of ten (10) weeks or less duration, we shall have the right to distribute without charge and without royalty obligation to you an *additional* ______ percent (__%) of the total records intended for re-sale. No royalties (whether artist, producer, or mechanical royalties) shall be payable on (i) records given away for promotional purposes or sold at below stated wholesale prices; (ii) so-called cut-outs, scrap or surplus records; and, notwithstanding any provision to the contrary herein contained, (iii) any record sold at a price of less than ______ Dollars ($__.00).

(f) On net sales of full price units sold through normal retail channels of distribution outside the United States, we shall pay you a royalty equal to fifty percent (50%) of our net receipts, not to exceed the royalty rate payable on United States retail sales of full price units.

(g) On net sales of records sold through record clubs, mail order or other direct-to-consumer methods, including broadcast packages, direct transmission, (including telephone, satellite, cable, point of sale manufacturing or any other means of direct transmission to the consumer over networks or through the air, now known or hereafter devised) or other methods utilizing television advertising, we shall pay you at the rate of fifty percent (50%) of our net receipts for sales by our licensees and one-half (1/2) of the otherwise applicable royalty for sales by us or our affiliates, provided that record club sales shall also be subject to the "free goods" provisions of Subparagraph (e), above. On net sales of records sold as "premiums" (i.e., records sold at less than customary prices in connection with the sale of unrelated products or services), we shall pay you fifty percent (50%) of the otherwise applicable base rate, in no event to exceed fifty (50%) of our net receipts therefrom, provided that we shall not sell records or Masters delivered hereunder as "premiums" without consulting you in accordance with the terms of Subparagraph 6(i), below.

(h) With respect to third party licenses of Masters wherein we are paid a royalty, or other licenses or uses of Masters not otherwise described herein and for which we are paid on a flat fee or net receipts basis, including, without limitation, in or on motion pictures, television or soundtracks derived therefrom, we shall pay to you fifty percent (50%) of our net receipts therefrom. With respect to Videos featuring your performances of musical selections embodied on videograms distributed to the home video market, we shall pay you a royalty of __________ percent (__%) of the wholesale price (less taxes) on net sales of videograms by us and fifty percent (50%) of our net receipts from licensees, the foregoing rates to be deemed be inclusive of master use and synchronization royalties, and such royalties shall be credited to your account prospectively following recoupment of video production costs. With respect to any other method of exploitation of Videos, we shall negotiate and agree upon the royalty payable on a case by case basis, provided, however, that our failure to agree shall not prevent us from exploiting the Videos. In regard to royalties payable to you hereunder, including, without limitation, in connection with "joint recordings" and "compilations," we shall have the right to prorate royalties according to your participation therein or thereon or, if applicable, according to the number of Masters actually contained in LPs in relation to all master recordings contained thereon. "Net receipts" as used in this Agreement shall mean receipts as computed after deduction from gross of all copyright, union and other applicable third party payments, including, without limitation, distribution fees and manufacturing costs, and any costs which are deducted from or recouped by monies otherwise payable to us, provided that we shall not "double dip" by deducting any such costs more than once.

(i) Notwithstanding anything to the contrary herein contained, and to the extent not otherwise defined or delineated herein, we agree to use good faith efforts to consult with you regarding any of the following which occur during the Term, provided that our inadvertent failure to so consult with you, or your unavailability to be so consulted shall not be deemed a breach of this Agreement;

(i) any "coupling" of any Master featuring your performances with master recordings featuring the performances of other artists or any joint recordings with other artists; and

(ii) the release of any "outtakes," demo recordings, rejected master recordings or "live" recordings (individually and collectively "Outtakes"); and

(iii) editing or remixing any Masters delivered to us hereunder, except with respect to non-disc configurations and singles; and

(iv) any so-called "premium" use of the Masters (as defined above); and

(v) any master use and/or master use synchronization licenses and interactive use licensing, and any so-called "B-sides" or EPs.

(j) Except as otherwise set forth herein, there shall be a ________ percent (__%) packaging deduction for standard audiocassettes, and EPs. There shall be a ________ percent (__%) packaging deduction for compact discs, recordings in digital pre-recorded tape form, new technology/new mediums of exploitation, and any other new form or configuration of recording or new form of package, container or box, and a ________ percent (__%) packaging deduction for audiovisual records, vinyl albums, maxi-singles and 7-inch singles.

(k) All artist royalties shall be deemed "all in," that is, inclusive of producer royalties, or any other third party royalties other than mechanical copyright royalties. In the event that you so request and, further provided that we so agree, we shall pay any such producer or other third party royalty participant on your behalf pursuant to the producer or other third party agreements delivered to us at the time of your delivery of the applicable Masters. Any royalties paid to producers or third party royalty participants on your behalf shall be deducted from royalties (excluding mechanical copyright royalties) or other sums payable to you hereunder. Additionally, for the recoupment of any advances or charges under this Agreement, the royalty rates herein shall be reduced by the amount of the applicable royalty rates contained in the agreement with such producer or other third-party royalty participant. Any advances payable by us to third parties which are not recouped by us from royalties payable to them may be recouped by us from any and all artist royalties or other sums [excluding mechanical copyright royalties] payable by us to you under this Agreement or any other recording artist agreement between you and us or our affiliates. All producer royalties shall be reduced, computed, calculated and paid, and shall be subject to the same category variations as are the royalties payable to you hereunder.

7. Accountings

(a) We shall send to you statements for royalties payable hereunder on a semi-annual basis, within ninety (90) days after the end of each semi-annual period, together with payment of royalties, if any, earned by you hereunder during the semi-annual period for which the statement is rendered, less all advances and other charges under this Agreement. We shall have the right to retain, as a reserve against charges, credits, or returns, such portion of payable royalties as shall be reasonable in our best business judgment, not to exceed __________ percent (__%) except in the case of seasonal (i.e., Christmas, Easter, and similar) product wherein the reserve rate shall be __________ percent (__%) and Singles (including Long-Play Singles), for which the reserve shall be ________ percent (__%). We may also retain larger reserves in respect of enhanced CDs, as well as other mediums of records, now or hereafter known or developed. Reserves shall be held for _______ (__) accounting periods. You shall reimburse us on demand for any overpayments, and we may also deduct the amount thereof from any monies payable to you hereunder. Royalties paid by us on records subsequently returned shall be deemed overpayments.

(b) No royalties shall be payable to you on sales of records by any of our licensees or distributors until payment on those sales has been received by us in the United States, or has been credited to us as a final credit against a prior advance. Sales by a licensee or distributor shall be deemed to have occurred in the semi-annual accounting period during which that licensee or distributor shall have rendered to us accounting statements and payments for those sales.

(c) Royalties on record sales outside of the United States shall be computed in the national currency in which our licensees pay us, shall be credited to your royalty account hereunder at the same rate of exchange at which our licensees pay us, and shall be proportionately subject to any withholding or comparable taxes which may be imposed upon our receipts.

(d) If we shall not receive payment in United States dollars in the United States for any sales of records outside of the United States, royalties on those sales shall not be credited to your royalty account hereunder. We shall, however, at your written request and if we are reasonably able to do so, accept payment for those sales in foreign currency and shall deposit in a foreign bank or other depository, at your expense, in that foreign currency, that portion thereof, if any, as a shall equal the royalties which would have been payable to you hereunder on those sales had payment for those sales been made to us in United States dollars in the United States. Deposit as aforesaid shall fulfill our royalty obligations hereunder as to those sales. If any law, ruling or other governmental restriction limits the amount a licensee can remit to us, we may reduce your royalties hereunder by an amount proportionate to the reduction in our licensee's remittance to us, provided that if you are in an unrecouped position, we shall credit your account with the full amount of royalties that would otherwise be due you hereunder.

(e) We will maintain books and records which report the sales of records, on which royalties are payable to you. You may, but not more than once a year, at your own expense, examine those books and records, as provided in this Paragraph 7(e) only. You may make those examinations only for the purpose of verifying the accuracy of the statements sent to you under Paragraph 7(a). All such examinations shall be in accordance with GAAP procedures and regulations. You may make such an examination for a particular statement only once, and only within two (2) years after the date that a statement is rendered to you under Paragraph 7(a). You may make such an examination only during our usual business hours, and at the place where we keep the books and records to be examined. If you wish to make an examination you will be required to notify us at least thirty (30) days before the date when you plan to begin the examination. We may postpone the commencement of your examination by notice given to you not later than five (5) days before the commencement date specified in your notice, but if we do so, the running of the time within which the examination may be made will be suspended during the postponement. If your examination has not been completed within one (1) month from the time you begin it, we may require you to terminate it on seven (7) days' notice to you at any time, and we will not be required to permit you to continue the examination after the end of that seven (7) day period. You will not be entitled to examine any manufacturing records or any other records that do not specifically report sales or other distributions of records on which royalties are payable to you. You may appoint a certified public accountant to make such an examination for you, but not if (s)he or his/her firm has begun an examination of our books and records for any person except you unless the examination has been concluded and any applicable audit issues have been resolved. The running of the time within which the examination may be made will be suspended until such applicable audit issues are resolved, and the point in time at which the audit issues are resolved shall be determined by us in good faith and communicated through written notice to you. Such certified public accountant will act only under a Letter of Confidentiality which provides that any information derived from such audit or examination will not be knowingly released, divulged or published to any person, firm or corporation, other than to you, your representatives or to a judicial or administrative body in connection with any proceeding relating to this Agreement.

(f) If you have any objections to a royalty statement, you will give us specific notice of that objection and your reasons for it within two (2) years after the date that a statement is rendered to you under Paragraph 7(a). Each royalty statement will become conclusively binding on you at the end of the two (2) year period, and you will no longer have any right to make any other objections to it. You will not have the right to commence a legal action against us for royalties on records sold during the period a royalty accounting covers, unless you commence the suit within that two (2) year period, provided that, if you make timely objection within the aforesaid two (2) year period, you may commence suit thereon within the later of the aforesaid two (2) year period, or within six (6) months after we have responded to your objections(s), but in no event later than two (2) years and six (6) months after the date on which we are required to send you the applicable statement. If you commence suit on any controversy or claim concerning royalty accountings rendered to you under this agreement in a court of competent jurisdiction (as provided herein), the scope of the proceeding will be limited to determination of the amount of the royalties due for the accounting periods concerned, and the court will have no authority to consider any other issues or award any relief except recovery of any royalties found owing. Your recovery of any such royalties will be the sole remedy available to you by reason of any claim related to our royalty accountings. Without limiting the generality of the preceding sentence, you will not have any right to seek termination of this Agreement or avoid the performance of your obligations under it by reason of any such claim.

(g) We shall have the right to deduct from any amounts payable to you hereunder that portion thereof as may be required to be deducted under any statute, regulation, treaty or other law, or under any union or guild agreement, and you shall promptly execute and deliver to us any forms or other documents as may be required in connection therewith.

(h) Each payment made by us to you under this Agreement, other than union scale payments, shall, at our election, be made by a single check payable to you. All payments herein are contingent upon us receiving properly completed W-9 and/or 1001 IRS tax forms, as applicable.

8. Mechanical Copyright Royalties; Publishing

(a) Any selections recorded in any Masters which are written, owned, or controlled, in whole or in part, directly or indirectly, by you or any person or company with whom you are affiliated ("Controlled Compositions"), are hereby irrevocably and non-exclusively licensed to us at ________ percent (___%) of the so-called minimum statutory rate which shall be deemed to be the statutory rate in effect in the United States at the time of the initial United States release of the first Master embodying a selection, without regard to so-called "long song" rates (the "minimum statutory rate"). In the event a licensee pays us mechanical copyright royalties on a less favorable basis, such less favorable basis shall be applicable to you hereunder. Notwithstanding anything to the contrary herein contained, to the extent that we are required to pay more than _______ percent (__%) of the so-called minimum statutory rate on any Controlled Composition or more than _________ percent (__%) of _____ (__) times the minimum statutory rate on any album, or more than ________ percent (__%) of the minimum statutory rate for a Controlled Composition on a midline album or an album distributed through so-called "record clubs," or __________ percent (__%) of the minimum statutory rate for a Controlled Composition on a budget album, we shall have the right to deduct any such amounts from any monies payable to you under this Agreement or any other agreement between you and us or our affiliates.

(b) With respect to the territory of Canada, you hereby irrevocably and non-exclusively license to us any and all Controlled Compositions in the same manner (and subject to the same limitations) as your license to us of said Controlled Compositions for the United States, except that the Canadian equivalent to the United States minimum statutory rate shall be _______ percent (__%) of the Canadian statutory per selection rate or, if there is no statutory rate in Canada at the time of the initial Canadian release of the applicable Master, _______ percent (__%) of the per selection rate then generally recognized by major record companies in Canada.

(c) Mechanical copyright royalties shall be paid on net sales and in all respects on the same basis and subject to the same limitations and reductions as artist royalties, and no mechanical royalties shall be payable on arrangements of music in the public domain, free goods, and the like. Notwithstanding the foregoing, if any Controlled Composition which is an arrangement of music in the public domain is credited by your performing rights society, we shall pay a mechanical royalty rate therefor in the same proportion or ratio used by your performing rights society in determining the credits for public performance of the work, provided you furnish us with satisfactory evidence of that proportion or ratio. We shall not be obligated to pay more than one (1) mechanical copyright royalty with respect to the use of any particular Controlled Composition on any particular record hereunder. Additionally, you hereby grant us at no fee, royalty, or other cost, an irrevocable and non-exclusive worldwide license to print the title and lyrics of any Controlled Composition(s) on album packaging and marketing materials throughout the world.

9. Warranties; Suspension; Termination

(a) You warrant, represent, covenant, and agree that you have the right and power to enter into this Agreement, to grant the rights herein granted by you, and to perform the services agreed to be performed by you hereunder, and that no selection to be recorded by you hereunder (or materials, ideas or other properties furnished or designated by you, including but not limited to your name or any group name) is subject to any restriction whatsoever, or is violative of the rights of any person, firm or corporation, including without limitation, contract rights, copyrights and rights of privacy. With respect to the Controlled Compositions referred to in Paragraph 8, above, you warrant: that you have the full right, power and authority to grant and to vest in Publisher all rights in the Controlled Compositions, free and clear of any and all claims, rights and obligations whatsoever; that all of the Controlled Compositions and all other results and proceeds of the services of you hereunder, including all of the titles, lyrics, and music of the Controlled Compositions and each and every part thereof, delivered and to be delivered by you hereunder are and shall be new and original and capable of copyright protection throughout the entire world; that no Controlled Composition shall, either in whole or in part, be an imitation or copy of, or infringe upon, any other material, or violate or infringe upon any common law or statutory rights of any party; that you have not sold, assigned, leased, licensed or in any other way disposed of or encumbered any Controlled Composition, in whole or in part, or any rights herein granted, nor shall you sell, assign, lease, license or in any other way dispose of or encumber any of the Controlled Compositions, in whole or in part, or any of said rights, except under the terms and conditions hereof. You expressly covenant and agree that each member of you has as of the date of this Agreement attained the age of majority, and you agree to indemnify us and hold us harmless from and against any and all claims and demands by any current, former or future members of you who may not have attained the age of majority.

(b) During the Term hereof, you shall not enter into any agreement which would interfere with the full and prompt performance of your obligations hereunder, and you shall not perform for the purpose of making audio or video phonograph records for any party (including yourself) other than us. During the Term hereof, you shall not at any time record, manufacture, distribute or sell, or authorize or knowingly permit your performances to be recorded by any party for any purpose without an express written agreement prohibiting the use of such recording on audio or video phonograph records. After the expiration of the Term hereof, you shall not record any selection recorded hereunder (or otherwise subject to this Agreement) for any other party for a period equal to the later of five (5) years after the delivery of the applicable Master to us, or two (2) years after the expiration or termination date of the Term hereof. In the event you make any sound recordings for motion pictures, television, radio or any medium, or if you perform as a member of the cast in making sound recordings for a live theatrical presentation [none of which you shall do without our prior written consent therefor and our approval over the terms thereof, which consent and approval we may withhold for any reason in our sole discretion], you shall do so only pursuant to a written contract prohibiting the use of such recordings, directly or indirectly, for phonograph record purposes.

(c) You further warrant and agree that during the Term you shall diligently, competently and to the best of your ability pursue on a full time basis your recording and performing career. If your voice or ability to perform as an instrumentalist becomes materially impaired, or if you fail, refuse, neglect or are unable to comply with any of your material obligations hereunder (including, without limitation, failure to timely fulfill your recording commitment), then, in addition to any other rights or remedies which we may have, we shall have the right, exercisable at any time by notice to you: (i) to terminate this Agreement without further obligation to you as to unrecorded Masters, or (ii) to extend the then current Contract Period of the Term for the period of such default plus such additional time as is necessary so that we shall have no less than nine (9) months following our release in the United States of the LP constituting your recording commitment for the then-current Contract Period [or one hundred twenty (120) days following the fulfillment of any other material obligation] within which to exercise our option, if any, for the next succeeding Contract Period. Our obligations hereunder shall be suspended for the duration of any such default.

(d) If at any time during the Term you shall commit any act or become involved in any situation or occurrence which brings you and/or us into public disrepute, contempt, scandal or ridicule or which tends to shock, insult or offend the community at large or any substantial group or class thereof, or which reflects unfavorably on our reputation, then we shall have the right (without limiting our other rights and remedies) to terminate this Agreement without further obligation to you except to pay any royalties due with respect to Masters which were recorded hereunder prior to such commission or involvement.

(e) If, because of an act of God, inevitable accident, fire, lockout, strike, or other labor dispute, riot or civil commotion, act of public enemy, enactment, rule, order or act of any government or government instrumentality (whether federal, state, local or foreign), failure of technical facilities, illness or incapacity of any performer or producer, or other cause of a similar or different nature not reasonably within our control, we are materially hampered in the recording, manufacture, distribution or sale of records, or our normal business operations become commercially impractical, then without limiting our rights, we shall have the option by giving you notice to suspend the Term of this Agreement for the duration of any such contingency plus such additional time as is necessary so that we shall have no less than thirty (30) days after the cessation of such contingency in which to exercise our option, if any, for the next following option period. During any such suspension, you shall not render your services as a recording artist (except pursuant to the "sideman" and producer exclusions contained in this Agreement) to any other person, firm or corporation. In the event of a suspension owing to a "force majeure" (as opposed to a suspension specifically related to you), which suspension exceeds six (6) consecutive months, you may terminate this Agreement upon thirty (30) days written notice to us but only if such "force majeure" does not affect a substantial portion of the United States recording industry or the suspension is not lifted within ten (10) days of the receipt of the written notice.

(f) Notwithstanding anything to the contrary contained herein, any or all of the individuals comprising you may render non-musical performances in motion pictures and/or television productions, provided that no such performance interferes with the full and prompt performance of your obligations under this Agreement, and further provided that no such performance includes or otherwise makes reference (directly or indirectly) to your Group Name (as defined below) or your musical recording, writing or performing services. Each or any of you (but not together on the same recording) shall also have the right during the Term hereof to perform as a producer or as a background sideman, background vocalist or background instrumentalist for the purpose of making phonograph record master recordings which are recorded by featured artist(s) other than you and are released by record companies other than us on the following terms and conditions:

(i) Such performance shall be only in a background capacity (unless as a producer) and under no circumstances shall you perform as a featured artist, including, without limitation, in a duet, trio, quartet or so-called "step-out" performance;

(ii) No such performance shall interrupt, delay or interfere with your rendition of services hereunder or with any professional engagement to which you are committed which is intended to aid in the promotion of the phonograph records embodying Masters hereunder;

(iii) No such performance shall be rendered in connection with the recording of any musical composition embodied on a Master theretofore or thereafter delivered by you hereunder.

(iv) Your name, likeness, photograph and biographical material concerning you, shall not be utilized in any manner in connection with the manufacture, sale or other exploitation of any such phonograph records embodying your performances or in connection with the advertising thereof, except that your name (but if you are a group, *not* your group name) may be printed on the liner notes of [and, if performing as a producer, in all places where producer credits are customarily placed on and with respect to the exploitation of] any album embodying your such performances in type no larger or more prominent than that used for any other background musician, background vocalist or background instrumentalist whose performances are embodied therein, and in such event, we shall receive a courtesy credit in the customary manner set forth below (except that with respect to your performances as a producer, there shall be no size or location restriction of your individual name, nor shall you be required to provide said courtesy credit to us where your name is used *solely* as a producer):

"________________ appears courtesy of ________________"

10. <u>Indemnification</u>

We each agree to indemnify the other and save and hold the other harmless from any and all claims, damages, liabilities, costs, losses and expenses (including legal costs and reasonable attorneys' fees) arising out of or connected with any claim, demand or action which is inconsistent with any of the warranties, representations, covenants or agreements which we have each made in this Agreement, and we agree to reimburse each other on demand for any payment made or incurred by either of us with respect to the foregoing, provided the claim concerned has been settled (with the indemnitor's consent) or has resulted in a final judgment against the other or its licensees. Pending the determination and settlement of any such claim, demand or action, or if you shall otherwise fail to faithfully perform all of the material terms and conditions hereof, we shall have the right at our election, to withhold in an interest bearing account payment to you of any monies (including royalties) otherwise payable to you under this Agreement or any other agreement between you and us or our affiliates, in an amount reasonably related to that claim, demand or action and our estimated costs and expenses (including legal costs and reasonable attorneys' fees) in connection therewith [or, if such withholding by us is a result of your failure to faithfully perform all of the material terms and conditions hereof, we may withhold all royalties otherwise due and owing to you hereunder], unless you have made bonding arrangements satisfactory to us which assure us of reimbursement for all damages, liabilities, costs and expenses (including legal costs and reasonable attorneys' fees) which we may incur as a result of that claim or your failure of performance. We agree to release any monies withheld if for one (1) full year following such withholding no action is commenced on any claim concerned or no settlement discussions have taken place and no further demand has been made on said claim, subject to our future right to withhold if litigation or settlement negotiations are commenced. We shall promptly notify you of any action commenced on such a claim, and you may participate in the defense of any such claim through counsel of your sole choosing and at your sole expense, subject to our right to control the defense of such claim.

11. Notices

The respective addresses of you and us for all purposes hereunder are set forth on page 1 hereof, unless and until notice of a different address is received by the party notified of that different address. All notices shall be in writing and shall either be served by personal delivery (to an officer of our company if to us), by mail or by overnight or local courier, in each case with all charges prepaid. Notices shall be deemed effective when personally delivered or mailed, all charges prepaid, except for notices of change of address, which shall be effective only when received by the party notified. A copy of each notice to us shall be simultaneously sent to ____________ _____.

12. Assignment

We may, at our election, assign this Agreement or any of our rights hereunder or delegate any of our obligations hereunder, in whole or in part, for any reason, including, without limitation, to any person, firm or corporation owning or acquiring all or a substantial portion of our stock or assets, to any person, firm or corporation that is related to us as an affiliate, subsidiary or otherwise, or to any person, firm or corporation into which or with which we might merge or consolidate. You may not delegate any of your obligations or assign any of your rights hereunder, except that you shall have the right, at your election, to assign your right to receive royalties hereunder to no more than one (1) then-current assignee thereof which is identified to us in an appropriate letter of direction signed by you. Any assignee of royalties otherwise payable directly to you hereunder shall not be a third-party beneficiary of this Agreement and shall have no right under this Agreement or otherwise to commence or prosecute any claim, demand or action against us as a result of our payment or failure to pay any royalties to that assignee.

13. Unique Services

You expressly acknowledge that your services hereunder, as well as the rights and privileges granted to us hereunder, are of special, unique, and intellectual character which gives them peculiar value, and that in the event of a breach by you of any term, condition, or covenant hereof, we will be caused irreparable injury. You expressly agree that in the event you shall breach any provision of this Agreement, we shall be entitled to seek injunctive relief and/or damages, as we may deem appropriate, in addition to any other rights or remedies available to us, and we shall have the right to recoup any such damages resulting from any such breach from any monies which may be payable to you under this agreement or under any other agreement between you and us or our affiliates.

14. Failure of Performance

Except with respect to the exclusivity provisions hereof (for which there shall be no cure period), the failure by either of us to perform any of our respective obligations hereunder shall not be deemed a breach of this Agreement unless the party claiming breach gives the other party written notice of such failure to perform and such failure is not corrected within thirty (30) days from and after the receipt of such notice, or, if such breach is not reasonably capable of being cured within such thirty (30) day period, the party receiving notice does not commence to cure such breach within such thirty (30) day period and proceed with reasonable diligence to complete the curing of such breach thereafter. Notwithstanding the foregoing, each of the following shall constitute an event of default which shall (without limiting our other rights and remedies) entitle us to terminate the Term of this Agreement immediately following (and without giving you an opportunity to cure) the occurrence of any such event:

(a) If you commence a voluntary case under any applicable bankruptcy, insolvency or other similar law now or hereafter in effect, or if you consent to the entry of any order for relief in any involuntary case under such law, or if you consent to the appointment of or taking possession by a receiver, liquidator, assignee, trustee or sequestrator (or similar appointee) of you or any substantial part of your property, or if you make an assignment for the benefit of creditors or take any act (whether corporate or otherwise) in furtherance of any of the foregoing;

(b) If a court having jurisdiction over your affairs or your property enters a decree or order for relief with respect to you or any of your property in an involuntary case under any applicable bankruptcy, insolvency or other similar law now or hereafter in effect, or if such a court appoints a receiver, liquidator, assignee, custodian, trustee or sequestrator (or similar appointee) of you or for any substantial part of your property or orders the winding up or liquidation of your affairs and such decree or order remains unstayed and in effect for a period of sixty (60) consecutive days.

15. Group Member Provisions

(a) The word "you" as used in this Agreement refers individually and collectively to the members of the group (whether presently or hereafter signatories to or otherwise bound by the terms and provisions of this Agreement) currently professionally known as "______________" and presently consisting of the following individuals: (i) ___________; (ii) _________; (iii) ___________; and, (iv) ______________. Individuals who are or become members of the group, in addition to those presently members of the group, may become members of the group only with our prior written approval. Additional members shall be bound by the terms of this Agreement relating to you, and you shall cause any such additional member to execute and deliver to us such documents as we may deem necessary or desirable to evidence that individual's agreement to be so bound. You shall not, without our prior written consent, record any Masters embodying the performances of any additional member prior to your delivery to us of those documents, and if you do so, those Masters, if we so elect, shall not apply towards the fulfillment of your recording commitment, and you shall fully indemnify us from and against any and all claims and demands made by any such unapproved additional members. All of the terms, conditions, warranties, representations, and obligations contained in this Agreement shall apply jointly and severally to each individual member of the group, and no change in the name of the group shall affect or otherwise limit our rights hereunder. A breach of any term or provision of this Agreement or a disaffirmance or attempted disaffirmance of this Agreement, for any reason whatsoever, by any member or members of the group shall, at our election, be deemed a breach by the entire group.

(b) We shall have the irrevocable and exclusive right (but not the obligation) during the Term hereof to record as soloists any of the above-referenced individuals or any other individuals comprising you (whether as "_______ _______" or any other name by which you and any new members may be known) subject to the terms and conditions of this Agreement, except that the recording budgets/funds and advances (if any) shall be determined in accordance with Subparagraph 15(d) below.

(c) In the event any individual member of the group shall, during the Term hereof, cease to be an actively performing member of the group (any such individual being hereinafter sometimes referred to as a "Leaving Member"), you shall promptly give us written notice thereof by certified or registered mail, return receipt requested. You shall, at our election, designate a replacement member for such Leaving Member and we shall have the right to approve any such replacement member. You shall cause any such individual so approved by us as a replacement member to be bound by all of the terms and provisions of this Agreement, and you shall, upon our request, cause such individual to execute and deliver to us such documents as we may deem necessary or expedient to evidence such individual's execution and delivery to us of any such documents. Pending such individual's execution and delivery to us of any such documents, we shall have no obligation to pay you any amounts which would otherwise be payable to you hereunder.

(d) We shall have the irrevocable option to contract for the exclusive recording services of any Leaving Member. Such option may be exercised by us by written notice given to such Leaving Member at your address hereunder no later than ninety (90) days after the date upon which we shall have received the written notice required to be served by you pursuant to Subparagraph (c). If we shall so exercise such option with respect to any such Leaving Member, such Leaving Member shall be deemed to have executed an exclusive recording contract with us pursuant to which such Leaving Member agrees to render his exclusive recording services to us subject to the terms and conditions of (and only for the then-remaining term of) this Agreement, except that the recording budgets and any advances (if any) shall be determined by us after good faith negotiation with such Leaving Member, but in no event to exceed those in respect of the initial period hereof. At our request, you shall cause any such Leaving Member to execute and deliver to us any and all documents as we may deem necessary or expedient to evidence the foregoing, including without limitation, an exclusive recording agreement with us relating to his recording services. We shall have the right to recoup from any royalties payable under this paragraph with respect to such Leaving Member a pro rata portion of any unrecouped advances and charges incurred under this Agreement prior to the date such Leaving Member ceased being an actively performing member of the group.

(e) Notwithstanding any of the foregoing, in the event the group shall completely disband, we shall have the right, at our election, in addition to all of our other rights or remedies which we may have in such event, to terminate this Agreement by written notice to you and shall thereby be relieved of any and all obligations hereunder except our obligations with respect to Masters recorded hereunder prior to such termination. In the event we elect to so terminate this Agreement, subparagraph (d) above shall be deemed applicable to each member of the group as if each such member were a Leaving Member.

(f) You hereby warrant, represent and agree that:

(i) You are the sole and exclusive owner of all rights in and to the professional name of "___________" (the "Group Name"), including, without limitation, the right to utilize and to permit others to utilize the Group Name for purposes of trade, and otherwise without restriction, in connection with the Masters recorded by you hereunder, the phonograph records derived therefrom, and our record business, and including the exclusive rights in and to the "Group Name.com" or any other similar domain registration designation (e.g., Group Name.net, Group Name.org., etc.) for Internet and other so-called "e-commerce" usage. You further warrant that our use of the Group Name in connection with our record business will not unfairly compete in any manner with any third parties, and you agree that in the event that we are required to expend any sums of money in connection with any dispute over the rights in and to the Group Name, we shall (without limiting our other rights and remedies) have the right to deduct all such sums from any and all royalties or other sums payable by us to you under this Agreement or any other agreement between you and us or our affiliates.

(ii) during the term hereof, the Group Name shall not be changed without our prior written consent.

(g) In the event any member of the group shall become a Leaving Member, such Leaving Member shall not have the right during the Term or thereafter to use any professional name utilized by the group (including without limitation, the Group Name, or "Formerly of" the Group Name) or any name similar thereto, or to prevent, prohibit or interfere with our and your use of the Group Name or any other professional name utilized by the group.

16. No Sales Warranty.

You hereby acknowledge and agree that we have not made and do not hereby make any representation or warranty of any kind or nature with respect to the quantities of albums which may be sold or the prices at which the same may be sold or the proceeds which will or may be derived by you or us pursuant to this Agreement. You acknowledge and agree that the extent of the sales and the amount of proceeds which may be derived therefrom is entirely speculative, and you further agree that our judgment in regard to any matter affecting the sale, distribution and exploitation of Masters hereunder shall be binding and conclusive upon you. You warrant, covenant and agree that you will not make any claim, nor shall any liability be imposed upon us based upon any claim that more sales could have been made than were made by us or our licensees, distributors, etc.

17. Life and Disability Insurance.

We may at any time during the Term obtain, at our cost, insurance on your life, and/or disability insurance that may affect you. We or our designees shall be the sole beneficiary of that insurance, and neither you nor any person, firm or corporation claiming rights through or from you shall have any rights in that insurance or the proceeds thereof. You agree to submit to such physical examinations and to complete and deliver such forms as we may reasonably require, and you shall otherwise cooperate with us fully for the purpose of enabling us to secure said life insurance. You shall have the right (at your sole cost and expense) to have a licensed medical doctor present at any such physical examinations. We agree to keep confidential the results of any such physical exam(s).

18. Promotional Activities.

From time to time at our request, and whenever the same will not unreasonably interfere with your touring and performing, you shall appear at photographic sessions in connection with the creation of artwork, poster and cover art to be used for the advertising, marketing and promotion of records hereunder; appear for interviews with representatives of the media and our publicity personnel; and advise and consult with us regarding your performances hereunder and your touring plans and schedules. At our request and subject to your availability, you shall make personal appearances on radio and television and elsewhere, and you shall record taped interviews, spot announcements, trailers and electrical transcriptions, all for the purpose of advertising, exploiting and/or promoting the Masters hereunder. You shall not be entitled to any compensation for such services, except as may be required by applicable union agreements, provided, however, we shall reimburse you for the reasonable (but not first class) travel and living expenses incurred by you pursuant to a budget approved in advance by us, which such reimbursements shall not be recoupable hereunder.

19. Artist Product Purchases

Upon request by you, we shall sell and deliver to you your requirements in the United States of any and all recordings produced under this Agreement, provided that you pay for those purchases in cash within thirty (30) days following the date of invoice at the rate of __________ Dollars ($__.00) per cassette and ________ Dollars ($__.00) per CD, plus freight, which such product shall be non-royalty-bearing; provided, however, you may pay to us your artist and mechanical copyright royalties over and above the aforesaid price, and we shall credit the same to your respective accounts and pay said royalties (if applicable) in accordance with our regular accountings. We shall have the right to deduct any and all delinquent amounts owing to us hereunder from any and all royalties or other sums (including advances) payable to you hereunder or under any other agreement between you and us or our affiliates. You warrant and agree that such product sold to you shall be resold by you only to individual consumers directly (and not for resale by them) at your concerts in the United States or to individual consumers through your own personal mailing lists (but not over the so-called "Internet") in the United States, and not at any other times, by any other means or at any other place. With respect to product purchases outside of the United States from our then current retail trade licensees or distributors (including importers), we agree to allow you to negotiate the terms thereof directly with such party, provided that we shall have a prior right of reasonable approval over such terms and the quantity purchased. All such purchases by you shall be at your sole expense and shall be for sales by you only to individual consumers directly (and not for resale by them) at your concerts in that particular country in which such purchase has been made or to individual consumers through your own personal mailing lists (but not over the so-called "internet") in that particular country in which such purchase has been made, and not at any other times, by any other means or at any other place. Such product shall not be sold by you in any other manner.

20. Tour Support

In the event that we provide any so-called "tour support" to you hereunder (whether in the form of cash, clothing, tour marketing or other property, and whether paid directly to you or to another on your behalf), you agree that __________ percent (__%) of said tour support shall be deemed an advance recoupable at our discretion from artist or mechanical royalties payable to you under this Agreement or any other agreement between you and us or our affiliates.

21. Confidentiality

You hereby warrant, represent and agree that this Agreement, and each of the terms and conditions hereof and thereof shall remain wholly confidential and that any matter relating to this Agreement or the respective terms hereof shall not be disclosed to or discussed with any person or entity, other than your counsel, personal manager or accountant, or otherwise as may be required by law.

22. Miscellaneous

(a) This Agreement contains the entire understanding of the parties hereto relating to the subject matter hereof and cannot be changed or terminated except by an instrument signed by the party to be bound. A waiver by either party of any term or condition of this Agreement in any instance shall not be deemed or construed as a waiver of such term or condition for the future, or of any subsequent breach thereof. All remedies, rights, undertakings, obligations, and agreements contained in this Agreement shall be cumulative and none of them shall be in limitation of any other remedy, right, undertaking, obligation or agreement of either party. The headings of the paragraphs hereof are for convenience only and shall not be deemed to limit or in any way affect the scope, meaning or intent of this Agreement or any portion thereof.

(b) It is understood and agreed that in entering this Agreement, and in rendering services pursuant thereto, you have and shall have, the status of an independent contractor and nothing herein contained shall contemplate or constitute you our employee, agent, partner or joint venturer.

(c) Those provisions of any applicable collective bargaining agreement between us and any labor organization which are required, by the terms of such agreement, to be included in this Agreement shall be deemed incorporated herein.

(d) This Agreement has been entered into in the State of ______________ and the validity, interpretation and legal effect of this Agreement shall be governed by the laws of the State of ______________ applicable to contracts entered into and performed entirely within the State of ______________, without regard to conflicts of laws principles. The venue for any controversy or claim arising out of or relating to this Agreement or breach thereof, shall be the appropriate state and federal courts located in ______________, ______________. Accordingly, you and we each submit to the jurisdiction of such courts. Any process in any action or proceeding commenced in the courts in the State of ______________ or elsewhere arising out of or relating to any such claim, dispute or disagreement may, among other methods, be served upon you or us by delivering or by mailing the same via registered or certified mail to the addresses contained herein. The prevailing party in any such dispute arising hereunder shall be entitled to recover from the other party its reasonable attorneys' fees in connection therewith in addition to the costs thereof.

(e) If any part of this Agreement shall be determined to be invalid or unenforceable by a court of competent jurisdiction or by any other legally constituted body having jurisdiction to make such determination, the remainder of this Agreement shall remain in full force and effect.

(f) You have been represented by independent legal counsel or have had the unrestricted opportunity to be represented by independent legal counsel of your choice for purposes of advising you in connection with the negotiation and execution of this Agreement. If you have not been represented by independent legal counsel of your choice in connection with this Agreement, you acknowledge and agree that your failure to be represented by independent legal counsel in connection with this Agreement was determined solely by you.

(g) This Agreement may be executed in one or more counterparts, each of which shall be deemed an original (including facsimile signatures), but all of which together shall constitute but one and the same instrument.

If the foregoing accurately reflects our understanding and agreement, please sign where indicated below.

Sincerely,

____

By: ___________________________
An Authorized Signatory

ACCEPTED AND AGREED:

"You"

The individuals comprising "__________," personally and individually, whether under this or any other personal or professional names:

______________________________ Social Security Number:

B

Suggested Reading

Beall, Eric. *Making Music Make Money: An Insider's Guide to Becoming Your Own Music Publisher.* Boston: Berklee Press, 2004.

Franz, David. *Producing in the Home Studio with Pro Tools.* Boston: Berklee Press: 2003.

Gladwell, Malcolm. *The Tipping Point: How Little Things Can Make a Big Difference.* Boston: Little, Brown, and Company: 2002

Goodman, Fred. *The Mansion on the Hill.* New York: Vintage Books: 1997

Passman, Donald. *All You Need To Know about the Music Business.* New York: Simon & Schuster: 2000

Sloman, Larry "Ratso." *On The Road with Bob Dylan.* New York: Three River Press: 1978.

Spellman, Peter. *The Self-Promoting Musician.* Boston: Berklee Press, 1999.

————. *The Musician's Internet.* Boston: Berklee Press, 2001.

"From the Field" Bios

The following people graciously let me interview them while I was researching this book. Many of the highlights of these interviews are quoted verbatim, with their names attached to them. And many more of their insights served to inspire my own writing. Their input is deeply appreciated.

David Bither, Senior Vice President of Nonesuch Records

David Bither began at Elektra Records, where he ultimately became General Manager, and then joined at Nonesuch Records in 1995. He has worked with a diverse roster of artists ranging from Steve Reich to Wilco, Bill Frisell to the Kronos Quartet, Ry Cooder to Caetano Veloso.

Loren Chodosh, Attorney

Loren Chodosh has been a lawyer since 1983. She was a partner at Levine Thall and Plotkin until 1995, when she opened her firm in TriBeCa. Her practice is artist-oriented, and she represents, for the most part, the creative side of the music business equation (rather than acting as outside counsel to major labels). She has worked with artists including the Cars, Live, Moby, Foreigner, and Shawn Colvin.

Sean Coakley, Founder of Songlines, Ltd.

Sean Coakley's radio promotion company, Songlines Ltd., gets radio airplay at Triple-A and Americana stations. Before starting this company, he worked in various capacities for INXS, Rooart Records, ATCO, and Arista, in promotion and product development. He has won the "Indie of the Year" award six times.

Sue Devine, Senior Director of Film & Television Music at ASCAP

Sue Devine works with both emerging and more established artists (Angelo Badalamenti, Carter Burwell, Howard Shore) in ASCAP's Film/TV Department and in the general Membership Department. Ms. Devine provides career development support for emerging artists. She programs Film/TV seminars and events for ASCAP writers and for filmmakers. She also launched *ASCAP Presents... (Not So) Quiet on the Set*, a showcase of acoustic artists and bands for the music industry in NYC and for the film industry at the Sundance Film Festival's Music Café.

Prior to ASCAP, Ms. Devine was operations manager of Arlo Guthrie's record label, Rising Son Records, where she produced a live concert video of Arlo Guthrie and Pete Seeger. She also worked with filmmakers as the Program Manager at the Independent Feature Project (IFP).

Chris Eselgroth, Designer

Chris Eselgroth was senior designer at Mammoth Records where he worked on packages for artists including Squirrel Nut Zippers, Seven Mary Three, the Dirty Dozen Brass Band, Victoria Williams, and Fu Manchu. In 2000, Chris started Foureyes Studios, in Durham, North Carolina, which concentrates on music packaging and photography.

Larry Goldfarb, Promoter, Manager, and Club Booker

Larry Goldfarb has spent over thirty years in the music business as promoter, manager, and club booker. He has worked with artists such as Nina Simone, Tom Waits, Smokey Robinson, Donovan, and Keith Jarrett. Larry has helped sign six acts from the Philadelphia area to major record labels including Susan Werner, Jeffrey Gaines, and Ben Arnold. He has been booking the Tin Angel club since its inception in 1992.

Tor Hansen, President, Redeye Distribution

Tor Hansen founded Redeye Distribution and Yep Roc Records in 1996 after working in the label, distribution, and the retailing sectors of the music industry. He began at Rounder Records Distribution in Cambridge, MA, and then moved into music retailing as Director of Merchandising at Hear Music Inc., and also at Planet Music, Borders Group Inc. As a distributor, he has worked with labels and artists including John Mayer, Jeru, Supersuckers, Little Feat, Burning Spear, and the Pernice Brothers. As a label, he has worked with a roster to include artists Nick Lowe, Paul Weller, Doyle Bramhall, Los Straitjackets, and Caitlin Cary.

David Henry, Producer, Cellist, Engineer, Owner of True Tone Recording, Nashville

David has worked with artists ranging from folkies like Rod Picott, Kasey Chambers, and Allison Krauss, to more AAA and alternative acts such as Josh Rouse, David Mead, Guster, Yo La Tengo, and Cowboy Junkies. David attributes his success as a Nashville producer to his versatility as a musician both in and out of the studio.

Steve Jurgensmeyer, Creative Director of Rounder Records

Steve Jurgensmeyer was the Art Director at Rykodisc for over ten years. He has also served as Creative Director at a number of Web design and development firms in the Boston area. He is currently Creative Director at Rounder Records, the largest independent and preeminent roots label in the country.

Mike Kappus, President/Owner of The Rosebud Agency (Marketing/Booking)

Mike Kappus is founder and owner of the Rosebud Agency and manager of J. J. Cale, Loudon Wainwright III, and Robert Cray. As manager, executive producer, or producer, Kappus' work with John Lee Hooker, Robert Cray, Pops Staples, and John Hammond yielded at least one Grammy nomination or win for eighteen of nineteen eligible projects with those artists. Started in 1976, Rosebud's intentionally limited roster has included artists from Muddy Waters to Captain Beefheart, as well as the Blind Boys of Alabama, ¡Cubanismo!, BeauSoleil, Marcia Ball, Charlie Watts, and the Dirty Dozen Brass Band. Kappus won his fourth Manager/Agent of the year award in 2003 from the Blues Foundation—an award that no other individual has won more than once. Rosebud's office, reflecting Kappus' environmental commitment, is the world's first solar powered booking agency.

Matt Kleinschmidt, The Music Syndicate

Matt Kleinschmidt is a former college-station DJ and general manager of RLC-WVPH FM. He currently works at The Music Syndicate, a company that leverages fan support to help launch new bands.

Paul Kolderie, Producer/Engineer

Paul Kolderie was a founding partner of Boston's Fort Apache Studios in 1986. He served as chief engineer there until 1990, working on records by the Pixies, Throwing Muses, Dinosaur Jr., Buffalo Tom, the Lemonheads, and many others. He teamed with Sean Slade to produce, engineer, and mix records throughout the nineties, notably *Pablo Honey* and *The Bends* by Radiohead, *Live Through This* by Hole, *No Depression* and *Still Feel Gone* from Uncle Tupelo, four albums by Morphine, and five from the Mighty Mighty Bosstones. He recently reopened Fort Apache's third location, in Cambridge, MA, as Camp Street Studios. His recent projects include the Joe Jackson Band's *Volume Four*, Consonant, S.T.U.N., Juliana Hatfield, the Tarbox Ramblers, the Explosion, Piebald, and Hey Mercedes.

Nathaniel Krenkel, Sony/ATV Music Publishing

Nathaniel Krenkel started working for Sony in 1997 as a talent scout. As an A&R executive, he has worked with Belle and Sebastian, Bright Eyes (Desaparecidos), Jason Morphew, Jesse Harris (Norah Jones), the Red King, Thin Lizard Dawn, Chris and Drew Peters, Si*se, and Shudder to Think.

Liz Linder, Photographer

Liz Linder has been making photographs for over twenty years. Her commercial work focuses on musicians, artists, families, and corporate bodies. Her photographs are used for CD art, marketing, artist packaging, and brochures, and appear in a variety of publications nationally. She is internationally exhibited, and her work is maintained in personal and corporate collections across the country. Her work can be seen on the Web at www.lizlinder.com.

Peter Lubin, Veteran A&R Executive

Peter Lubin is a veteran A&R executive in the recording industry. Mr. Lubin was Vice President of Mercury Records in 1980, and signed artists including the Moody Blues, Peter Gabriel, Michelle Shocked, and Robert Cray. He also worked closely with a wide variety of artists such as Rush, Kool & the Gang, the Scorpions, Def Leppard, John Mellencamp, and the Everly Brothers. He signed the Refreshments—the ninth-best-selling new artist of 1996.

Moving to Elektra Entertainment in 1998, where he eventually became Senior Vice President of A&R, he acquired the Pixies and the Breeders for the Elektra Entertainment, and was instrumental in the acquisition of They Might Be Giants and Phish. He also worked closely with Elektra artists Jackson Browne, Simply Red, and Huey Lewis, among others.

Mr. Lubin is a past Governor of the New York chapter of The National Academy of Recording Arts and Sciences (NARAS). He is an active lecturer, and currently serves as a consultant to various artists, labels, and companies.

Sheryl Northrop, Founding Partner of The Baker/Northrop Media Group

Sheryl Northrop has worked in entertainment publicity and related media for almost two decades and is a founding partner in The Baker/Northrop Media Group, a Los Angeles-based music PR company. Northrop has, throughout her career, created highly successful PR campaigns for both artists and corporate clients, including Lisa Loeb, Marc Broussard, the Clarks, Caitlin Cary, Robert Cray, Loudon Wainwright III, Pete Seeger, June Carter Cash, Casey Kasem, Dominic Chianese (*The Sopranos*), Susan Tedeschi, Delbert McClinton, Suzy Bogguss, Warner Music Group, Sundance Channel, HBO, and many others. She is a former lecturer at UCLA Extension, where she co-taught the principles of music publicity for several years.

Sean O'Connell, Founder of Music Allies

Sean O'Connell has worked in the music business for over twelve years. After launching a non-commercial radio station, Sean started his music business career in concert promotion and music management before segueing into radio promotion. O'Connell was formerly the Head of Promotion for Rykodisc. He was also the Director of Marketing and Business Development for ETC Music (a technology startup) and promoted national recording artists for the independent promotion company Songlines.

Jeff Price, Co-Founder, General Manager, President of spinART Records

Jeff Price's independent record label spinART has been in strategic relationships with Sony, Warner Bros., Sire, Polygram Music Publishing and others. SpinART has distributed over 130 releases since its inception, including such bands/artists as Frank Black, the Pixies Apples In Stereo, Vic Chesnutt, Jason Falkner, Richard Thompson, Echo & the Bunnymen, Ron Sexsmith, Paul Kelly, the Fastbacks, John Doe, Lilys, Eyes Adrift, Clem Snide, and others. It is currently distributed via the Warner Bros.–owned distributor ADA.

Jason Rio, Manager

Jason Rio manages artists through Asquared Management (a division of Aware Records). His clients include Liz Phair (Capitol), Brendan Benson (Star Time/V2), Motion City Soundtrack (Epitaph), and The Working Title (Universal). Prior to joining Asquared/Aware in 2002, he was a partner in the management firm, DBMI, where he worked with artists such as Remy

Zero and the Verve Pipe. Besides management, Rio has also spent time as a tour manager and a college concert promoter.

Carla Sacks, Publicist

Carla Sacks founded her publicity firm, Sacks & Co., in 1995. She has planned and executed the press campaigns for both major and debuting artists, as well as for entire record labels. Her clients have included the popular artists Natalie Merchant, Grant Lee Phillips, Emmylou Harris, Dolly Parton, Semisonic, Bob Mould, Kristin Hersh, Cowboy Junkies, Mark Isham, and Robert Earl Keen. She has been at the forefront of Latin and World music building profiles for Loreena McKinnett, Buena Vista Social Club, Cubanismo, Chiekh Lô, Oumou Sangare, Afel Bocoum, Luaka Bop artists (including Zap Mama, Tom Zé, and the Cuba Classics Series), Natalie MacMaster, Los Van Van, Oumou Sangare, Donal Lunny, James Galway, and Phil Coulter. Her current and past corporate clients include Nonesuch/World Circuit, 4AD, Luaka Bop, Arts at St. Ann's, and Sony Wonder.

John Soares, Photographer

Boston-based photographer John Soares has been called the "King-Daddy of Inventiveness." He has produced powerful images of Johnny Cash, Tony Bennet, John Haitt, No Doubt, Suzanne Vega, Shawn Colvin, and others. He has also been published in *Rolling Stone*, *The New Yorker*, *Communication Arts*, *Print*, and Creative Edge books. John shoots for a lot of major magazines and has won a bunch of big awards. www.soaresphotos.com.

David Wykoff, Attorney

David Wykoff practices law in Nashville, representing performing musicians and others in the music industry. He specializes in contract negotiation and dispute resolution. David has practiced law since 1990. Before then, he was a correspondent for *Billboard*, *Rolling Stone*, and many other magazines.

About the Author

Producer and musician **George Howard** founded his first independent label, Slow River Records, in 1993. In 1995, Slow River entered into a co-venture with Rykodisc, one of the world's largest independent labels. In 1999, he was made president of Rykodisc and was fortunate to work with a diverse roster of artists and artist catalogs including Kelly Willis, Robert Cray, Medeski, Martin & Wood, Morphine, Frank Zappa, Pork Tornado, Josh Rouse, Bill Hicks, Richard Buckner, the Tom Tom Club, Catie Curtis, Future Bible Heroes, Sophie B. Hawkins, and the Slip, among others. He has produced records for many artists, including Kelly Joe Phelps, Chuck E. Weiss (with Tom Waits), Jess Klein, Matthew (with Paul Q. Kolderie), and Peter Bruntnell. He recently started Essex River Works, a production, marketing, and publishing company. He teaches about the recording industry at Northeastern University and is a frequent lecturer at Berklee College of Music and other colleges.

Index

BERKLEE PRACTICE METHOD

0-634-00650-9 **Bass** by Rich Appleman & John Repucci
0-634-00652-5 **Drum Set** by Ron Savage & Casey Scheuerell
0-634-00649-5 **Guitar** by Larry Baione
0-634-00651-7 **Keyboard** by Russell Hoffmann & Paul Schmeling
0-634-00795-5 **Alto Sax** by Jim Odgren & Bill Pierce
0-634-00798-0 **Tenor Sax** by Jim Odgren & Bill Pierce
0-634-00791-2 **Trombone** by Jeff Galindo
0-634-00790-4 **Trumpet** by Tiger Okoshi & Charles Lewis
0-634-00794-7 **Vibraphone** by Ed Saindon
0-634-00792-0 **Violin** by Matt Glaser & Mimi Rabson
Book/CD $14.95 (each)

BERKLEE INSTANT SERIES

0-634-01667-9 **Bass** by Danny Morris
0-634-02602-X **Drum Set** by Ron Savage
0-634-02951-7 **Guitar** by Tomo Fujita
0-634-03141-4 **Keyboard** by Paul Schmeling & Dave Limina
Book/CD $14.95 (each)

IMPROVISATION

Blues Improvisation Complete Series by Jeff Harrington
0-634-01530-3 Bb Instruments
0-634-01532-X C Bass Instruments
0-634-00647-9 C Treble Instruments
0-634-01531-7 Eb Instruments
Book/CD $19.95 (each)

A Guide to Jazz Improvisation Series by John LaPorta
0-634-00700-9 C Instruments
0-634-00762-9 Bb Instruments
0-634-00763-7 Eb Instruments
0-634-00764-5 Bass Clef
Book $16.95 (each)

MUSIC TECHNOLOGY

Arranging in the Digital World by Corey Allen
0-634-00634-7 Book/MIDI Disk $19.95

Finale: An Easy Guide to Music Notation by Tom Rudolph & Vince Leonard
0-634-01666-0 Book/CD-ROM $59.95

Producing in the Home Studio with Pro Tools Second Edition by David Franz
0-87639-008-4 Book/CD-ROM $34.95

Recording in the Digital World by Tom Rudolph & Vince Leonard
0-634-01324-6 Book $29.95

POP CULTURE

Inside the Hits by Wayne Wadhams
0-634-01430-7 Book $29.95

Masters of Music: Conversations with Berklee Greats by Mark Small and Andrew Taylor
0-634-00642-8 Book $24.95

MUSIC BUSINESS

Getting Signed! An Insider's Guide to the Record Industry by George Howard
0-87639-045-9 Book $26.95

How to Get a Job in the Music & Recording Industry by Keith Hatschek
0-634-01868-X Book $24.95

Making Music Make Money: An Insider's Guide to Becoming Your Own Music Publisher by Eric Beall
0-87639-007-6 Book $26.95

Mix Masters: Platinum Engineers Reveal Their Secrets for Success by Maureen Droney
0-87639-019-X Book $24.95

The Musician's Internet by Peter Spellman
0-634-03586-X Book $24.95

The New Music Therapist's Handbook, Second Edition by Suzanne B. Hanser
0-634-00645-2 Book $29.95

The Self-Promoting Musician by Peter Spellman
0-634-00644-4 Book $24.95

SONGWRITING / ARRANGING / VOICE

Arranging for Large Jazz Ensemble by Ken Pullig
0-634-03656-4 Book/CD $39.95

Complete Guide to Film Scoring by Richard Davis
0-634-00636-3 Book $24.95

The Contemporary Singer by Anne Peckham
0-634-00797-1 Book/CD $24.95

Essential Ear Training by Steve Prosser
0-634-00640-1 Book $14.95

Jazz Composition: Theory and Practice by Ted Pease
0-87639-001-7 Book/CD $39.95

Melody in Songwriting by Jack Perricone
0-634-00638-X Book $19.95

Modern Jazz Voicings by Ted Pease & Ken Pullig
0-634-01443-9 Book/CD $24.95

Music Notation by Mark McGrain
0-7935-0847-9 Book $19.95

Reharmonization Techniques by Randy Felts
0-634-01585-0 Book $29.95

The Songs of John Lennon by John Stevens
0-634-01795-0 Book $24.95

The Songwriter's Workshop: Melody by Jimmy Kachulis
0-634-02659-3 Book $24.95

Songwriting: Essential Guide to Lyric Form & Structure by Pat Pattison
0-7935-1180-1 Book $14.95

Songwriting: Essential Guide to Rhyming by Pat Pattison
0-7935-1181-X Book $14.95

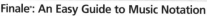